DISTILLING THE FRENZY

ABOUT THE AUTHOR

Peter Hennessy is Attlee Professor of Contemporary British History in the School of History and Patron of the Mile End Group at Queen Mary, University of London. He is also an Honorary Fellow of St John's College, Cambridge, the London School of Economics and St Benet's Hall, Oxford. He was elected a Fellow of the British Academy in 2003. In 2010 he was appointed an independent crossbench peer in the House of Lords where he sits as Lord Hennessy of Nympsfield. In 2011 he joined the Chief of the Defence Staff's Strategic Advisory Panel. He is author of Never Again: Britain 1945–51 *(which won the Duff Cooper and the NCR prizes),* Having It So Good: Britain in the Fifties *(winner of the Orwell Prize for political writing) and* The Secret State: Preparing for the Worst, 1945–2010.

BY THE SAME AUTHOR

States of Emergency
(with Keith Jeffery)
Sources Close to the Prime Minister
(with Michael Cockerell and David Walker)
What the Papers Never Said
Cabinet
Ruling Performance
(edited with Anthony Seldon)
Whitehall
Never Again: Britain 1945–1951
The Hidden Wiring: Unearthing the British Constitution
Muddling Through: Power, Politics and the Quality of Government
in Postwar Britain
The Prime Minister: The Office and Its Holders since 1945
The Secret State: Whitehall and the Cold War
Having It So Good: Britain in the Fifties
The New Protective State: Government, Intelligence and Terrorism (editor)
Cabinets and the Bomb
The Secret State: Preparing for the Worst, 1945–2010

PETER HENNESSY

DISTILLING THE FRENZY

WRITING THE HISTORY OF ONE'S OWN TIMES

Biteback Publishing

First published in 2012 by
Biteback Publishing
Westminster Tower
3 Albert Embankment
London SE1 7SP

ISBN 978-1-84954-215-9

10 9 8 7 6 5 4 3 2 1

A CIP catalogue record for this book is available from the British Library.

Set in Minion by Soapbox.

Printed and bound in Great Britain by
CPI Group (UK) Ltd, Croydon CR0 4YY

CONTENTS

IN MEMORY OF JOHN RAMSDEN
1947–2009

FRIEND, GUIDE AND ACE
CONTEMPORARY HISTORIAN

INTRODUCTION

DISTILLING THE FRENZY:
THE PSYCHODRAMATIC AND THE PROSAIC

Madmen in authority, who hear voices in the air, are distilling their frenzy from some academic scribbler of a few years ago.
J. M. KEYNES, 1936[1]

WHAT Albert Einstein called 'a holy curiosity'[2] in human beings takes a vast variety of forms as does the power of imagination with which it is twinned. My imagination, such as it is, is heavily historical and has been, in terms of my conscious memory, since the late 1950s at the very least. I suspect, though cannot know, that the hippocampus – the memory sector – of my brain is the most developed though, inevitably, for a postwar baby born in 1947, it is now fraying more than a tad. And I always had a certain sympathy with that extraordinary scholar-politician Enoch Powell, when he declared, as he often did in one form of words or another, to a student audience at Trinity College, Dublin in 1964, that 'the life of nations, no less than that of men, is lived largely in the imagination.'[3]

Yet, in that same speech devoted to Britain's history as an imperial power, Mr Powell went on to claim that 'all history is myth. It is a pattern which men weave out of the materials of the past. The moment a fact enters into history it becomes mythical, because it has been taken and fitted into its place in a set of ordered relationships which is the creation of a human mind and not otherwise present in nature.'[4]

How much débris passes through what my friend Sir Mark Allen calls 'the nit-comb of history'[5] is a haunting one for historians. Benjamin Disraeli captured this anxiety in his novel *Sybil, or the Two Nations* in 1845 when he wrote of the historians of England: 'Generally speaking, all the great events have been distorted, most of the important causes concealed, some of the principal characters never appear, and all who figure are so misunderstood and misrepresented, that the result is a complete mystification …'[6] Inevitably, the scholar's capacity to capture and reconstruct the past before applying his or her historical imagination will always and everywhere be seriously limited.

Enoch Powell knew as much as any man or woman I've known about the power of historical imagination to move and stir individuals and audiences. Indeed, he became an instant household name when he did just that during a speech on immigration in Birmingham in April 1968.[7]

Even on less sensitive topics there was always an air of the psychodramatic about Mr Powell when he came into BBC Broadcasting House for a Radio 4 *Analysis* discussion I was chairing, whether it be with Tony Benn on the royal prerogative[8] or Roy Jenkins and Denis Healey on Cabinet government.[9] He taught me a lesson, for example, when I read his speech to the Royal Society of St George on St George's Eve in April 1964. Using the historical threads that bound him, he possibly revealed more of himself that evening than on any other public occasion[10] when his distillation of historical imagination took him back to the late Middle Ages:

> Backward travels our gaze, beyond the grenadiers and the philosophers of the eighteenth century, beyond the pikemen and the preachers of the seventeenth, back through the brash, adventurous days of the Tudors, and there at last we find them … in many a village church, beneath the tall tracery of a perpendicular East window and the coffered ceiling of the chantry chapel. From brass and stone, from line and effigy, their eyes

look out at us, and we gaze into them, as if we would win some answer from their inscrutable silence.

Tell us what it is that binds us together; show us the clue that leads through a thousand years; whisper to us the secret of this charmed life of England, that we in our time may know how to hold it fast.[11]

Imagine these thoughts, those images, intoned in that extraordinary West Midlands accent rising up, sentence by sentence, as if its deliverer were a kind of classically educated air-raid siren.

In contrast, the distillation of my frenzy is deeply prosaic and covers but a tiny patch of our past in terms of its concentration – Britain post-Victory in Europe. It spans the generation that stood firm during the Second World War, finally prevailed with its allies then bred me and my generation. Mine is not a thing of effigy and line, of 800-year-old village churches (much as I, too, love them). Mine is an early welfare state Britain, an age of relative political consensus, possessing a strong sense of a stoical, admirable recently shared past of great and sustained collective effort. Buckled to this was a postwar austerity, an absence of conspicuous consumption, out of which would come a juster, healthier, better-educated and more socially harmonious country when easier times returned. That was the aspiration. That is still my sustaining myth – my gold standard – which I profoundly hope will not prove to be the high-water mark of institutionalised decency in British history (though I strongly fear it might).

There are, no doubt, a whole sheaf of my sustaining myths running through the pages that follow. I am especially prone to them in those passages of personal history where, as Seamus Heaney put it, 'hope and history rhyme.'[12] For example, when talking to Steve Kelly, a fellow member of my postwar generation, about his forthcoming study of Britain in the 1950s I found myself saying that in the early to middle part of that decade – in the afterglow of the 1953 Coronation, the successful ascent of Everest by a British and Commonwealth team, the UK crafting the first commercial jetliner (the Comet), pioneering civil nuclear power, mixing quite naturally, it seemed, the deeply ancient and the highly modern – the feeling was 'that one really did belong to a success-story nation.'[13]

It *did* feel good. And the rockier patches in Britain's fortunes since that boyhood formation have very definitely not felt good. And, as during the summer riots of 2011, they still don't. I am not, as Anthony Trollope described his fictional Whig-Liberal Prime Minister, Plantagenet Palliser, the Duke of Omnium, one of those for whom 'patriotism ... was a fever.'[14] But I have always taken it badly when things run wrong for our country, especially when an element of own-goal scoring is involved.

In fact, writing the history of one's own times is a thing of 'paradox', as Julian Barnes caught it, with a Disraelian touch, in his Booker Prize-winning *The Sense of an Ending* in 2011:

> The history that happens underneath our noses ought to be the clearest, and yet it's the most deliquescent. We live in time, it bounds us and defines us and time is supposed to measure history isn't it? But if we can't understand time, can't grasp its mysteries of pace and progress, what chance do we have with history – even our own small, personal, largely undocumented piece of it?[15]

Yet the pitfalls of writing the history of one's own country within very largely the compass of one's own memory and experience of it are trumped by the perpetual fascination of its curiosity-filled pursuit undertaken, one can only hope, in the spirit of Spinoza, who declared in 1677 that 'I have striven not to laugh at human actions, not to weep at them, nor to hate them, but to understand them.'[16] For even if you have lived through the years you are describing there has to be an element of what Sir Keith Thomas called 'retrospective ethnography of ... approaching the past in a way an anthropologist might approach some exotic society' in his marvellous reconstruction of early modern England, *The Ends of Life*.[17]

The opportunity to 'backward travel my gaze' I owe to the Trustees of the annual Wiles Lectures at Queen's University, Belfast who invited me to take to the podium in May 2012. I am very grateful to Professor Peter

Gray, Head of the School of History and Anthropology at Queen's, for making the arrangements run so smoothly and for the pleasure of working with him. The invitation was especially welcome because I have always relished giving seminars at Queen's, having benefited from forty years of friendship and wisdom generously given by Professor Keith Jeffery (we jointly authored our first book, *States of Emergency*, thirty years ago[18]). And I enjoy immensely the companionship of sitting on the crossbenches of the House of Lords with Professor Lord Bew.

The pleasure of accepting the Trustees' invitation was made more exquisite still as it enabled me to cast that backward gaze over those aspects of writing the history of one's own country in one's own times that have intrigued me most. The range of topics within these pages reflects the two historical streams that have carried me along in a cataract of boredom-avoidance, first as a journalist and later as a university teacher: the wider themes of Britain's place in the world plus the defence, diplomatic and intelligence efforts that go with it; the mechanics of the state and parliamentary activities that keep us, we hope, a clean and decent and relatively efficient political society as we do so; the utility of history to government and governed alike; and the need to help create what Walter Bagehot called 'the instructed imagination'[19] vital to those in authority who seek to rise above the commonplace.

I am grateful for lecture and seminar invitations that have enabled me to mount dry runs for a number of chapters inside these covers in addition to the immense stimulus provided by the Wiles Trustees: to the Gresham Society for their invitation to deliver the 2011 Peter Nailor Lecture (chapter 3); to Lady Quinlan, the former Lord Speaker, Baroness Hayman, the Mile End Group and the Trustees of the Michael Quinlan Lecture plus Lord Guthrie of Craigiebank and the Liddell Hart Trustees to deliver the 2011 Sir Michael Quinlan and Sir Basil Liddell Hart lectures respectively (chapter 4); to Baroness Garden of Frognal and the Royal Institute of International Affairs (Chatham House) for the invitation to deliver the Sir Timothy Garden 2011 Lecture (chapter 5); to Professor Christopher Andrew and Dr Peter Martland and the Cambridge Intelligence History

Seminar and to Professor Len Scott of the Department of International Politics at the University of Aberystwyth (chapter 6); to Charles Dormer and the King's School, Grantham for the invitation to deliver the 2011 Burghley Lecture (chapter 7); to the Marquess of Salisbury and the University of Hertfordshire for the invitation to deliver the Chancellor's Lecture 2012 (chapter 8); and to Vice Admiral Charles Style and the Royal College of Defence Studies for the invitation to deliver the 2011 Churchill Lecture (chapter 10).

I am immensely grateful to Sean Magee of Biteback Publishing, who has now published me in three imprints and brings his very special version of fun and enjoyment to the collaboration. I must thank the late John Ramsden, to whose memory *Distilling the Frenzy* is dedicated. John was the truest of friends. I don't think he entirely approved of my injecting the personal into every possible paragraph of my writing. But he tolerated it and could be very funny about it. I miss him greatly.

My gratitude also goes to Matt Lyus, without whose word-processing gifts no book of mine would appear; old friends at the National Archives in Kew; and new friends in the House of Lords Library at Westminster.

PETER HENNESSY,
Walthamstow, Mile End and Westminster,
April 2012

1

THE HUMAN FOOTNOTE:
HISTORY AND AUTOBIOGRAPHY

This is the material of history, naked and unformed.
MICHEL DE MONTAIGNE, 1580[1]

SITTING in his tower in the Dordogne in south-west France crafting his essay 'Of Books', Montaigne was writing about the power of rumour in the shaping of history. 'Each man', he declared, 'can make his profit of it according to his understanding.'[2] I have a natural appetite for rumour's twin – gossip – as will become evident on several pages to come. But Montaigne's line about 'the material of history, naked and unformed' is a fine description of all of us, not just professorial historians, the moment we spring from the womb. We live our own history even if most of us never write or otherwise record it. We are all human footnotes to our own times.

It is, I suspect, a fascinating exercise for anyone to find the morning paper which captures the previous day of their birth. Reading *The Times* for Saturday 29 March 1947 I am struck by how many of the themes it contains which will shape this book. Several of my particular frenzies were already there waiting to be distilled when I drew my first breath in the North Middlesex Hospital alongside the North Circular Road in Edmonton, Middlesex.

The lead story in the paper reported that the Foreign Ministers of the great powers were seriously falling out in Moscow about the future of Germany with the British Foreign Secretary, Ernie Bevin, taking on Vyacheslav Mikhailovich Molotov, Stalin's grim, stony-faced Foreign Minister who turned being negative into an art form, as the chilling atmosphere frosted into a forty-year Cold War ('Foreign Ministers Far from Accord'); the western powers were attempting to bail out Greece in the midst of its civil war ('American Appeal to U.N.: Support for Aid to Greece') as the cash-strapped British government handed over the lead external role in that country to the United States; the UK's overextended imperial and global role produced a rash of stories from Palestine ('Pipe-Lines Damaged at Haifa: Terrorists' Attack with Bombs'), Egypt ('Bomb in Cairo'), Hong Kong ('Chinese Threat to Aircraft: Defence of Sovereignty'). There were some lighter imperial touches with King George VI and his family touring South Africa on the White Train ('Royal Party on Fruit Farm: Labourers' Greeting. From Our Special Correspondent ROYAL PILOT TRAIN, March 28').[3]

Now the Cold War and the British Empire (a few, scattered residuals apart) are gone, though the overextension of Britain's global commitments is not. But it is the economic news of Saturday 29 March 1947, the subject of the paper's first leader, that offers (that day's Boat Race and Grand National apart) perhaps the most enduring of our national frenzies – our shaky economic position.

On my birthday, the Attlee government had announced the appointment of a businessman, who had served in Whitehall during the war, Sir Edwin Plowden, to the new job of Chief Planning Officer and head of the Central Economic Planning Staff.[4] *The Times* was deeply sceptical about the progress to date of Labour's big idea of the day (justifiably, as it turned out), declaring:

> Believing almost passionately in the virtue of planning they have so far failed to plan effectively. They have succeeded neither in realizing the symmetrical efficiency of their own theoretical propositions, nor in

applying to peace-time requirements the practical lessons of civilian and service planning during the war.

Under the headline 'Mr Attlee's Opportunity', however, *The Times*' leader-writer allowed himself a burst of near-evangelical optimism about the possibility of eventual economic and productive well-being for the war-ravaged British economy if the Plowden appointment signified the getting of a grip:

> If Mr ATTLEE and his chief colleagues have both the will and the capacity to seize the chance offered to them, they can transform the quality of government almost over-night. Their opportunity is nothing less than the salvation of Britain: it is in direct proportion to the magnitude of the difficulties with which they are confronted.

By *Times* standards, this was almost millenarian. (I say this as someone who was to write *Times* leaders in the early 1980s.)

Friday 28 March 1947 did represent a new birth – mine. Sadly, the same could not be said for the British economy. We still await salvation-level transformation and successive sets of ministers, from Attlee, Bevin, Stafford Cripps and Herbert Morrison onwards, have been denied the hosannahs of a grateful nation for setting us on an enduring and sustainable trajectory of economic growth and competitiveness.

I was born into a medium-sized Catholic family in north London though both my Mum's and my Dad's roots were in the north-west of England, Thornton-Cleveleys (near Blackpool) and Liverpool respectively. I had the great boon of being the youngest of four with three elder sisters to help bring me up, a factor to which my wife has always attributed what she regards as my overconfidence (I think she is probably right). The home was blessed with plentiful affection but not lubricated by a regular or adequate flow of money. Dad was an intelligent man, but he lacked application, and was not, I suspect, the easiest of employees. As a result, he did not reach the professional level to which his gifts might have lifted him. We relied a good deal on Mum going out to work as typist, sometimes on the evening shift at the newly nationalised British Road Services depot in Muswell Hill which laid on, I recall, rather good Christmas parties.

We also depended on the welfare state, which Dad, as a high Tory, affected to disdain as he did pretty well everything a Labour government introduced (though the wartime coalition and the Attlee administration which followed were post the Beveridge Report,[5] responsible for first putting in train the reforms on whose benefits and services we relied as a family). As a result, I've always sustained a tendresse for those 1940s welfare statutes and for the politicians across the parties who enacted them. I remember hearing Barbara Castle recalling Nye Bevan saying to her of the welfare state in the late 1940s: 'Barbara, if you want to know what all this is for, look in the perambulators.' Rob Shepherd and I were filming her for our 1994 Channel 4 television series, *What Has Become of Us?* That's me, I thought. And it was. And I increasingly became aware that we were the best-provided-for generation in the history of our country (of which more in the conclusion to this book).

The state was quite a shaper of mine, and most people's, postwar childhoods. So, in my case, was the church, as it still is (I lapsed from the Catholic Church from between the ages of seventeen and fifty-four; but never ceased to believe). My mother ran the Brownie pack associated with St Mary Magdalene in Whetstone. The parish priest, Fr Gerry Ryan, was a great family friend. He would slip me a few bob at jumble sales in the scout hut to buy a parking lot's worth of second-hand Dinky toys. The Cubs he would take to London for the annual Tyburn Martyrs Walk. As we marched we would stamp on the stretches of black rubber in the road which, in those days when the traffic passed over them, would cause the lights to change, causing a pleasingly rapid pyrotechnic effect of red, green and amber. This was followed by a service in Westminster Cathedral and refuelling in a Lyons Corner House before we caught the Northern line home to Finchley Central and points north to High Barnet.

There is a frustrated sailor in me which might flow from Cub pack trips down the reeking Thames, oil smeared and jetsam littered, from

Westminster Pier to Greenwich through a Port of London groaning with freighters at their moorings. More likely it comes from Fr Ryan taking us to Navy Days in Portsmouth. HMS *Victory*, naturally, but also, in 1954, the last of the Royal Navy's battleships, HMS *Vanguard*, huge and fascinating. Fifty five years later, there in the Ward Room of the Trident submarine HMS *Vanguard* (I was on board with friend and producer Richard Knight for the making of *The Human Button* documentary for BBC Radio 4[6]) was a photo of the very *Vanguard* on whose deck I had trodden as a seven-year-old. When I mentioned this, the younger officers gave me a look as if I'd come from a deep and distant past somewhere between their deterrent patrols and the Battle of Jutland (which, in a way, I suppose I had).

Perhaps most subliminally of all, our journeys to tea with Fr Ryan's family in Fareham took us on the ferry from Portsmouth to Gosport and past HMS *Dolphin* crowded with its squadrons of submarines, several of them, no doubt, veterans of World War II. How I wish I'd looked more closely and freeze-framed the scene in the pictorial section of my hippocampus more effectively than I have.

Church was not just a significant element in mine and the family's social life (my older sisters were Brownies, then Girl Guides, then members of Catholic youth clubs). I believed, too. The lot. Looking back, there was no room for caveats in the pre-Vatican II Roman Catholic Church. When we sang 'Faith of Our Fathers' at Benediction, I really meant it. Until puberty, I fancied becoming a monk. And, as much as I have come in later life to admire the sixth-century Rule of St Benedict as a guide to the use of time[7] (very patchily applied in my case), I would not have thrived in the cloister. My appetite for gossip alone would have represented, as we Catholics used to say, a constant 'occasion of sin'.

As to the autobiographical antecedents of other ingredients in the book, I have to confess that although memory stretches back to 1950, it is largely confined to my pram when outdoors and our flat in Granville Place in Finchley alongside what further up its path mutated into the Great North Road. It did not, to my great regret, embrace my one political hero, Clement Attlee, then the occupant of No. 10. I certainly absorbed the

Churchillian presence during his last premiership as I did, in vivid terms, the Coronation of 1953. I can recall the blue posters in Finchley during the 1955 general election for Sir John Crowder (Mrs Thatcher's predecessor as MP) and Sir Anthony Eden, then in the brief spring of his short and tragic premiership. But the first Prime Minister I watched carefully was Harold Macmillan (of whom more later). Indeed, my record as a political forecaster peaked in January 1957 when I was certain Mr Macmillan would emerge (which is what Leaders of the Conservative Party did until 1965) as Eden's successor rather than Rab Butler, largely, I suspect, because our household newspaper, the *Daily Express*, encouraged me to think that way.

The Bomb, and the question of Britain as a nuclear weapons power, was very live in the UK into which I was born but only on the country's innermost and heavily secrecy-protected circuits in Whitehall. A few weeks before I drew breath, on 8 January 1947, Attlee and a super-secret Cabinet committee, GEN 163, had authorised the manufacture of an atomic bomb.[8] Not until May 1948, in a carefully worded answer to a planted parliamentary question in the House of Commons, did his Minister of Defence, A.V. Alexander, announce that research into atomic weapons was under way[9] with the press (Chapman Pincher on the front page of the *Daily Express* apart[10]) scarcely giving it a glance.[11]

The first British atomic test took place off the north-west coast of Australia on 3 October 1952. But my proper recall only begins with Chapman Pincher's coverage of the vastly more powerful H-bomb tests, American and Russian, in the early 1950s with the photos of huge mushroom clouds that accompanied them. Harry Pincher, who became a friend of mine thirty years later, was enormously well connected in Whitehall's Civil Service, military and scientific circles. Rather to my surprise in 2011 in his dramatically titled *Treachery: Betrayals, Blunders and Cover-Ups*, published at the age of ninety-four, Harry, in a special section on 'sources', names his helpers.[12]

You did not need a degree in physics to understand the immense surge in destructive power those mushroom clouds over Hiroshima and Nagasaki signified. Though it was not until the Lower Sixth at my

Gloucestershire grammar school in Stroud did I first read of the US–UK–Canadian Manhattan Project, which led to those bombs (I simply can't remember which book it was; but the nuclear question has fascinated me from that day to this).

The Bomb, its possession, its sustenance and, each generation or so, its upgrading is very much part of the wider debate about Britain's attempts to retain a place in the world out of proportion to its geographical, demographic and economic size – its continuing aversion to slipping into the mediocrity of being a medium-sized power tucked inside a huge regional organisation called the European Union (about which it has harboured doubts from its very limited, early 1950s initial incarnation the European Coal and Steel Community – a national neuralgia that has persisted throughout my lifetime and which, I'm sure, will see me out).

The place-in-the-world question has gripped me since the Suez autumn of 1956. Apart from other factors, I have read the newspapers every morning since then. Being a devotee of the cinema as a boy (the Odeon, Temple Fortune in north London, seemed perpetually to vibrate to the sound of the Rolls-Royce Merlin engine housed in Spitfires, Hurricanes or Lancasters), I had acquired the conviction that we Brits did not lose wars. It was not difficult, therefore, to glean from *Radio Newsreel* on the BBC's Light Programme each evening or the *Daily Express* every morning that something was not quite right with our attempt to get back the canal from Colonel Nasser. One of the least cheering patches of my pursuit of the papers disgorged by the 30-Year Rule at the National Archives in Kew was working through the Suez files. And the tragic demise of Sir Anthony Eden, so gallant an anti-appeaser in the late 1930s, was, to my mind, made triply so when I realised that in his last appearance in the House of Commons on 20 December 1956, he had simply lied when Denis Healey pressed him about Anglo-French-Israeli collusion ahead of the invasion of Egypt a few weeks earlier. 'There were no plans got together [with Israel] to attack Egypt,' Eden said.[13]

Parliament did not impinge upon my imagination as much as it should have when I was a boy. To be sure, the newspapers reported the House of Commons with a length and a regularity that is now gone. But my generation grew up without the benefit of hearing Parliament at work (radio was allowed in on 3 April 1978) let alone seeing MPs or peers on their feet (the cameras first turned on 21 November 1989). Great parliamentary occasions would be reported on radio and television by oral sketch-writers, some of whom (the BBC's Christopher Jones in particular) took it to an art form.

Not until as late as 1964 did Parliament as a functioning institution begin to bite into my curiosity. Bernard Crick's classic *The Reform of Parliament*[14] was first published that year and it did the rounds a bit in the Lower Sixth at Marling School. On 31 July 1964, the very last day of the 1959 parliament, my friend Bob Gardiner and I were given a day off school so that we could travel up to London and sit in the Strangers' Gallery at the House of Commons.

We thought it was to be Sir Winston Churchill's last day in Parliament but, in fact, that had already taken place four days earlier.[15] I was struck by the smallness and intimacy of the chamber; its physical atmosphere, the vacuousness of the last-day behaviour down below. We ate in the café where the policemen dined too. I can remember peeing into an adjacent pedestal to Manny Shinwell (a particular hate of my father's – though this may be conflating a later experience when Bob and I visited Parliament in the early days of the first Wilson government). We travelled back to Stroud on a very late train from Paddington. I half remember thinking about a political life that day; but the path which eventually took me to the other chamber was, naturally, quite unforeseeable that summer night as Bob Gardiner and I talked about Harold Wilson's prospects in the coming general election. Bob was staunch Labour. He was a contemporary of mine too at Cambridge and became first a schoolteacher and then a Baptist minister. I wasn't a Labour man. In fact, I stood for the Conservatives in Marling School's mock election the following October and won.

A proper immersion in Parliament had to wait until a brief spell in 1976 as the *Financial Times*' Lobby Correspondent (I didn't take to the lobby system of mass briefing and soon reverted to a more solitary operation on the Whitehall beat). After their creation in 1979, I took a continued interest in the government department-shadowing House of Commons select committees, which Bernard Crick's 1964 volume had recommended and foreseen.[16] The House of Lords I knew held high-quality debates and ran some very thoughtful select committees. But, for obvious reasons, I now wish I had followed its work more consistently and closely. Since becoming an independent crossbench peer in November 2010, I've found it the most agreeable form of adult education I've ever encountered as well as an exquisite provider of weapons-grade gossip on an almost daily basis.

There has been another, enduring stimulus for my interest in the governing and legislating institutions, the tribes that people them and the processes they deploy – Anthony Sampson and his early anatomies of Britain. Anthony brimmed with curiosity until the very end of his days (he died in December 2004). As I came to know him as well as his books (I received the second in the line, *Anatomy of Britain Today*,[17] as a sixth-form prize in 1965) it dawned on me that Anthony's secret as a super-successful operator behinds the lines was a special Sampsonian equation:

Curiosity + courtesy = confidences.[18]

As his fellow *Observer* journalist Neal Ascherson said at his memorial service in St Martin-in-the-Fields: 'I never knew such an artist at questioning. Anthony was the most skilful, relentless listener in the world.'[19] I have never matched Anthony at that. Never will – I'm too loquacious. But I'll try harder in future. It's a gold standard to which every scholar of his or her own time should aspire; part of the contemporary historian's craft.

2

STAYING BEHIND, CATCHING UP AND LOOKING FORWARD:
THE CONTEMPORARY HISTORIAN'S CRAFT

Never underestimate the vital importance of finding early in life the work that for you is play.
PAUL SAMUELSON, UNDATED.[1]

PAUL Samuelson shaped the minds of countless young economics students across the globe with his best-selling textbooks. He also promulgated an employment law which has certainly applied to me. I only wish it had gilded the employment prospects of millions more individuals than it has in finding work which was also play. This I managed to do as a journalist and Whitehall-watcher for twenty years and as a full-time academic at Queen Mary, University of London, for another nineteen. And certainly the House of Lords, for me, has been a House of pleasure and fascination since I first slipped onto the red benches in late 2010.

The economist with whom this volume begins, the incomparable Maynard Keynes, singled out two particular branches of learning in that quotation from which the title of this book is drawn. The 'ideas of economists and political philosophers', the great polymath of King's College, Cambridge, declared, both when they are right and when they are wrong, are more powerful than is commonly understood. Indeed the world is ruled by little else. Practical men, who believe themselves to be quite exempt from any intellectual influences, are usually the slaves of some defunct economist. Madmen in authority, who hear voices in the air, are distilling their frenzy from some academic scribbler of a few years back.[2]

I like to think that if Keynes were writing today he might have brigaded historians with his economists and political philosophers. For several members of our recent political class like to talk, in their toe-curling, post-modern fashion, about the need to create a convincing 'narrative' with which to beguile and manipulate the electorate. Parties compete not just for votes but for *their* interpretation of the recent past as if the blessing of history could bring a kind of benediction to what Victor Rothschild once vividly depicted as 'the promises and panaceas that gleam like false teeth in the party manifestoes'.[3]

Contemporary history well researched and written for what the American political scientist Gabriel Almond called the 'attentive public'[4] should be the antidote to the virus of crude, political capture. Though we contemporaries have our own *déformations professionelles*, too, unless we are very careful. For example, there always lurks the danger of an agreed view amongst a few authors, a kind of informal, authorised version. This sits alongside another scholarly vice – that of current retrospection, which can lead to what Edward Thompson famously described as the 'enormous condescension of posterity'.[5]

Before digging further into the caveats and the concerns, how do I see those of us who make our living by taking our students and our readers back into the more recent layers of compost that made them and their country what they are? We are, I think, a scholarly equivalent of those 'stay behind' groups the British Secret Intelligence Service and the American CIA had ready lest the Red Army really did move westward and, without the mutual annihilation of a nuclear war, succeed in occupying parts of western Europe with Warsaw Pact and Soviet forces.[6] Paul Addison caught this stay-behind impulse in his fine work of postwar British social history, *No Turning Back*, when he lingered on the significance of placing a photograph amidst its pages of himself as a fourteen-year-old member of Lower Five Modern at King Edward VI school in Lichfield in May 1957. Paul asked:

> Would I, if I could, put the clock back to Britain as it was in 1957? Hardly: the gains we have made since then outweigh the losses. I have to admit, however, that the passage of time has left me with a sense of disorientation I can never quite suppress. At some barely conscious level of my imagination the England of which I was a part in the late 1950s is forever the norm, and almost everything that has happened since a puzzling deviation.

'Much as I like to think of myself as fully adult,' Paul went on, 'I know that somewhere at the back of my mind lurks a schoolboy forever putting up his hand to ask why smoking is banned in the cinema, or why passengers on the railway are referred to as "customers", or why so many couples live together without getting married.'[7]

I know exactly how Paul feels. The difference between us is no more than four or five years, 200 or so miles and the names of our grammar schools. For Addison read King Edward VI, Lichfield, 1957. For Hennessy read Marling School, Stroud, 1961. I suspect we contemporary historians all have an equivalent and it's a useful spot from which to peer back and forward, to sniff the air (still plenty of coal smoke despite the Clean Air Act 1956) and gaze upon the cars, the steam locomotives, the clothing (on wet days we all draped ourselves in grey pacamacs; even the Queen[8]). Harold Macmillan as Prime Minister, the first I read about every day and whose ripe and decidedly overdone style I came to admire, is as vivid for me today as David Cameron (more so, to be honest). It was still a time to look up if you heard a jet engine in the sky or to peer with intense curiosity as the A-road your Dad's Austin A35 was well, hardly zipping, along crossed one of the rare, new patches of motorway. It was an era when Cliff Richard, mercifully, was soon to be superseded by the Beatles, of whom we had yet to hear a chord or a whisper.

So, natural stay-behinders we are. We are also avid catcher-uppers – purveyors of catch-up, now-it-can-be-told history especially, in my case, once immensely secret files are declassified at the National Archives in Kew. Indeed, I like to think the twin phenomena of stay-behind and catch-up are the tests of whether our books work for readers of our own age, give or take a decade or two either way (people with whom we share what Melvyn Bragg calls 'generational kinship'[9]). In the space of a chapter you want them to say: 'Ah! That's just how I remember it', and, 'Well, that I *never* knew! How did they manage to keep it a secret for so long?'

Stay-behind and catch-up are a great help in preventing the past being displayed, in the words of the philosopher Anthony Kenny, as 'present contemporary prejudices in fancy dress'.[10] The job of the historian is to put back into the past the same uncertainty we feel today about the future – an indispensable requirement.[11] Closely related to that criterion is another Tony Kennyism which he uses as a justification for studying the history of philosophy in his great survey, *A New History of Western Philosophy*. We may, he writes, 'wish to understand the people and societies of the past, and read their philosophy to grasp the conceptual climate in which they thought and acted'.[12]

We historians, too, have to go back and immerse ourselves into that same 'conceptual climate', to reconstruct what people – leaders and led alike – knew up to that point, the memories and experiences that shaped their fears, expectations and mentalities. And to avoid discounting, or, worse, still, as Spinoza warned, deriding the belief systems that moved them (this is particularly true of religious faiths in an age where sympathy for such convictions is not universally spread across the scholarly trades).

As well as the concepts and the beliefs that made the climate of consciousness, we need to stretch the meteorological metaphor still further, to apply the best biographical techniques to those individuals who, in Churchill's famous description of Joe Chamberlain, made the political weather.[13] And not just the highly visible politico-weather-makers either. We must reach into the lives of the usually invisible scene-shifters – not least the scientists and technologists who shaped what we do, with what and how in the material manifestations of our lives.

Many of these requirements we contemporaries share with our brother and sister historians who go back further than we do deep into the past where oral archives cannot be compiled by interviewing survivors and veterans or even photos and recordings found to help us recall what they looked and sounded like. For some colleagues, the removal vans full of historical tools have a long, long journey to get them back to the centuries where the pull of fascination is greatest for them. For me it had to be the era in which there *were* roads and removal vans for real. Why? Because of the special curiosity of shared, lived moments, events, transformations, air breathed, noises heard; the powerful desire to make sense of your own time and to place configurations upon it while avoiding excessive patterning, mono-causal explanations or the condescending and patronising urge to tell the veterans how they should have felt if only they had thought about it harder. Nothing, I suspect, irritates a survivor more than to be told their proud memories of the Blitz or the largely stoically shared privations of the World War II home front are to some degree mythical.

Enough of the health warnings. May I now turn to the reasons for plying the contemporary branch of the historians' trade? For the *soi-disant* practical in authority, the justification for investing in more than a dash of historical reading has never been better argued than in Richard Neustadt and Ernest May's *Thinking in Time*, which grew out of their celebrated course for policy-makers at Harvard's Kennedy School of Government and was published in 1986.[14] Above all, they wanted their clients, and those to whose service they would return once the course was over, to practice their decision-taking while 'seeing time as a stream'[15] in whose flow they were caught whether they wished to be or not.

In presenting their flow theory, Neustadt and May were firmly in the tradition of the great, if terrifying, unifier of Germany, Otto von Bismarck, the most accomplished shaper of European events of his generation,[16] who famously declared: 'The river of history flows as it will, and if I put my hand in it, this is because I regard it as my duty, not because I think I can change its course.'[17] Bismarck, as Henry Kissinger noted when reviewing Jonathan Steinberg's fine recent life of the Iron Count, treated politics '[like a physicist, [he] analysed the principal elements of each situation and then used them in an overall design.'[18]

Neustadt and May promulgated their own version of disaggregation in a way that I find convincing. For them, thinking in time has three components. One is recognition that the future has no place to come from but the past, hence the past has predictive value. Another element is recognition that what matters for the future in the present is departures from the past, alterations, changes, which prospectively or actually divert familiar flows from accustomed channels, thus affecting that predictive value and much else besides. A third component is continuous comparison, an almost constant oscillation from present to future to past and back, heedful of prospective change, concerned to expedite, limit, guide, counter or accept it as the fruits of such comparison suggest.[19]

For some would-be movers of the world, such thinking comes naturally – the product of well-stocked minds and a natural gift for historical allusion and comparison. Kissinger himself would be an American example; Harold Macmillan a British (more on Macmillan in chapter 7). Both were prone to grand designs. Both were not short of critics. And, like Bismarck himself, such thinkers-in-time are always open to the retort 'and a fat lot of good it did them'.

If a politician in power, however, found the Neustadt–May thesis persuasive, what could they do about it? This came up during a session at the Royal College of Defence Studies in London in April 2011 addressed by the former Cabinet Secretary to three Prime Ministers (Thatcher, Major and Blair), Lord Butler of Brockwell. His theme that evening was 'What's wrong with government?' and I was his discussant. During the discussion, the senior military asked about the degree to which ministers possessed a sense of historical context. Robin Butler, who had led the inquiry into intelligence and Iraqi weapons of mass destruction in 2003–4,[20] replied: 'The people who took the Iraq decisions were ignorant of history and did not even want to be told about it.' 'Every department should have a historical adviser,' he continued, adding that even if such an adviser was not expert in every aspect of a department's range they would know who was and to whom to turn.[21]

History, I am convinced, has a high and continuous utility for policy-makers both ministerial and official; though it can never be more than a necessary, but not a sufficient, condition of seriously increasing the chance of better outcomes (more on this in chapter 7). And I would argue that the latent capacity of history to guide becomes the greater in the contemporary period, especially as a scene-setter and a context-provider. This I shall attempt to illustrate in the coming chapter with the very British example I mentioned earlier – the running postwar theme of Britain's place in the world.

3

AN INSTINCT TO INTERVENE:
BRITAIN'S PLACE IN THE WORLD

The British and the French are the only countries in the European Union with
the instinct to intervene … We are always looking for different playing fields.
LORD HURD OF WESTWELL, 16 JUNE 2011.[1]

AT the gathering in the Travellers' Club in Pall Mall during which
Douglas Hurd, who served a long tenure as Foreign Secretary under
Margaret Thatcher and John Major 1989–95, made that observation,
he also noted that 'at international meetings people are not bored by
what the British have to say. They are interested.'[2] A few weeks earlier,
I had heard a highly distinguished former US Secretary of State say he
emphatically did not want the UK to cease being a nuclear weapons
power in the near future as the United States would always wish Britain
'to be part of the conversation' when the world discussed disarmament
and without a weapon the UK would not be there.[3]

Three months later, on 8 September 2011, the Foreign and
Commonwealth Secretary, William Hague, summoned a mixture
of parliamentarians, journalists, scholars and old diplomatic hands
to the huge and exquisite Grand Locarno Room in the Foreign and
Commonwealth Office for what the invitation described as 'a major
address on the role of the Foreign Office'.

The line which set the tone for his whole speech was that 'the nation that is purely reactive in foreign policy is in decline.'[4] There it was, undiluted and caveat free, the special impulse, the authentic voice of a country quite unprepared for mediocrity in the shape of foreign policy quiescence.

Mr Hague's predecessors, Lord Curzon, Austen Chamberlain, Ernest Bevin, Anthony Eden, the great ghosts whose shades one can still sense in that still dazzling palazzo of a building designed by Sir Gilbert Scott and opened by Benjamin Disraeli in 1868,[5] would all have approved his words. Indeed, they would have thought he could think and speak no other.

As for Mr Hague's boss, David Cameron, the words *he* used a few weeks later at the Conservative Party conference in Manchester would have left the ancestors glowing with posthumous pride. 'Britain', the Prime Minister declared, 'never had the biggest population, the largest land mass, the richest resources, but we had the spirit ... Let's turn this time of challenge into a time of opportunity. Not sitting around, watching things happen and wondering why. But standing up, making things happen and asking why not.'[6]

Aspirational disarmament generally has never been a simple business for Britain during its long slippage from pre-1914 superpowerdom, and, on present trends, it is unlikely to become so. The 'instinct to intervene' is a particularly difficult and important frenzy for contemporary historians to distil. This was very evident during that spring 2011 evening on strategy at the Royal College of Defence Studies, which, naturally given where we were and who we were with, had a particular interest in Britain's place in the world, its continuing desire to cut a dash in international affairs and the mismatch between that impulse and the stretched resources available to sustain it. Libya was vivid in our minds. As was Afghanistan. The previous autumn's Strategic Defence and Security Review – and Iraq, as we have seen, still hung heavy over the room.

One senior participant, Vice Admiral Charles Style, the RCDs's Commandant, observed he had been in the naval service for thirty-seven years and for all of them – apart from a short, post-Falklands boost – he and his colleagues had been managing decline: 'In the end, it begins to screw up your mind,' he said.[7] Another participant wondered if, in these days of freedom of information, a truly no-holds-barred review exercise could summon up the required levels of realism and candour.

I recalled the absurd line (given the defence cuts in the Strategic Defence and Security Review that accompanied it[8]) in the October 2010 National Security Strategy, *A Strong Britain in an Age of Uncertainty*, which declared in its 'Introduction':

> The National Security Council has reached a clear conclusion that Britain's national interest requires us to reject any notion of the shrinkage of our influence.[9]

Another participant suggested the impulse to react, as David Cameron has done as Prime Minister, when Benghazi was about to fall to Gaddafi's forces, was 'hard wired' into him and, perhaps, the country he led.

Thinking about it the following weekend it reminded me of comparable appetites a century ago captured in the words of Lord Rosebery, Liberal Prime Minister 1894–95, distinguishing in 1899 between what he called 'sane Imperialism, as distinguished from what I [Rosebery] might call wild-cat Imperialism'[10] (though I think he went a bit far the following year in his rectoral address at Glasgow University when he said of the British Empire: 'No one outside an asylum wishes to be rid of it.'[11]) Replace in the 1899 quote the word 'Imperialism' with the words 'liberal and humanitarian intervention' and you find, I think, the comparator and the impulse behind that hubristic and self-delusory sentence in the 2010 National Security Strategy, itself a classic example of what a friend of mine, a former officer of the Secret Intelligence Service, called 'the itch after the amputation'.[12]

I'm sure there is much in that, but, in some of its aspects it's almost a divine and a laudable discontent. Why? Because one can define patriotism (as I do in my own case, for example) as a desire for one's country to be greater than the sum of its parts. And this wish applies to a wide range of the activities contained within our islands including punching in the world's scholarly and intellectual markets heavier than the weight of our accumulated little grey cells. This variety of patriotism, in my judgement, is also part of the impulse to provide a strategy for the UK which increases the chances of that where diplomacy, intelligence, defence policy and procurement, trade, aid and the instruments of soft power such as the BBC World Service and the British Council mingle and fuse. For these reasons, I am a supporter of the practice of publishing regular national security strategies and defence and security reviews.

Furthermore, one must not be too unkind about the current set of ministers dealing with Britain's place in the world. It is hard for a country that was a great power for such a time as ours to alter a nervous system long in the making. As Charles de Gaulle wrote a few years before he became the first President of the French Fifth Republic in the late 1950s: 'France is not really herself unless she is in the front rank.'[13] A British version of this kind of Gaullism plays powerfully still in the UK. The appetite for being a territorial, imperial power has long abated. But when it comes to being a great power (or a 'pocket superpower', as that shrewd observer of us Brits, Stryker McGwire, formerly of *Newsweek*, liked to put it[14]), the fires are not entirely banked.

Nor should they be. For as Sir Jeremy Greenstock, former Ambassador to the United Nations and later Director of the Ditchley Foundation, put it in a lecture to the Order of St Michael and St George (the diplomatic and intelligence section of the honours system) in June 2011: 'It is probably inevitable that we shall continue to lose relative power as others grow. But there is still a lot to play for.'[15] So there is especially if we take the non-heroic, unflashy approach to diplomatic influence as prescribed by that arch-realist in the Foreign Office and No. 10 the great Marquess of Salisbury in the late nineteenth century in terms of 'a series of microscopic advantages; a judicious suggestion here, an opportune moment and a foresighted persistence at another...'[16]

That said, the Strategic Defence and Security Review of October 2010 was, in my view, the least satisfactory of the eleven defence reviews that have now been conducted since the end of the Second World War. Briefly, its ten predecessors were:

1. The Harwood Review, 1949 (Labour). This was neither announced nor published; it emerged in 1980 at the National Archives under the Thirty-Year Rule. It was an attempt to keep the defence estimates at an average of £700 million a year over the three years 1950–52. It was swiftly swept away by the Korean War-inspired rearmament.[17]

2. The Chiefs of Staff Report on Defence Policy and Global Strategy, 1952 (Conservative). The chiefs stressed the overwhelming primacy of the Cold War threat ('The Free World is menaced everywhere by the implacable and unlimited aims of Soviet Russia'). It foresaw 'a prolonged period of Cold War' and urged that the priority of the UK should be '(i) Action required to win the Cold War. (ii) Playing our part in deterrents against war. (iii) Preparations for War'.[18] This, too, was never published and emerged eventually at the National Archives.

3. The Sandys Review, 1957 (Conservative), which foreshadowed the end of National Service, substantial cuts in conventional forces and a reliance upon nuclear deterrence as the country moved from the age of atomic bombs to thermonuclear weapons.[19]

4. Healey, Mark I, 1964–66 (Labour), which is primarily remembered for the cancellation of the TSR2 as the replacement for the V-bombers and the planned alternative purchase of US-made F111s.[20]

5. Healey, Mark II, 1968 (Labour), following the sterling devaluation of November 1967; Harold Wilson announced a planned withdrawal of British forces from east of Suez and the cancellation of the F111 order.[21]

6. The Mason Review, 1974–75, (Labour). UK defence to concentrate on NATO central front in Germany, anti-submarine warfare in the eastern Atlantic, home defence and the nuclear deterrent with reductions in out-of-NATO area deployments, RAF transports and amphibious capability.[22]

7. The Nott Review, 1981 (Conservative). Drastic reductions in the Royal Navy's surface fleet, including the loss of an aircraft carrier and two amphibious assault ships while replacing Polaris with Trident as the carrier of the UK nuclear deterrent.[23] Drastically revised as a result of the Falklands War of April–June 1982.

8. *Options for Change*, 1990 (Conservative). Post-Cold War rethink reduced size of the Army by a third, announced the withdrawal of six RAF squadrons from Germany and the slimming of the Royal Navy's destroyer/frigate fleet from forty-eight to forty.[24]

9. Defence Costs Study, 1994 (Conservative). Use of outsourcing, the civilianisation of previously military functions and the Private Finance Initiative to shed 18,700 military and civilian jobs by 2000 and to put the *Front Line First*.[25]

10. *The Strategic Defence Review*, 1998 (Labour) plus the SDR 'New Chapter', 2002 (Labour). Restructuring of the Army. Increase in joint capability with a 'tri-service' approach, greater use of new technology, spells out the number of overseas operations the UK could conduct at any one time with or without allies. 'New Chapter' prepared in response to international terrorism and 'asymmetric threats' post-9/11.[26]

All these reviews had a strong element of cost-push behind them and a desire to reduce the proportion of GDP absorbed by defence (see tables opposite and overleaf). Aspirations were perpetually outstripping resources. But the October 2010 coalition marque was rushed. It looked and smelt like a fistful of spending reviews overlaid by a thin patina of strategy. It cried out for rethinking and revision from the moment it was published (a view expressed, after I had drafted these words, by the all-party House of Commons Defence Committee in its August 2011 report *The Strategic Defence and Security Review and the National Security Strategy*[27]). The force requirements of the Libyan operation five months later made this plain for all to see and talk soon began of its being reopened as the difficulties of what one insider called during the early days of Operation Ellamy 'a slow war of attrition by inches' became apparent.[28]

In fact, the most accomplished review of the postwar years lay beyond the standard defence review genre (which is why it does not feature in the list of ten) and fell into a class of its own. It was called *Future Policy Study* and it was commissioned in great secrecy by Harold Macmillan in June 1959 and tasked with a candid assessment of where the UK would be in the world by 1970 on current policies.[29] This, for me, remains the model of how to handle the Place in the World question because it's the only post-1945 example of an all-in approach that covered the range of moving parts and their relationship one to another in terms of Britain's security, well-being and capacity to influence others.

PERCENTAGE OF UK GDP SPENT ON DEFENCE

1955/56	4.7%	1984/85	5.1%	1998/99	2.5%
1971/72	4.7%	1985/86	4.9%	1999/2000	2.4%
1972/73	4.3%	1986/87	4.6%	2000/01	2.4%
1973/74	4.2%	1987/88	4.3%	2001/02	2.5%
1974/75	4.7%	1988/89	3.9%	2002/03	2.5%
1975/76	4.8%	1989/90	3.9%	2003/04	2.5%
1976/77	4.7%	1990/91	3.9%	2004/05	2.4%
1977/78	4.5%	1991/92	4.1%	2005/06	2.4%
1978/79	4.3%	1992/93	3.8%	2006/07	2.4%
1979/80	4.4%	1993/94	3.5%	2007/08	2.4%
1980/81	4.7%	1994/95	3.2%	2008/09	2.6%
1981/82	4.8%	1995/96	2.9%	2009/10 (est. outturn)	2.7%
1982/83	5.0%	1996/97	2.8%		
1983/84	5.0%	1997/98	2.5%		

I am very grateful to the House of Lords Library for collecting these figures.

The House of Lords Library drew my attention to Michael Dockrill's *British Defence since 1945* (Blackwell, 1988), p.151, for figures covering the period 1948–54. They are:

1947/48	7.1%	1950/51	7.9%	1953/54	9.2%
1948/49	6.5%	1951/52	9.8%		
1949/50	6.6%	1952/53	9.7%		

The immediate postwar figures were:

1945/46	33.9%	1946/47	22.0%

John Baylis, *British Defence Policy: Striking the Right Balance*, (Macmillan, 1989), p.143.

If I were Chief Historical Adviser to the Prime Minister, a yet-to-be-created post to which I do *not* aspire (and not merely because I am an independent crossbench peer), I would urge David Cameron to commission a no-holds-barred equivalent of Harold Macmillan's *Future Policy Study* with instructions that it be suffused with the purpose of drawing up the 'cold rules for national safety' which the great historians of Empire, Robinson and Gallagher in their classic work *Africa and the Victorians*, said each political generation had to compile for itself.[30] This cannot be done, in my judgement, without a stiff dose of Neustadt and May's 'thinking in time' and 'seeing time as a stream' by carrying with you into your horizon-scanning and future strategy endeavours a living sense of those who trod the same path as you along that long road of review since Victory in Europe Day in May 1945. It should open by making the case for the UK as a serious player in world affairs (no longer an 'of course' proposition) and by a burst of candour about what this means in share-of-GDP terms. Its prose should provide an equally vivid portrait of what a less globally ambitious UK would look like in terms of armed forces, equipment, defence spending and intelligence capability.

Such a review, unless a seriously shrivelled Britain was to be the outcome, would also require a genuine infusion of grand strategy, which is not the same as generating stratagems, to draw a distinction the defence analyst Robert Fox likes to make.[31] This indispensable function, as the House of Commons Public Administration Committee noticed in the autumn of 2010 in its *Who Does UK National Strategy?* investigation, is effectively balkanised not just across Whitehall but, to an outsider's eye, even within critical departments like the Ministry of Defence and is made worse, in my view, by an unnecessarily high degree of tension between the senior Civil Service and the military about who does what inside that joint headquarters. This was the subject of a study commissioned in 2010 by the new Chief of the Defence Staff, General Sir David Richards, and led by Major General Mungo Melvin, whose essence was caught in General Melvin's farewell lecture on 'Soldiers, Statesmen and Strategy' at the Royal United Services Institute in November 2011.[32]

If Clausewitz could somehow manifest himself in London today he would have a difficult time finding who was in charge of grand strategy (although the word 'strategy' itself is ubiquitous and almost as devalued a piece of linguistic litter as the word 'vision'). A visiting Clausewitz, were he capable of retrospectively penetrating those committee rooms, intelligence sections and Chiefs of Staff suites where our ten postwar defence and security reviews have been crafted, would, I think, see successive generations of our guardians of national security in pursuit of two, related holy grails:

1. The careful management, and, where possible, disguise of decline by keeping as many capabilities as possible in being, or, failing that, sustaining a capacity to regenerate them.

2. The sculpting from the assets, human, physical and structural, in the armed forces, the Civil Service, the Diplomatic Service and the intelligence agencies, a system whereby the maximum value can be squeezed out of them. This has been the impulse behind a parallel, though rarely synchronised, series of organisational reports alongside the defence reviews. These include the 1958 review of the Chiefs of Staff's functions;[33] the Ismay–Jacob report, *The Higher Direction of Defence*

(1963),[34] which led to the creation of a unified Ministry of Defence the following year;[35] the 1984 changes to the Chief of the Defence Staff's role and the abolition of the three service departments;[36] the 2011 Levene Report on defence reform;[37] the Trend–Greenhill reforms of the Joint Intelligence Committee in 1968, which created the Assessments Staff in the Cabinet Office;[38] and a pair of reviews of the Foreign Office by Lord Plowden in 1964[39] and Sir Val Duncan in 1969[40] as well as the 1977 Central Policy Review Staff's *Review of Overseas Representation*.[41]

There will, I suspect, be a fistful of similar inquiries to come before I find myself in some great celestial archive where no-one is ever denied access to any file. If asked 'can history be any help to the next set of strategic inquisitors?' I would answer 'possibly'; 'probably', even. If asked 'in what way?' I would reply that first of all, is the assumption that our 'pocket superpower' impulse is likely to continue unabated to the point where we reconcile ourselves to being a medium-sized power with no particular wish to exert ourselves in terms of reach, capability and expense over any other country, tucked up inside a big regional grouping (the European Union) and part of a longstanding military alliance (NATO)? If the answer was 'no', I would be seriously surprised and, I must admit, not a little regretful. I would then say postwar history has little with which to help because we are now dealing with a government *mentalité* I don't recognise.

If the answer was 'yes', but a slimmer, better-organised and targeted version of the status quo, I would not be surprised. The first thing I would say is that, as a country, we should not continue as if, in terms of place-in-the-world, we were operating on the principle of the old Venetian proverb directed to the fluid precariousness of their city midst the lagoon, *Sempre crolla ma non cade* ('It is always collapsing but it never falls down'[42]).

How can matters be so organised in future that we avoid the perils of overstretch and the depressing, often searing, recitative of relative decline? First would come the history in the form of an examination of the ingredients that have competed for time, attention, money and capability (both human and physical) since 1945:

1. Permanent demands or 'musts' (air defence of the UK; home defence of the UK; nuclear deterrent; security of the eastern Atlantic; NATO commitments).
2. For the years 1945–80, the military requirements of disposing of the British Empire (with some residuals still exerting demands, e.g. the Falkland Islands, Gibraltar).
3. Periodic need to bring military aid to the civil ministries (e.g. Green Goddess fire engines during industrial action by the Fire Brigades Union) or the civil power (Northern Ireland during the 'Troubles').
4. Unexpected crises that cannot be met with inaction (Northern Ireland in 1969, Argentinian invasion of the Falkland Islands in 1982): without either dereliction of duty, harm to national self-image and international image of the UK (or both).
5. Crises that can be met with inaction (but at a price in terms of the factors listed above). Libya could have been an example of this in 2011 but turned out not to be.
6. The wouldn't-it-be-nice-to-help if we had the money, the people and the kit (the list of these is nearly endless).
7. The sustenance of top flight diplomatic and intelligence services, a considerable overseas aid programme and a substantial investment in 'soft power'[43] (e.g. the BBC Overseas Service, the British Council).

So, in the light of the recent, post-1945 past, the test for strategy-making is two-fold:

1. How can its formation be best organised to reconcile/decide between the vector of forces created by functions 1 to 7?
2. How can it help run a system that sustains a 'capacity to act' in the words of the 1998 *Strategic Defence Review*,[44] that is greater than the sum of its parts? The 'capacity to act' impulse became especially acute in the aftermath of the 2010 review as, in Sir Kevin Tebbit's words, 'we had a Strategic Defence and Security Review which says we want to continue to do high-intensity things a long way from our shores but with less.

This puts great strain on both our Armed Forces and on industry. You can't turn capabilities on and off like a tap. You can lose them. One's fed up with managing decline but managing without sufficient resources.' Sir Kevin is a former Permanent Secretary at the Ministry of Defence and now a leading figure in the UK-based defence industry.[45]

We have never as a country in my lifetime pulled off this pair of requirements. It's high time we did. As William Hague said in his Grand Locarno Room speech in September 2011: 'The world is not conducting a seminar on foreign policy. Out there are nations advancing their own national interest, ideas which promote violent extremism, wars we must prevent, new threats we must anticipate...'[46] And, if we are to seriously crank up our chances of doing so, history – contemporary history especially – will be one of the key levers of said cranking. At the very least, it will remind the future guardians of our national security, during the darkest hours of the next Strategic Defence and Security Review, that we have been here before and they are not alone; that the ghosts of many of the best Whitehall, the armed forces and the intelligence services ever reared will be flitting through their committee rooms, emitting inaudible if sympathetic sounds and with more than a touch of irony upon their countenances, as the latest manifestation of our enduring great power impulse bumps and grinds alongside our always limited capacity to fund it.

Finally, let's make a quantum leap of the imagination – to a future Prime Minister and Cabinet who collectively decide that the instinct to intervene has to stop and charges its National Security Council officials, the Foreign and Commonwealth Office, the Ministry of Defence and the secret agencies to concentrate on home defence; on making the UK a hard target against people, states, factors and actions that could seriously harm the country.

What would such a threat assessment – external and internal – look like? With the help of my friend Alan Petty and some necessarily anonymous Whitehall insiders, who have long experience with national

POSSIBLE THREATS
TO THE UK

Serious collapse of UK/EU/
world economy

Hostage crisis with
wider repercussions

Serious industrial
disturbance

Serious revival of
Ireland-related
terrorist attacks

Terrorist acts
arising from
jihadist/lone
obsessive

Terrorist attacks
on infrastructure
or iconic site /
building

Social
unrest/riots

INTERNAL

Serious nuclear
accident civil or
military

Serious prison
disturbances with
outside repercussions
(e.g. Muslim prisoners
seize control of a wing)

Serious climate event
within the UK

EXTERNAL

Financial Shock / collapse
triggered by events beyond
UK control

Indo-Pakistan
(possibly nuclear war)
with instant repercussions
for the UK

Epidemics

Unanticipated mass
immigration

Taking of UK hostages abroad

External state-to-state attack
(e.g. Iranian missile)

Invasion of UK sovereign
territory (Argentinian attacks
on Falkland Islands)

Severe climate event
overseas with repercussions for
global trade

Threat (direct or implied) by
a nuclear-equipped state

Severance of special US–UK
nuclear and intelligence
relationships

Attack or threat of attack by
a CRBN capable terrorist group

Serious and widespread cyber
attacks (Chinese; Russian;
other including national
infrastructure targets)

State-to-state war in the Middle
East with serious repercussions
for UK (e.g. swift and steep rise
in oil prices)

Revival of a mini Cold War
after a change in regime and
attitudes in Moscow

Internationally inspired /
directed terrorism (including a
9/11-style aerial attack)

security matters, I have attempted such an audit and depicted it in the accompanying diagram, which I hope is largely self-explanatory.

This circle of anxieties and possibilities may strike you as vastly overdone, even verging on the chill-your-bones fictional *oeuvre* begun with such effect 106 years ago by William Le Queux in his 1906 bestseller *The Invasion of 1910*, in which the Kaiser's armies are successfully put ashore in Norfolk while England dozed through the small hours of a late summer Saturday night and Sunday morning on 1–2 September 1910.[47]

As Alan Petty pointed out, as we compiled our two-edged circle on a warm August lunchtime in the House of Lords, it reminded him of Philip Larkin's poem 'Aubade', in which the gloomy sage writes about waking up at four in the morning with too much wine in him and thinking about where and when he will die, 'the anaesthetic from which none come round'. The Larkin line caught on Alan's memory was that unlike our deaths 'Most things may never happen'.[48] And the greatest threat of my lifetime – the Cold War mutating into World War III – was avoided (of which more in the next chapter).

But the point about the cartography-of-threats exercise is that some of them might – and in particularly malign and simultaneous combination. If you accept that, two things stand out:

1. Even with the instinct to intervene curbed, the world and its woes won't ignore these shores nor is domestic security guaranteed.
2. Finding ways to avert such threats and/or the resilience to withstand them if they happen is a costly business requiring a serious slice of gross domestic product even if we have found ways of keeping the defence spending proportion below 2 per cent (too low, in my view, given current commitments and aspirations).

If I was a Le Queux-style thriller-writer, I'd have a crack at all this in novel form. I'm not; so I won't. This, at least, you have been spared!

4

CHILD OF THE URANIUM AGE:
THE SHADOW OF THE BOMB

Preserve us all from a baptism of uranium ...
MONSIGNOR RONALD KNOX, 1945.[1]

A DECADE after Ronald Knox wrote those words in his book *God and the Atom* in frustration at the failure of the English Catholic bishops to give a lead after the bombs had fallen on Hiroshima and Nagasaki,[2] each member of the British Cabinet was presented with the Strath Report, a top secret study of what ten 10-megaton Russian hydrogen bombs would do to the United Kingdom. The level of destruction, it said, 'would remain beyond the imagination until it happened.'[3]

I possess a vivid imagination. But, for all the hours spent in the archives on those terrifying 'what if...' assessments and transition-to-war exercises and scenarios,[4] I still can't grasp fully what World War III and a nuclear assault on these islands would have brought, let alone the fate of the rest of the world. In certain locations I come close. The old World War III War Cabinet bunker, codenamed TURNSTILE in the 1960s, is one. It lies beneath the Cotswolds under Box Hill near Corsham in Wiltshire.[5] Another is the missile compartment on a Royal Navy Vanguard class Trident submarine. When I was photographed by my friend and BBC Radio 4 producer Richard Knight, alongside tube number 4 with Commander Richard Lindsay, HMS *Vanguard*'s captain, in October 2008 a few days before the boat left is Faslane base in the west of Scotland for a patrol in the North Atlantic (reproduced on the back cover of this book), the white forest around us contained missiles whose warheads contained a combined destructive power greater than all the explosives used by every combatant everywhere in World War II from its beginning to its end. There, understandably, you feel what you are – a child of the uranium age – particularly if that age, give or take a year, also marks out your own time on earth.[6]

Growing up in the shadow of the Bomb, marrying, having one's own children while the Cold War lengthened, has left me with a fascination for the inside story of the UK nuclear weapons programme – the politicians, scientists, Chiefs of Staff, airmen, sailors and soldiers and the industrial workforce that has gone and still goes into the formidable combined enterprise of making and sustaining Britain a nuclear-tipped nation. Given the sensitivity of its archival spoor, the story is a classic example of catch-up history and some of it, understandably, will never reach the National Archives.

The shadow of the Bomb meant that the Cold War was like no other conflict the world has ever faced. Clement Attlee recognised this in 'The Atomic Bomb', the first paper he wrote for his Cabinet Committee on Atomic Energy, GEN 75, at the end of August 1945, less than a month after the weapons had been dropped on Hiroshima and Nagasaki. 'It must be recognised', he wrote,

> that this weapon has rendered much of our postwar planning out of date ... For instance a redistribution of industry ... is quite futile in face of the atomic bomb. Nothing can alter the fact that the geographical situation of Britain offers a Continental Power such targets as London and the other great cities. Dispersal of munitions works and airfields cannot alter the facts of geography ... Again it would appear that the provision of bomb proof basements in factories and offices and the retention of A.R.P. [Air Raid Precautions] and Fire Services is just futile waste.

It was plain to Attlee what this meant in terms of policy: 'The answer to an atomic bomb on London is an atomic bomb on another great city.'

Attlee finished by telling his ministers on GEN 75 that they were like no other set of politicians to have sat in the Cabinet Room:

> No government has ever been placed in such a position as is ours today. The Governments of the UK and the USA [with Canada, the partners in the World War II Manhattan Project] are responsible as never before for the future of the human race.[7]

Never before had the British people been in such a position, certainly once the Soviet Union had tested its bomb in August 1949 and we had tested ours in October 1952.

Why? Because of the destructive magnitude of the atomic bombs, and, from the early to mid-fifties, from the immensely more powerful hydrogen bombs. As a friend of mine formerly high in British intelligence put it: 'The Cold War was a strategic threat on steroids thanks to nuclear weapons.'[8] And because, as A. J. P. Taylor expressed it in 1969: 'A deterrent may work ninety-nine times out of a hundred. On the hundredth occasion it produces a catastrophe. There is a contemporary moral here for those who like to find one.'[9] Joe Nye, the American scholar-diplomat, rightly stressed 'the crystal ball effect of nuclear weapons'.[10] The Cold War was the first conflict in which the endgame – massive, mutual nuclear exchange – was plain for all to see and foresee it we did.

In April 2010, the second Earl of Stockton (the first being Harold Macmillan) came down the Mile End Road to the School of History at Queen Mary, University of London, to present the Macmillan Prizes to those students who had won distinctions on our MA in Twentieth Century History programme. We talked a little about his grandfather's constantly urging economic expansion upon a cautious Treasury during his premiership especially in 1963 when, with his Chancellor of the Exchequer, Reggie Maudling, Macmillan launched what became known as the 'dash for growth'.[11] 'Ah,' said Alexander Stockton, 'that was a mistake. Politicians fossilise the crisis of their youth and, for Grandfather, it was unemployment.'[12]

I was intrigued by that notion and wondered, though I am a crossbencher in the House of Lords, not a party politician, what my equivalent would be. What have I 'fossilised' from my youth? I knew straightaway what it was – a rolling forty-year east–west crisis called the Cold War which, at its most perilous moments, threatened Ronald Knox's 'baptism of uranium' in a matter of days and perhaps hours if one side made a catastrophic miscalculation about the intentions of the other. Even at the very end, when the hardliners' coup in Moscow spanning 18–21 August 1991 looked as if it were about to reverse all the Cold War endgames played out since the fall of the Berlin Wall in November 1989, there was a final moment of peril. As my friend Rear Admiral Simon Lister, then Naval Attaché in the British Embassy in Moscow, put it twenty years later: 'For three days we didn't know who had the nuclear button.'[13]

When we had that conversation about the Moscow events on 1991 in the ward room of HMS *Neptune*, the Royal Navy's base at Faslane, over lunch on 15 August 2011 after a morning spent aboard HMS *Astute*, the lead boat of the Navy's latest hunter-killer submarine class, I was specially aware of the huge, interlocking effort it took – and takes – for Britain to remain the kind of top-of-the-range submarine nation the country has to be every hour of every day if it is to remain a serious and sustained nuclear weapons power. Admiral Lister, as Director, Submarines, was central to the whole enterprise.

In terms of high policy at the summit of government there are two threads that have constantly linked the Prime Ministers' worlds to that of Simon Lister and his equivalents in both the Royal Air Force and the Royal Navy since Clem Attlee outlined his first thoughts to his Cabinet Committee on Atomic Energy in August 1945. The most enduring dates from the late 1940s and is the link between No. 10, the Cabinet Room and the weaponeers and the armed services tasked to carry the bombs, and, later, the missiles. The second, in place since the first atomic bomb was delivered to the RAF in December 1953, is the firing chain down which the Prime Minister's authorisation of nuclear release passes.

As a historian, it is the theme of Cabinets and the Bomb and the firing chain and the fall-backs that have most fascinated me – an absorption enhanced by the gradual exposure of the documentary trail over the past thirty to forty years. I have been particularly interested in those patches of our postwar political and economic history when decisions have had to be taken whether or not to become a nuclear-tipped power; whether or not to carry on being so; whether or not to upgrade the system; whether or not to pursue the nuclear tipping independently or with a very substantial and almost certainly irreversible dependence on the United States.

The periods when the question of Britain and the Bomb goes on heat – we are living through one at the moment – are especially revealing of the difficulties and dilemmas of sustaining the nuclear element of the UK's place in the world, not least because (as we shall see shortly) such sequences usually coincide with bouts of economic stress too. We have, however, a template to guide us at such moments thanks to my old friend and mentor the late Sir Michael Quinlan, former Permanent Secretary at the Ministry of Defence, the leading Whitehall defence intellectual of the postwar years.[14]

CHRONOLOGY

1940

March	Otto Frisch and Rudolf Peierls, a pair of émigré scientists at Birmingham University, complete their memorandum 'On the Construction of a "Super-bomb": Based on a Nuclear Chain Reaction in Uranium', showing that far less uranium than previously thought, if it could be enriched, would be needed to make a bomb of great destructive power producing 'radiations [which] would be fatal to living beings even a long time after the explosion'.

April	The Ministry of Aircraft Production establishes the Maud Committee to examine the feasibility of a uranium bomb on the basis of the Frisch–Peierls Memorandum.

1941

July	The Maud Committee 'considers that the scheme for a uranium bomb is practicable and likely to lead to decisive results in the war. It recommends that this work be continued on the highest priority and on the increasing scale necessary to obtain the weapon in the shortest possible time.'

1942

30 July	Sir John Anderson, minister for 'Tube Alloys' (the weapon's cover name), minutes Churchill advising that the scale and cost of the atomic bomb project requires the UK to 'move our design work and the personnel concerned to the United States. Henceforth, work on the bomb project would be pursued as a combined Anglo-American effort.'

1943

19 August	Churchill and Roosevelt sign the secret Quebec Agreement establishing 'First, that we will never use this agency [the atomic bomb] against each other. Secondly, that we will not use it against third parties without each other's consent. Thirdly, that we will not either of us communicate any information about Tube Alloys to third parties except by mutual consent.' Collaboration between the US and the UK to be overseen by a Combined Policy Committee meeting in Washington.
December	First members of a nineteen-strong UK team of British scientists arrive at Los Alamos in New Mexico, where the bomb is designed and built in immense secrecy.

1944

19 September Hyde Park *aide-mémoire* of conversation between Roosevelt and Churchill at the President's home in upstate New York recording the decision that the 'matter should continue to be regarded as of the utmost secrecy; but when a "bomb" is finally available, it might perhaps, after mature consideration, be used against the Japanese, who should be warned that this bombardment will be repeated until they surrender' and that 'full collaboration between the United States and the British Government in developing tube alloys for military and commercial purposes should continue after the defeat of Japan unless and until terminated by joint agreement.'

1945

1 July Churchill gives UK approval for atomic bombs to be dropped on Japan.

16 July World's first atomic explosion takes place at the Trinity test site in New Mexico.

26 July Attlee forms a government. Labour majority of 146 in the House of Commons.

6 August Atomic bomb dropped on Hiroshima.

9 August Atomic bomb dropped on Nagasaki.

14 August Japan surrenders.

28 August Attlee circulates memorandum on 'The Atomic Bomb' to GEN 75, his Cabinet Committee on Atomic Energy. He tells ministers that 'no government has ever been placed in such a position as is ours today. The Governments of the UK and the USA are responsible as never before for the future of the human race' and that 'the answer to an atomic bomb on London is an atomic bomb on another great city.'

18 December GEN 75 authorises the construction of an atomic pile at Windscale to produce plutonium.

1946

August　　　　US Congress passes the McMahon Act, prohibiting the
transmission of nuclear information to another country.

25 October　　During a GEN 75 meeting, Dalton (Chancellor of the Exchequer)
and Cripps (President of the Board of Trade) argue that UK
economic recovery could not afford the £30m–40m needed over
five years to build a gaseous diffusion plant for the production of
uranium 235. Bevin insists: 'We've got to have the bloody Union
Jack on top of it' [i.e. the atomic bomb], and prevails.

1947

8 January　　GEN 163 meets for the first and only time to authorise 'that
research and development work on atomic weapons should be
undertaken' in conditions of the utmost secrecy. The decision is
taken by Attlee and five ministers. The group does not include
Dalton and Cripps.

1948

12 May　　　Minister of Defence, A. V. Alexander, tells the House of
Commons that 'research and developments continue to receive
the highest priority in the defence field, and all types of modern
weapons, including atomic weapons, are being developed.' He
adds that it would not be 'in the public interest' to say more.

1949

29 August　　The Soviet Union detonates its first atomic device in Kazakhstan.

23 September　Truman announces the news of the Russian test in Washington.

1950

31 January　　Truman makes public his decision taken that day that the US
will manufacture 'the so-called hydrogen or superbomb'.

3 February　　British nuclear physicist Klaus Fuchs charged with passing
nuclear secrets to the Soviet Union.

23 February   General election: Attlee government returned to office with a majority of five.

1 March   Fuchs sentenced to fourteen years' imprisonment.

1951

25 October   General election: Churchill and the Conservatives returned to power with a majority of seventeen.

21 November   Churchill briefed on Attlee governments' work on atomic bomb.

12 December   Churchill briefed on how Attlee governments concealed the cost of the atomic bomb from Parliament.

14 December   Churchill authorises bomb test in Australia.

1952

18 February   Churchill announces that the UK will test an atomic bomb later in the year.

3 October   First British atomic device detonated in the Monte Bello Islands off north-west Australia.

1 November   US tests first hydrogen bomb at Eniwetok in the Pacific. At 10.4 megatons, its power is twice that of all the explosives used in the Second World War.

1953

12 August   Soviet Union tests an H-bomb. (In fact, it was a hybrid device, not a true thermonuclear explosion.)

7 November   First Blue Danube atomic bomb arrives from Aldermaston at RAF Wittering.

1954

1 March   US explodes a 15-megaton H-bomb at Bikini Atoll in the Pacific.

22 March   *Lucky Dragon* returns to Japan from a Pacific fishing voyage with its crew suffering from radiation sickness.

13 April	Churchill tells ministers on the GEN 464 Cabinet Committee he would like the full Cabinet to authorise the manufacture of a British H-bomb.
1 June	Chiefs of Staff brief Churchill and members of his Defence Policy Committee on the danger of the USA starting a 'forestalling' war against the Soviet Union. They also claim that a UK armed with its own H-bomb could 'be on terms with the United States and Russia'.
16 June	Churchill's Defence Policy Committee authorises an H-bomb programme.
7 July	Cabinet breaks up in disarray after discussing proposed talks with the Russians and the making of a British H-bomb. Some ministers complain at lack of consultation.
8 July	Cabinet discusses morality and cost of an H-bomb.
26 July	Cabinet agrees to the manufacture of a British H-bomb.

1955

13 January	Joint Intelligence Committee states that the only warning of an H-bomb attack on the UK will probably be the presence of Russian bombers on RAF and allied radar screens.
17 February	Defence White Paper reveals government's intention to make an H-bomb.
5 April	Churchill resigns. Eden Prime Minister.
26 May	General election: Conservatives increase majority to fifty-nine.
22 November	Soviets test a 1.6-megaton hydrogen bomb.

1956

July	First operational Valiant bombers arrive at RAF Wittering.
5 November	Soviet Prime Minister, Bulganin, threatens rockets on Paris and London if Anglo-French invasion of Egypt is not halted.

1957

9 January	Eden resigns.

10 January	Queen appoints Macmillan Prime Minister.
4 April	Sandys Defence White Paper published, stressing the primacy of nuclear deterrence and foreshadowing the end of National Service.
15 May	UK tests a thermonuclear device at Christmas Island in the Pacific. It yields 300 kilotons, 30 per cent of the megaton target.
3 October	Bevan heckled at Labour Party conference for arguing this is not the time for Britain to renounce the H-bomb.
24 October	President Eisenhower agrees to amend the McMahon Act to enable a US–UK exchange of nuclear weapons information during talks in Washington with Macmillan.
8 November	Britain's first megaton H-bomb explodes off Christmas Island, yielding 1.8 megatons.

1958

15 January	Meeting at Canon Collins's home near St Paul's Cathedral sees birth of the Campaign for Nuclear Disarmament (CND).
17 February	CND holds its first meeting in Westminster Central Hall.
4 April	4,000 protesters leave Trafalgar Square for the Atomic Weapons Research Establishment at Aldermaston.
7 April	They arrive.
30 June	US Congress repeals those sections of the McMahon Act that prevented nuclear weapons collaboration with the UK.
4 August	US and UK governments conclude the Agreement for Co-operation on the Uses of Atomic Energy for Mutual Defence Purposes.

1959

7 June	Secret meeting at Chequers of military, officials and diplomats chaired by Macmillan rules out unilateral nuclear disarmament and concludes that 'in terms of foreign policy the British contribution to the western deterrent had paid a handsome dividend up to now, but we should have to consider whether

it would continue to do so.' Macmillan commissions a *Future Policy Study* to forecast Britain's place in the world by 1970.

8 October   General election: Conservatives increase majority to 100.

1960

13 February   France tests its first atomic bomb in the Algerian Sahara.

24 February   *Future Policy Study* completed. It concludes: 'Our purpose should be to maintain a strategic nuclear force which is accepted by the Americans, and by the [NATO] Alliance as a whole, as a significant contribution to the western deterrent … This would not mean (except in the view of one of those associated with this study [Sir Dermot Boyle, Chief of the Air Staff]) that we were aiming to provide a force capable by itself of deterring Russia.'

13 April   Cabinet told that its Defence Committee, on the advice of the Chiefs of Staff, had decided to abandon the Blue Streak rocket. Cabinet concurs and the decision is announced in the House of Commons the same day.

20 June   Cabinet approves the purchase of the untested US stand-off Skybolt missile, which, if it worked, would have a British nuclear warhead and prolong the deterrent capability of the RAF's V-bombers into 'the later 1960s', thereby filling the gap left by the cancellation of Blue Streak.

1962

11 December   Kennedy administration announces the cancellation of Skybolt.

18 December   Macmillan flies to Nassau to meet President Kennedy in an attempt to persuade his administration to supply submarine-launched Polaris missiles as a replacement for Skybolt.

21 December   Cabinet, chaired by R. A. Butler in Macmillan's absence, considers telegrams from the Prime Minister in Nassau and asking 'for the advice of the Cabinet' on the acceptability of the terms proposed for the purchase of Polaris.

26 December	Macmillan asks Minister of Defence to prepare a paper on UK-designed and built alternatives to Polaris if the Nassau agreement collapsed.
31 December	At a meeting of ministers and officials, chaired by Macmillan, Ted Heath says the Skybolt cancellation and the Polaris purchase exposed to the public 'the extent of our dependence on the United States'. If the two governments disagreed strongly on policy, the US might cancel the arrangement. The Minister of Defence, Peter Thorneycroft, says the UK would not be able to afford to develop 'a reinsurance system of its own' from scratch.

1963

3 January	Full Cabinet discusses the Nassau deal and authorises the purchase of Polaris, and the arrangement whereby it could be withdrawn from NATO into national service 'if the supreme interests of the country required it'. Macmillan says that, unlike Skybolt, 'Polaris would extend the effectiveness and credibility of the United Kingdom deterrent for an almost indefinite period'.
15 January	Amery, Minister of Aviation, briefs Thorneycroft on the long-term procurement runs and expense needed to develop a UK alternative to Polaris.
28 January	Thorneycroft rules out taking the exercise further.
6 April	Polaris Sales Agreement signed in Washington.

1964

September	Labour's general election manifesto says of Polaris: 'It will not be independent and it will not be British and it will not deter … We are not prepared any longer to waste the country's resources on endless duplication of strategic nuclear weapons. We shall propose the re-negotiation of the Nassau agreement.'
15 October	General election: Labour wins with a majority of five. Harold Wilson Prime Minister the following day.
16 October	China explodes an atomic device in Sinkiang Province.

11 November MISC 16 Cabinet Committee on 'Atlantic Nuclear Force' meets (Wilson; Patrick Gordon Walker, Foreign Secretary; Denis Healey, Defence Secretary). Discusses the idea of pooling the UK Polaris submarines with a number of US ones in an Atlantic nuclear force. Decides that 'three submarines would represent the minimum force which would be acceptable to us in the event of the dissolution of the NATO Alliance.' The Conservative government's proposed five submarines 'would not represent a nuclear force for a world-wide role, but would only meet the requirements of the European theatre.'

21–22 November Wilson summons a meeting of MISC 17, his Cabinet Committee on Defence Policy, to Chequers to consider the forthcoming defence review and the future of Polaris. Wilson tells his colleagues that 'of the five submarines which had been planned, two were at an advanced stage of development and short of scrapping it would be impracticable not to complete them.' Debate focuses on desirability of a three- or four-boat force.

26 November Full Cabinet briefed by Wilson on decision to commit 'such Polaris submarines as we might construct' to a proposed Atlantic Nuclear Force ... The precise number of these submarines would be for further consideration; but it was relevant to a decision that the construction of some of them was already sufficiently advanced to make it unrealistic to cancel the orders. On the other hand the number to be retained would be smaller than the number which the previous Government had envisaged and would be such as to make it clear that we no longer contemplated the maintenance of an independent nuclear force. The Cabinet approves the Prime Minister's proposals.

1965

6 January Healey circulates a paper to the Cabinet's Defence and Overseas Policy Committee arguing that a fleet of four Polaris submarines is preferable to three, and as the fourth boat is already under construction, 'cancellation at this stage would involve the payment of cancellation charges'.

29 January Cabinet's Defence and Overseas Policy Committee meets (Wilson plus six ministers). Decision taken to build four Polaris submarines partly to ensure that one boat will always be on station when the Royal Navy assumes the main deterrent role in the late 1960s.

1966

March Labour manifesto says the party 'stands by its pledge to internationalise our strategic nuclear forces' through the proposed Atlantic Nuclear Force (which never materialised).

31 March General election: Labour returned with a majority of ninety-six.

28 September First meeting of Wilson's new Cabinet Committee on Nuclear Policy (PN). Discussion on whether UK 'could no longer count on United States co-operation in nuclear defence matters unless we retained a nuclear weapons capability.'

1967

3 August Healey implements PN committee decision that 'in accordance with the Nassau Agreement our POLARIS missiles will be assigned' to NATO's Supreme Allied Commander Europe, 'as soon as the first submarine becomes operational, i.e., in 1968. Ultimate United Kingdom control of the POLARIS force will not be affected, since control of the firing chain will remain in UK hands; in particular, no submarine commander will be authorised to fire the POLARIS weapons without the Prime Minister's specific authority.'

30 October HMS *Resolution*, first of the Polaris missile-carrying submarines, is commissioned.

18 November The pound is devalued by 14 per cent from $2.80 to $2.40 against the US dollar.

1 December   Paper goes to PN on future options for Polaris. Should it be improved to enable the missiles to penetrate the anti-ballistic missile screen the Russians were thought to be planning to protect Moscow? The Ministry of Defence and the Foreign Office say yes. The Treasury and the Department for Economic Affairs urge 'abandonment' of 'the whole of our nuclear capability as quickly as possible. Given our difficult economic situation, the capability is a misuse of the resources it will consume.'

5 December   PN meets. Polaris to continue but 'further studies should be undertaken to clarify the requirements and the costs of alternative programmes for hardening the Polaris warhead and of penetration aids for the Polaris system.' Inquiry to be held 'into the minimum scale of effort' that would be needed at the Atomic Weapons Research Establishment, Aldermaston.

1968

15 February   HMS *Resolution* successfully test-fires the first of the Royal Navy's Polaris missiles off Florida.

31 July   Lord Rothschild, in a minority dissenting note to the Kings Norton inquiry into the future of Aldermaston, recommends against improving Polaris as it 'will incur additional open-ended expenditure' as 'no technical considerations have been advanced which lead to the conclusion that hardening or the development of more sophisticated warheads would confer clear-cut and unequivocal advantages on the United Kingdom.'

24 August   France successfully tests an H-bomb at Fangataufa Atoll in the Pacific.

28 September   HMS *Repulse* commissioned.

15 November   HMS *Renown* commissioned.

1969

17 January   Joint Intelligence Committee reports that 'an ABM system is being constructed around Moscow' based on the Galosh missile which 'is expected to provide Moscow with a limited defence against ... Polaris missiles' picked up on radars in the Baltic and the Kola Peninsula.

14 June   Royal Navy Polaris submarines formally take over the primary deterrent role from the RAF V-force. HMS *Resolution* had slipped out of Faslane on 30 April.

4 December   HMS *Revenge* commissioned.

1970

18 June   General election: Conservatives returned with a majority of thirty. Heath becomes Prime Minister the following day and inherits Labour's work on a possible Polaris improvement programme codenamed 'Super Antelope'.

1972

26 May   Signing in Moscow of SALT I treaty limiting the USA and USSR to 200 anti-ballistic missile launchers to protect Washington and Moscow.

1973

12 September   Heath chairs a meeting of three ministers (Douglas-Home, Foreign Secretary; Carrington, Defence Secretary; Barber, Chancellor of the Exchequer) on the future of the deterrent. Funding for 'Super Antelope' research due to run out at the end of the month. Carrington says it's uncertain that the US Congress would approve the sale of Poseidon missiles to the Royal Navy. Heath says 'the maintenance of a credible nuclear deterrent must be regarded as of very great importance in the wider political context.' More money allocated to 'Super Antelope'.

30 October   The same Ministerial Group approves the development of 'Super Antelope' (later known as 'Chevaline'). Co-operation with France ruled out.

1974

28 February   General election produces a 'hung' result. Labour 301 seats; Conservatives 297; Liberals 14.

4 March   Heath resigns; Wilson appointed Prime Minister in a minority Labour government.

5 April   Wilson, after discussion with Callaghan (Foreign Secretary) and Healey (Chancellor), approves a 'Chevaline'-related test in Nevada planned by the Heath administration.

24 May   UK underground test, codenamed 'Fallon', in Nevada.

13 June   Joint Intelligence Committee reports heavy Soviet R and D and new construction work around Moscow to improve 'the deployed MOSCOW system'.

19 June   Defence Studies Working Party (part of Labour's 1974 defence review) reports that £50m has already been spent on 'Super Antelope' and that the project's cancellation 'would mean that our Polaris missiles could no longer be certain of penetrating Soviet ABM defences throughout the existing life of the submarines; and, although our ability to threaten undefended cities within range would remain, our ultimate determination to go to the limit in confronting the USSR would be in question and the main reason for possessing a strategic deterrent negated.'

15 July   Paper circulated to ministers on the Cabinet's Defence and Overseas Policy Committee arguing that 'peacetime capability' of Polaris needs improving if the UK strategic deterrent is to remain credible. The cost estimated at 'about £170m over the [ten-year] LTC [long-term costing] period'.

31 July   Wilson prepares a paper for the Cabinet on a recent British nuclear test in America. 'We knew from technical assessment [of] … the nature and rate of Soviet anti-missile defence development that our missiles would have to be given better penetration capability if we wished to retain a credible deterrent … We also specifically agreed that the decision to hold this test was without prejudice to the policy decision of whether to retain our nuclear deterrent which would be taken in the context of the defence review.' (The paper is not shown to the Cabinet until 12 September because of pressure of other business at last pre-recess Cabinet).

18 September Wilson chairs a meeting of the Defence and Overseas Policy Committee (including Callaghan; Healey; Short, Lord President; Mason, Defence Secretary; Lever, Chancellor of the Duchy of Lancaster). Decides not to lower 'the nuclear threshold'.

10 October General election; Labour returned with an overall majority of three. Its manifesto says: 'We have renounced any intention of moving towards a new generation of strategic nuclear weapons.'

20 November Wilson tells the full Cabinet that the DOPC 'had unanimously decided' the UK strategic nuclear deterrent 'should be retained'. Planned improvements 'necessary to ensure the continuing credibility of the present force were relatively cheap; they would not involve either a new generation of missiles or Multiple Independently Targeted Re-entry Vehicles'. Some dissenting views expressed, but Cabinet agrees.

1976

4 April Wilson resigns and Callaghan becomes Prime Minister.

December Substantial defence spending cuts, to meet the terms of an International Monetary Fund loan, fleetingly place 'Chevaline' and the Polaris system in jeopardy.

1977

Estimates of 'Chevaline' costs rise to £810m (£494m at 1972 prices). Callaghan and a small group of ministers decide to carry on nonetheless.

1978

January Callaghan sets up Ministerial Nuclear Policy Group (himself; Owen, Foreign Secretary; Healey, Chancellor of the Exchequer; Mulley, Defence Secretary) to consider possible Polaris replacement. Commissions an official Steering Group on Nuclear Matters chaired by the Cabinet Secretary, Hunt.

16 February The steering group commissions Nuclear Matters Working Party to produce a two-part report: on politico-military requirements for a future UK deterrent, led by Sir Antony Duff, a senior diplomat; and on the technical options, led by Professor Sir Ronald Mason, Chief Scientific Adviser to the Ministry of Defence.

13 December Callaghan's Ministerial Group meets to consider the Duff–Mason Report, which recommends Polaris be replaced by Trident. Owen argues for a cheaper, submarine-launched cruise missile system. Callaghan says: 'To give up our status as a nuclear weapon state would be a momentous step in British history,' but the decision should go to Cabinet after the general election. Full Cabinet unaware of this discussion.

21 December Ministerial Group meets.

1979

2 January Ministerial Group meets.

6 January Callaghan secures agreement from President Carter at a private meeting during the Guadeloupe summit that the US would supply Trident missiles if a UK Cabinet asked for them.

April Labour's manifesto states: 'In 1974, we renounced any intention of moving towards the production of a new generation of nuclear weapons or a successor to the Polaris nuclear force; we reiterate our belief that this is the best course for Britain. But many great issues affecting our allies and the world are involved, and a new round of strategic arms limitation negotiations will soon begin. We think it is essential that there must be a full and informed debate about these issues in the country before the necessary decision is taken.' Conservative manifesto states: 'The SALT [Strategic Arms Limitation Talks] increase the importance of ensuring the continuing effectiveness of Britain's nuclear deterrent.'

3 May   General election: Conservatives win a majority of forty-three.

4 May   Callaghan leaves instructions in Downing Street that Duff–Mason Report should be made available to Mrs Thatcher, who becomes Prime Minister that day. Mrs Thatcher swiftly convenes her MISC 7 Cabinet committee to examine Polaris replacement.

6 December   MISC 7 decides to opt for the Trident C4 missile.

1980

24 January Frances Pym (Defence Secretary) reveals 'Chevaline' programme to Parliament and says its costs have risen to £1bn (£530m in 1972 prices).

17 July   Thatcher tells the full Cabinet that MISC 7 has decided to opt for the Trident C4 missile (announcement made in Parliament by Pym on 15 July for fear of a leak in the *New York Times*). Government publishes *The Future United Kingdom Strategic Nuclear Deterrent Force*. Drafted by Michael Quinlan, it stresses the 'second centre of decision-making' argument ('We need to convince Soviet leaders that even if they thought at some critical point as a conflict developed the US would hold back, the British force could still inflict a blow so destructive that the penalty for aggression would have proved too high').

1981

November   MISC 7 reopens C4 decision. Decides to opt for the improved D5 January missile and a four-boat force.

29 November MISC 7 reopens C4 decision and considered a paper from John Nott (Defence Secretary) urging the purchase of the improved D5 missile and a four-boat force.

1982

January Full Cabinet briefed on MISC 7 deliberations and concurs.

November Ministry of Defence announces 'Chevaline' missiles operational at sea.

1993

14 August HMS *Vanguard*, the first Trident missile-carrying submarine, is commissioned.

1994

May HMS *Vanguard* launches first UK test firing of a Trident D5 missile off Florida.

December HMS *Vanguard* sails on first Trident operational patrol.

1995

7 January HMS *Victorious* commissioned.

1996

13 May HMS *Repulse* returns to Faslane at the end of the 229th and final Polaris operational patrol.

28 August Prime Minister John Major visits Faslane for decommissioning ceremony for HMS *Repulse* and the end of Polaris's twenty-seven years of continuous patrols.

10 December HMS *Vigilant* commissioned.

1999

27 November HMS *Vengeance* commissioned.

2003

11 December The Ministry of Defence publishes its White Paper *Delivering Security in a Changing World*, which notes that decisions on replacing Trident 'are not needed in this Parliament but are likely to be required in the next one'.

2004

January Prime Minister's Group on Nuclear Weapons Policy agrees funds to sustain capabilities of the Atomic Weapons Establishment, Aldermaston.

21 July The Defence Secretary, Geoff Hoon, unveils the White Paper *Delivering Security in a Changing World: Future Capabilities*. He tells Parliament that the government remains committed to keeping open the option to replace Trident until such time as a decision is required, 'probably in the next Parliament', and announces continued funding for the Atomic Weapons Establishment.

2005

13 April The Labour Manifesto is published, stating: 'We are ... committed to retaining the independent nuclear deterrent ...'

19 July Defence Secretary John Reid tells Parliament that an average of an additional £350m per annum will be invested in Aldermaston over three years to maintain its capability.

1 November John Reid informs the House of Commons Defence Committee that the government's working assumption is that the UK will keep its nuclear weapons as long as other nuclear states which present a potential threat keep theirs, but that that assumption will be tested before decisions are taken.

16 November The Official Group on the Future of the Deterrent meets for the first time under the chairmanship of the Cabinet Secretary, Sir Gus O'Donnell.

24 November	The Ministry of Defence submits evidence to the Commons Defence Committee inquiry into the future of the deterrent, on the strategic context.
14 December	The Official Group on the Future of the Deterrent meets for the second time under the chairmanship of Sir Nigel Sheinwald, foreign policy adviser to the Prime Minister.

2006

26 April	The Official Group on the Future of the Deterrent meets for the third time under the chairmanship of O'Donnell.
22 June	The Chancellor of the Exchequer, Gordon Brown, in his Mansion House speech, says the 'strength of national purpose' needed to maintain UK security requires 'retaining our independent nuclear deterrent'.
27 June	The Prime Minister's Group on the Future of the Deterrent meets for the first time.
28 June	The Prime Minister, Tony Blair, tells Parliament that a decision will be taken in 2006.
30 June	The Commons Defence Committee publishes its report *The Future of the UK's Strategic Nuclear Deterrent: the Strategic Context*.
12 July	Tony Blair confirms that Parliament will vote on the future of the deterrent.
26 July	The government responds to the Commons Defence Committee report on the strategic context.
18 September	The Official Group on the Future of the Deterrent meets for the fourth time under the chairmanship of O'Donnell.
17 October	The Official Group on the Future of the Deterrent meets for the fifth time under the chairmanship of Sheinwald.
10 November	The Official Group on the Future of the Deterrent meets for the sixth time under the chairmanship of O'Donnell.
15 November	The Prime Minister's Group on the Future of the Deterrent meets for the second time.
21 November	The Minister for Defence Procurement, Lord Drayson, gives

evidence to the Commons Defence Committee inquiry into the strategic nuclear deterrent, on the manufacturing and skills base.

23 November The Cabinet discusses future threats which might require the retention of nuclear weapons by the UK.

4 December Full Cabinet decides, without 'any dissenting voices', to authorise construction of a new generation of missile-carrying submarines to sustain UK deterrent over the period 2020–2050. A White Paper, *The Future of the United Kingdom's Nuclear Deterrent* (Cm 6994), is published that afternoon.

6 December The Commons Defence Committee announces its inquiry into the White Paper.

7 December President Bush and Tony Blair exchange letters arranging collaboration on Trident's 'life extension programme' under the terms of the 1958 agreement on nuclear co-operation and the 1963 Polaris Sales Agreement, and stating that 'any successor to the D5 system' will be compatible with UK submarine-carried launch systems.

19 December Tony Blair publishes the UK–US exchange of letters. The Commons Defence Committee publishes its report on the manufacturing and skills base.

2007

14 March House of Commons votes 409–161 to renew the Trident system (88 Labour MPs vote against).

2009

23 September Gordon Brown announces that the UK is prepared to consider reducing from four to three the number of its nuclear submarines. This reduction caught many in the MOD, FCO and Cabinet Office by surprise.

2010

May　　　　　Coalition programme for government states that 'we will maintain Britain's nuclear deterrent, and have agreed that the renewal of Trident will be scrutinised to ensure value for money. Liberal Democrats will continue to make the case for alternatives.'

12 October　　National Security Council agrees to delay the 'Main Gate' decision on the 'Successor' system until 2016, plus a range of changes listed below.

19 October　　'Value for money' study is published in the *Strategic Defence and Security Review*: cut the number of missile tubes from twelve to eight. Extend the service life of the Vanguard submarines into the late 2020s and early 2030s. 'Agreed to defer and potentially remove over £1 billion of future spending on infrastructure over the next 10 years.' Take the second investment decision known as 'Main Gate' around 2016. A delay of five years. Delivery of the first 'Successor' submarine in 2028. Reduce the number of warheads on board each submarine from forty-eight to forty. Reduce requirement for operationally available warheads from fewer than 160 to no more than 120. Reduce overall nuclear weapon stockpile to no more than 189.

3 December　　Liam Fox, Secretary of State for Defence, announces that the government's decision to prolong the life of the current Vanguard submarines by four years would cost an extra £1.2bn.

2011

18 May　　　　Treasury and MOD announce the signing off of the 'Initial Gate' decision covering the configuration of the 'Successor' boats' missile compartments and propulsion system, the Rolls Royce Pressurised Water Reactor, known as PWR 3. The actual signing off had taken place on 29 March 2011.

2011–12

18 May 2011   The coalition announces a new 'Trident Alternative Review' to be overseen by Nick Harvey, Liberal Democrat Minister for the Armed Forces. It was to be led by the Cabinet Office and tasked to examine credible alternatives to a submarine-based system; any credible submarine-based systems other than Trident; and any credible alternative postures other than continuous at-sea deterrence. This report is due to go jointly to the Prime Minister and Deputy Prime Minister in December 2012.

In March 2008, Michael Quinlan prepared his template for a seminar on 'Cabinets and the Bomb' sponsored by the British Academy in association with the National Archives and Queen Mary's Mile End Group. The chronology above is an extended version of the one produced for that occasion (and I am very grateful to Dr Catherine Haddon of the Institute for Government, James Jinks of the School of History, Queen Mary and the Mile End Group and James Rivington of the British Academy for their help with this).

That evening at the British Academy, surrounded by former Cabinet ministers, fellow defence officials, serving and retired, plus scientists and scholars of Cabinet government and politico-military history, Michael opened the proceedings by identifying eight themes which emerged from what he called the 'treasure chest' of declassified records we had before us ranging from the early 1940s to the mid-1970s, published later that year by the British Academy[15] as a non-partisan contribution to the current debate about Trident replacement. It followed the Blair Cabinet's decision so to do on the morning of 4 December 2006, 'without any dissenting voices' (as the Prime Minister's Press Secretary briefed the lobby correspondents shortly afterwards[16]). A White Paper, *The Future of the United Kingdom's Nuclear Deterrent*, was presented to Parliament that afternoon.[17]

Here are the Quinlan octet of factors that, in various flurries, go – or went in Cold War days – into the making of the politico-nuclear weather when the UK faces a big decision:

1. **Rationale**. Michael Quinlan picked out what he called discernible strands: prestige; seat at top table; influence with the United States; contribution to overall western deterrence.

2. **Challenge**. Within governments and Whitehall and without. Michael said: 'I find myself wondering just why challenges to nuclear-weapon status were more frequently recurrent, and went deeper, in Britain than in any of the other four Treaty-recognised possessors [USA, USSR/Russia, France and China].'[18]

3. **Cost**. 'A continued worry,' wrote Michael. And indeed it is today as it was in the Cabinet committee discussions presided over by Clement Attlee in 1945–47 which led to the decision in January 1947 to make a British bomb[19] (which was not divulged to Parliament until May 1948).[20] It's interesting to note, when examining the swathe of decision-taking from that version of austerity Britain (and, in the late 1940s, it really was austerity-on-stilts) to our own, just how often a decision to carry on as a nuclear weapons power or upgrade our delivery capability has coincided with economic crisis. This was true of the Polaris system in the mid-1960s rolling economic crisis of the first Wilson governments;[21] it was true when the decision was taken to improve the penetrability of Polaris with the 'Chevaline' improvement in the final days of the Heath government[22] and the decision of the last Wilson administration and the Callaghan government to carry on with 'Chevaline'.[23] It was true, too, in the fiscally stretched and recession-hit early 1980s when the first Thatcher government decided to replace Polaris with Trident.[24] It was true once more in the summer and autumn of 2011 as the new National Security Committee, created by David Cameron, sought to reconcile the diverging views of the coalition partners on a successor system to Trident (of which more in a moment).

4. **Attitude of the United States**. Put simply, and this is me not Michael, if a US President decided to pull the plug on the 1958 Agreement for Cooperation on the Uses of Atomic Energy for Mutual Defence Purposes or the Polaris Sales Agreement 1963,[25] the UK would very quickly be out of the nuclear weapons business. According to the

late Sir Hermann Bondi, Chief Scientific Adviser to the Ministry of Defence in the early 1970s, 'If the Americans tell us at one stage, "We will go on for another twelve years but not a day longer", we can adapt. If the Americans say tomorrow, "All we do now for you will stop", then it won't be many months before we don't have a weapon.'[26]

5. **France**. A powerful factor in British thinking since General de Gaulle finally achieved nuclear status for his country with the atomic test in the Algerian Sahara in February 1960. And it's linked to the question of American attitudes. So far, neither the leaderships of the USA or the UK has wanted France to be the sole nuclear weapons power in Europe.

6. **Ethics**. This covers a wide area from those who believe the possession, let alone the contemplation of use in any contingency, is inherently immoral to questions of both the circumstances of use and associated targeting for those involved in the formulation of policy.

7. **Institutional pressures**. Which armed service possessed the deterrent duty? The cost of remaining a nuclear weapons power to other budgets both within the deterrent-duty service, its impact upon the armed forces generally and the overall configuration of the defence budget.

8. **Secrecy**. This factor is much diminished. The ending of the Cold War helped naturally. But even before it had, Michael Quinlan's evidence on Polaris replacement to the House of Commons Defence Select Committee in 1980 was a breakthrough in relative openness[27], as was, in the same year, the so-called *Defence Open Government Document 80/23*,[28] which set out in public more fully than before the UK's deterrent rationale and which, though anonymous, bore all the hallmarks of Michael's distinctive pen. And it is to the credit of post-Cold War administrations of all parties that we now have vastly more information in the public domain including the size of the nuclear inventory.[29] As Lord Carrington, a veteran of nuclear policy decision-taking, talking of Cold War days, said at the British Academy seminar in March 2007: 'Unless you were quite senior in the government, you knew nothing about those things at all. You talk about Parliament being ignorant ... We were all ignorant about it.'[30]

Because of the special secrecy that attached to UK nuclear weapons policy-making, certainly over its first three to four decades, the release of the files under the Thirty-Year Rule represents a classic and important example of catch-up history – delayed freedom of information, if you like, or, perhaps, more vividly, the retrospective bugging of the Cabinet Room, the Chiefs of Staff suite, the Joint Intelligence Committee and other of Whitehall's more sensitive locations. A great deal of money has been sunk into the making and sustenance of Britain as a nuclear weapons power, and a dash of retrospective accountability through the release of such documents is no more than the taxpayers' deserts.

But the documentary trail, indispensable as it is, only takes you so far. This kind of retrospective eavesdropping doesn't capture personality, the more vivid interventions or turns of phrase in No. 10 or at Chequers, or round the Cabinet table. It cannot because the Cabinet Secretariat or the No. 10 Private Office staff are trained to be sparse and restrained in their note-taking, which is designed to record what is needed of discussions for the purposes of action to be taken, not to meet the needs of historical reconstruction or telling anecdote.

The most famous example of this is the meeting of Attlee's Cabinet Committee on Atomic Energy, GEN 75 in the Cabinet Office classification, on the afternoon of Friday 25 October 1946. This was the moment when the UK might have decided *not* to become a nuclear power before it had really started because the expense and the diversion of scarce scientific and engineering resources were too great for a recovering postwar Britain once the United States Congress had cut off nuclear collaboration with the McMahon Act of that year. Ernest Bevin, the great Foreign Secretary and dominant force in the Attlee Cabinet, was late for the meeting. He had been lunching well.

By the time he wheezed in, the economic ministers, Hugh Dalton from the Treasury and Stafford Cripps from the Board of Trade, were well on the way to talking out the bomb project on the aforementioned grounds of opportunity cost, arguing that the country could not afford to build the gaseous diffusion plant whose construction was the subject of the meeting. Bevin, we know from the testimony of Sir Michael Perrin, one of the Ministry of Supply team at the meeting (Supply was the bomb department after the war), engaged in one of his great and, in this case, historically significant eruptions. He was having none of it and he roared out in his strong West Country accent:

> That won't do at all ... we've got to have this ... I don't mind for myself, but I don't want any other Foreign Secretary of this country to be talked to or at by a Secretary of State in the United States as I have just had in my discussions with Mr Byrnes.

And here comes the passage that has resonated down the years:

> We've got to have this thing over here whatever it costs ... We've got to have the bloody Union Jack on top of it.

On the way back to the Ministry of Supply from No. 10, Lord Portal, the World War II Chief of the Air Staff and now Controller of Production of Atomic Energy, turned to Perrin and said: 'You know, if Bevin hadn't come in then, we wouldn't have had that bomb, Michael.'[31]

Here's how Denis Rickett's Cabinet Secretariat minutes capture this crucial, crunch moment:

> In discussion it was urged that we must consider seriously whether we could afford to divert from civilian consumption and the restoration of our balance of payments, the economic resources required for a project on this scale. Unless present trends were reversed we might find ourselves faced with an extremely serious economic and financial situation in two or three years' time.

On the other hand it was argued that we could not afford to be left behind in a field which was of such revolutionary importance from an industrial, no less than from a military point of view. Our prestige in the world, as well as our chances of securing American co-operation would both suffer if we did not exploit to the full a discovery in which we had played a leading part at the outset.[32]

The official note conveys the essentials; it eschews the atmospherics and Bevin's *force majeure*.

The great power impulse, Ernie Bevin's motive power that autumn afternoon in No. 10, was at work again when the Churchill Cabinet (and this time it was the full Cabinet, not a Cabinet committee, that took the decision[33]) authorised the great leap in terms of destructive power from fission to fusion, from the atomic bomb to the hydrogen bomb, in 1954. The atmospheric, as opposed to the desiccated account this time, was provided by Lord Plowden, first chairman of the Atomic Energy Authority, recalling in conversation with me in 1988 for the BBC Radio 4 historical documentary, *A Bloody Union Jack on Top of It*, his receiving

a minute from the Prime Minister, from Churchill, saying to let him know what it would cost, what effort would be necessary to develop and manufacture hydrogen bombs. And under the direction of Bill Penney, and the collaboration of Hinton and Cockcroft [the so-called 'Atomic Knights' who pioneered Britain's bomb project], I was given the answer to his question, and I went to see Churchill in his room in the House of Commons after lunch, and when I explained what the effort necessary would be, he paused for a time, and nodded his head, and said in that well-known voice of his, 'We must do it. It's the price we pay to sit at the top table.' And having said that, he got up and tied a little black ribbon round his eyes, and lay down on his bed in his room, and went to sleep.[34]

The Chiefs of Staff, in fact, rather overdid the great power aspect in the run-up to the 1954 H-bomb decision. They pressed for it as a means of strengthening 'our position and influence as a world power' claiming that 'our scientific skill and technological capacity to produce the hydrogen weapon puts within our grasp the ability to be on terms with the United States and Russia'.[35] There was no way in the mid-to-late 1950s that the UK could hope to come anywhere near matching the growing nuclear arsenals of the United States and the Soviet Union. It was no longer a world of competing great powers and duelling European empires. There were two military superpowers and the rest. Britain was the biggest power of the rest, and nuclear weapons were a key element in that. But 'on terms', with the Soviet Union and the USA? No. Such thinking on the part of the chiefs was a prime example of what Stryker McGuire calls the UK 'pocket superpower' impulse.

Perhaps the most bizarre ministerial intervention uncaptured by the now declassified official papers is that of George Brown in the Cabinet discussions when Harold Wilson, having given a contrary impression during the 1964 general election,[36] had taken the decision, with a tiny Cabinet committee of three (the smallest ever), to carry on with the Polaris programme to sustain the British bomb once the V-bombers stepped down from the deterrent role.[37] The reasoning in Wilson's tiny MISC 16 group (just him and Patrick Gordon Walker, Foreign Secretary, and Denis Healey, Defence Secretary) was interesting when they met on Armistice Day 1964. Three Polaris-laden Royal Navy submarines 'would represent the minimum force which would be acceptable to us in the event of the dissolution of the NATO alliance'.[38] There it is – the 'standing alone' contingency, the memory of summer–autumn 1940 which Sir Frank Cooper, another long time MOD nuclear insider, reckoned always played powerfully on Prime Ministers' minds, as we shall see shortly.

The mercurial, occasionally liquid-fuelled and, therefore, unpredictable George Brown weighed in during a subsequent discussion in a full Cabinet on 26 November 1964 which, amongst other things, had to consider the question of three or four submarines.[39] Denis Healey took up the story when interviewed for *A Bloody Union Jack on Top of It*:

Jim [Callaghan, Chancellor of the Exchequer] wanted it down to three, just to save money, of course. But George Brown wanted it down to three on the grounds that with three boats we couldn't be sure of always having one on patrol, and therefore it couldn't be regarded as capable of being used independently.

This, I suspect, was not a line of argument that had been anticipated – remaining a nuclear power for some of the time, but not all of the time, thereby perhaps losing part of what some might see as the moral stigma of being a nuclear power. An unlikely figure, the Secretary of State for Education, the quiet and conciliatory Michael Stewart, saw off the Brown argument in a very British Nonconformist fashion. Denis Healey again:

I remember Michael Stewart saying at the time that it reminded him very much of when he was on the committee of the Fulham Co-op in the 1930s and they were discussing, being good Methodists all, whether, for the first time, they should stock wine. And they finally decided they would stock wine, but only very poor wine.[40]

A little dash of Methody plus the spirit of the co-operative movement apparently took care of that argument at least for the time being. It has surfaced again in our two post-Cold War decades in the shape of the contention that, even if the UK retains a nuclear force, we no longer need continuous at-sea deterrence (known in the business as CASD [Cazz-D]) – that is a submarine on patrol at all times, and, therefore, three boats rather than four are perfectly adequate.

CASD or no CASD is but one of the factors that has illustrated the fact that the UK, in the words of another former MOD Permanent Secretary, Sir Kevin Tebbit, has 'always been a reluctant nuclear power'. Though, as Sir Kevin added at a Royal United Services Institute seminar in September 2009, the Bomb has, so far, been treated by those involved in its provision and sustenance as 'the ultimate backbone ... Governments know there is a point beyond which they cannot be intimidated.'[41] This, too, was very much the late Hermann Bondi's view. He told Michael Quinlan that, in Michael's words, 'a nuclear state is a state that no one can afford to make desperate.'[42]

This was very much the line Tony Blair took in his 'Foreword' to the White Paper *The Future of the United Kingdom's Nuclear Deterrent*, published in December 2006 after the Cabinet had that morning endorsed his view that Britain should stay nuclear tipped up to the 2050s: 'We cannot', Mr Blair wrote,

> predict the way the world will look in 30 or 50 years' time ... we cannot be sure that a major threat to our vital interests will not emerge over the longer term ... I believe it is crucial that, for the foreseeable future, British Prime Ministers have the necessary assurance that no aggressor can escalate a crisis beyond UK control.[43]

Yet, in one of the more fascinating passages in his memoirs, Tony Blair gives a classic illustration of what I would call the paradox of the double reluctance – reluctant to pay the cost; but even more reluctant to bring the boats, the missiles and the warheads home forever lest the highly unlikely but utterly desperate contingency of a direct nuclear threat to these islands should manifest itself sometime in the future, perhaps suddenly, almost out of the blue, and an unforgiving country would remember on whose prime ministerial watch the British bomb was given up. For once given up, it would, I think, be impossible to restore – certainly without a great deal of time and a pile of public expenditure. Sir Frank Cooper, as we have seen, used to say that this factor would play powerfully as long as 1940 was remembered – when only a small amount of the latest technology (the Spitfires and the Hurricanes) crewed by a small number of immensely highly trained young men was all that stood between us and there not being a recognisable UK in 1941.[44]

Here's the section from Tony Blair's *A Journey*, published in September 2010:

We agreed the renewal of the independent nuclear deterrent. You might think I would have been certain of that decision, but I hesitated over it. I could see clearly the force of the commonsense and practical arguments against Trident, yet in the final analysis I thought giving it up too big a downgrading of our status as a nation, and in an uncertain world, too big a risk for our defence. I did not think this was a 'tough on defence' versus 'weak or pacifist' issue at all.

On simple, pragmatic grounds, there was a case either way. The expense is huge, and the utility in a post-cold war world is less in terms of deterrence, and non-existent in terms of military use. Spend the money on more helicopters, aircraft and anti-terror equipment? Not a daft notion.

In the situations in which British forces would be likely to be called upon to fight, it was pretty clear what mattered most. It is true that it is frankly inconceivable we would use our nuclear deterrent alone, without the US – and let us hope a situation in which the US is even threatening use never arises – but it's a big step to put that beyond your capacity as a country.

So, after some genuine consideration and reconsideration, I opted to renew it. But the contrary decision would have not have been stupid. I had a perfectly good and sensible discussion about it with Gordon [Brown], who was similarly torn. In the end, we both agreed, as I said to him: Imagine standing up in the House of Commons and saying I've decided to scrap it. We're not going to say that, are we? In this instance, caution, costly as it was, won the day.[45]

Gordon Brown's version of being 'torn' and his expression of the paradox of reluctance became apparent in September 2009 when, to the surprise of many during a non-proliferation session of the UN Security Council, he said that 'the United Kingdom will retain only the absolute minimum credible and continuing nuclear deterrent capability.' He went on to say that 'subject to technical analysis and progress in multilateral negotiations, my aim is that when the next class of submarines enters service in the mid-2020s, our fleet should be reduced from four boats to three.'[46] Neither the full Cabinet nor his own nuclear sub-committee of his National Security International Relations and Development Cabinet Committee were consulted. And rumour has it that only at the last minute did Whitehall doubters persuade Mr Brown to add the words 'credible and continuing' to his text after they had been informed of what he intended to say.[47]

Where are we now, post-general election and with coalitionism touching the Bomb for the first time? (Churchill kept his bomb decisions away from his War Cabinet during the wartime coalition government.[48]) The Coalition Agreement of 2010 declared:

> We will maintain Britain's nuclear deterrent, and have agreed that the renewal of Trident should be scrutinised to ensure value for money. Liberal Democrats will continue to make the case for alternatives.[49]

Continuous at-sea deterrence has been maintained and will be sustained under the coalition. The value for money study was completed in the run-up to the coalition's wider Strategic Defence and Security Review (SDSR). The Trident upgrade question sculled through the National Security Council's nuclear policy sub-committee, NSC(N), and, in terms of the political deal required by coalitionism, in meetings outside the committee between the Prime Minister, David Cameron, and the Deputy Prime Minister, Nick Clegg.[50]

The deal was caught in a paper which went to the full National Security Council on 12 October 2010 before being announced as part of the SDSR document, *Securing Britain in an Age of Uncertainty*.[51] It is:

- Defer decisions on a replacement to the current warhead.
- Reduce the cost of the replacement submarine missile compartment.
- Extend the life of the current Vanguard class submarines and re-profile the programme to build replacement submarines.
- Consequently, take the second investment decision (the so-called 'Main Gate' decision) finalising the detailed acquisition plans.

- Design and number of submarines around 2016 (i.e. after the next general election).
- Reduce the number of warheads on board each submarine from forty-eight to forty.
- Reduce the requirement for operationally available warheads from fewer than 160 to no more than 120.
- Reduce the number of operational missiles on each submarine.[52]

A dash of supporting detail:

- The value for money review will save £3.2 billion.[53]
- However, the delay in bringing into service the new submarines and running on the Vanguard boats to the late 2020s and early 2030s (between six and eight years longer than the Polaris-carrying Resolution class submarines were at sea) will add £1.2 billion to the eventual bill.[54]
- The new boats will have eight operational tubes rather than the sixteen on the current Vanguard submarines.[55]

On 29 March 2011 the Ministry of Defence and the Treasury finally signed off the so-called 'Initial Gate' agreement covering the configuration of the 'Successor' boats' missile compartments and their propulsion system.[56] It was arguments about the latter which had delayed it since the previous September.

The Treasury were finally persuaded that the cost of a new Rolls-Royce pressured water reactor 3 system (PWR 3), rather than carrying on with an improved model of the latest version of the PWR 2 installed in the new Astute hunter-killer class, was worthwhile in cost terms given the stringent health and safety requirements likely to apply in the 2030s, 2040s and 2050s. The Fukushima disaster in Japan thrust into everyone's minds the risks that can be incurred by running on reactors designed a generation-plus earlier.[57]

The decision of 29 March 2011 was not announced, however, until 18 May 2011 as government pronouncements fell into pre-election purdah until the local government polls and the referendum on the alternative vote system for Westminster had passed in early May. In addition to the statement by Liam Fox, Secretary of State for Defence, in the House of Commons that day,[58] the coalition published an *Initial Gate Parliamentary Report*.[59] The document noted that this would add £50 million to the cost of each 'Successor' submarine (whether the squadron will be three or four boats will be decided at the time of the 'Main Gate' decision in 2016). The reasons given justifying the extra cost were that fitting PWR 3 would provide 'superior performance over PWR 2' as it would significantly reduce periods in upkeep and maintenance. A particularly important issue was safety: 'As we move to a new class of submarine the requirement to continually improve our performance ... is only met through "PWR 3".'[60]

As for the 'white forest', there will be a Common Missile Compartment (CMC) with the next US generation of deterrent-carrying submarines to cater for the current Trident D5 missiles and any successors. 'The baseline design for a CMC is a 12 tube unit and work is ongoing with the US to look at how best to include our requirement for eight operational missiles into this design.'[61] The horizon for propulsion, hull design, missile systems, sonar, stealth – all the factors that go into the making of these huge vessels, their safety, endurance and undetectability – is deep into the 2050s.

More immediately, the question of Britain and the Bomb, I reckon, will remain live throughout the current parliament. And 2015, if the coalition endures that long, will be a nuclear election like 1964 and 1983 when Michael Foot took on Margaret Thatcher. What might be the outcome? So far, though the demise of the British bomb has occasionally seemed possible, no Prime Minister has wanted to risk history's verdict as the premier-who-gave-it-away (though I think Michael Foot would have stopped it had he become Prime Minister with a sufficient majority in the 1980s). So far, as Michael Quinlan put it during a seminar to coincide with the 'Secret State' exhibition I curated at the National Archives in May 2004, each set of decision-makers faced with the question of upgrading or carrying on has produced 'a set of rationales to clothe that gut decision'.[62] And carrying on, in my judgement, has been exactly that kind of 'gut decision' rather than an evidence-based one for all the paperwork and cost-benefit analysis that precedes the moment of final choice.

But maybe the next election will produce a different behaviour pattern. Certainly there are no Ernie Bevins left to press the case for 'a Union Jack on top of it' whatever the cost. But if public spending is still tight and growth spluttering, a construction bill of £20 billion and a through-life cost over fifty years of £80–100 billion might appear unmanageable. Then a number of possibilities flicker.

Cripps and Dalton could have their belated way. A decision might be reached that the economy can't bear the load. The Vanguard boats could be run on until they are no longer serviceable and that's it. Or they may swiftly be brought home to Faslane and decommissioned to save running costs.

It may be the hour of George Brown and Michael Stewart's interwar Fulham Co-operative Society; no more continuous at-sea deterrence with a replacement system cheaper and less top-of-the-range than Trident-carrying 'Successor' class submarines.

Or, if the Conservatives win an overall majority and govern solo, a more slimly configured version of the *status quo* with fewer missiles (as already announced) and warheads but four boats sustaining continuous at-sea deterrence and a 'Bloody Union Jack on Top of It' through to the 2050s which will give Britain 100 years of an operational bomb (the first one having been delivered to RAF Wittering in December 1953).

Who knows? The question is – and will remain for some time – on heat, and the Quinlan criteria will retain their salience.

There is, too, a special ingredient in the UK's rolling debate about the Bomb. It is, as Professor Sir Lawrence Freedman put it in late 2011, 'always about tangibles and intangibles'. The tangibles are all the other things 'you can buy with that money'. The intangibles? What might await us deep in the future. 'It's either completely useless,' said Lawrie Freedman. 'Or one day, it might be the only thing that saves our children and our grandchildren.' I agree very strongly with that – which is why I am a deterrent man.[63]

My guess, and it's only that, is that in some form or another, the UK will remain a nuclear weapons state. If we decided to finish, it would be a considerable moment, the rupturing of a long history that goes back to the pioneering days seventy-plus years ago during the Second World War and the repudiation of a sizeable 'gut instinct'. And, as that connoisseur of us Brits, Jean Monnet, remarked of the British people in the late 1970s – another time of financial stress, nuclear weapons debate and anxiety about our place in the world: 'They have not suddenly stepped aside from history'.[64] That, I think, still applies to us – nuclear weapons and all – and, in my judgement, it's set to continue.

My guess is that in the 2050s there will be a 'bloody Union Jack' on top of a British bomb aboard a Royal Navy submarine somewhere in the North Atlantic. New Prime Ministers will, early in their premiership, continue to be briefed by the Cabinet Secretary and the National Security Adviser on the four choices of 'last resort' letters they have to sign for placing inside the inner safe of each Trident and 'Successor' submarine, to be opened only when the captain is sure Britain has been reduced to a smoking, irradiated ruin by a devastating nuclear strike and neither the Prime Minister nor the two 'nuclear alternate' ministers he or she has selected can take or transmit a decision on whether or not to retaliate.

They face four choices:

1. Retaliate.
2. Don't retaliate.
3. If 2, put yourself under the command of the United States, if it's still there; or sail to Australia, if it's still there; or put in at a neutral port.
4. Captain of the boat to use his own judgement (though this fourth option has not been on the menu of choices presented to PMs in recent years).[65]

After the briefing, the Cabinet Secretary and the National Security Adviser leave the new man or woman in No. 10 alone with the draft letters and a shredding machine to destroy the unused ones for no-one must know what the PM's decision is. The new premier places the signed letters in four envelopes, one for each boat, and seals them before a Cabinet Office official travels to Faslane and oversees their installation into the inner safes.[66]

The moment you sign is when you really know you're Prime Minister. It is the most awesome and solitary decision of your entire premiership. That's when you truly live in the shadow of the Bomb.

5

THE THIN WISPS OF TOMORROW:
THE HORIZON-SCANNER'S CRAFT

A theorem: In matters of military contingency, the expected, precisely because it is expected, is not to be expected. Rationale: What we expect, we plan and provide for; what we plan and provide for, we thereby deter; what we deter does not happen. What does happen is what we did not deter, because we did not plan and provide for it, because we did not expect it.

SIR MICHAEL QUINLAN, 2008[1]

MICHAEL Quinlan never published his theorem. It was contained in one of the last papers he wrote before his death in 2009. He gave it a very Quinlanesque title – 'Shaping the Defence Programme: Some Platitudes'. It distilled well over fifty years of largely inside experience of Whitehall's – and Britain's – tales of the unexpected. Quinlan's Law should, like Harry Truman's 'The Buck Stops Here' in the late 1940s and early 1950s White House,[2] be converted into a set of plaques to be placed on the desks of all secretaries of state, permanent secretaries, military chiefs, secret service chiefs and Whitehall chief economists as an aid to chiefly wisdom and humility.

Alongside Quinlan's Law they should place a kind of sub-title plaque – 'The Thin Wisps of Tomorrow'. The phrase was minted by the great

French historian Fernand Braudel in the Introduction to his *A History of Civilisations*, published in 1987. This is what he wrote:

> When it comes to the present day, with all its different potential *dénouements*, deciding which are the really major problems essentially means imagining the last line of the play – discerning, among all the possible outcomes, those which are most likely to occur. The task is difficult, hazardous and indispensable ... forecasting the near future – the 'futurible', to use a frightful word beloved of certain economists. The 'futurible' is what now can legitimately be described in the future tense – that thin wisp of tomorrow which can be guessed at and very nearly grasped.[3]

Feeling for those 'thin wisps' is quite a powerful impulse in us mortals. Institutions often incorporate a permanent need, a particular human anxiety or aspiration and are driven by a desire for *certainty*.[4] Some reflect the desire to institutionalise social justice (the Department of Work and Pensions), altruism (the National Health Service), national protection (the Ministry of Defence) or public safety (the Home Office and Ministry of Justice). The last century, in fact, has seen a succession of government-led attempts to reduce *uncertainty* – the intelligence and security services are a classic example – by trying to anticipate events, good and bad, and to increase the chances of the good happening and to reduce the prospects of the harmful.

Today what is called 'horizon-scanning' is a trans-Whitehall activity on a substantial scale. Indeed, Braudel's 'thin wisps of tomorrow' problem has absorbed the energies of some of the best-primed clusters of grey cells in Crown service since, as we have seen, the prototypical Edwardian national security council – the Committee of Imperial Defence, the CID – came into experimental being in the early 1900s. The pursuit of top-of-the-range horizon-scanning has been a kind of holy grail for Whitehall ever since, though the subject has still to find its scholar/cartographer. A really good book cries out to be written on this.

For in its various guises, the horizon-scanners' craft has been central to the British state's preparations for the worst from that day to this.

What might be some of the key ingredients of this still-to-be-written history? By 1909–10, the CID had bequeathed two enduring legacies to the British way of government. The first was the British intelligence community, which emerged in something approaching its recognisably modern form as the Secret Service Bureau in 1909 following a CID report (it split into MI6, the modern Secret Intelligence Service, and MI5, today's Security Service, in 1911).[5] The second was the practice of a prototypical version of modern foresight/contingency planning in the shape of the 'War Book'.

The 'War Book' was the inspiration of a remarkable Royal Marine artillery officer, Maurice Hankey, who joined the CID's Secretariat in 1908 and became its Secretary in 1912.[6] As so often with the British way of horizon-scanning, it took a crisis and a scare to trigger action and follow-through. In this instance it was the Agadir crisis, when the Germans indulged in a dash of gunboat diplomacy off Morocco as part of a dispute with France in July 1911[7] (more on this in chapter 11), which 'hastily intensified the work already proceeding [inside the Committee of Imperial Defence] of formulation and codification of plans for immediate action by all departments in case of war,' as Franklyn Johnson, the historian of the CID, put it.[8]

It was another swathe of threats (largely home-grown ones in this instance, though the shadow of the Russian Revolution hung heavy over the guardians of national security at the time) that stimulated the next bout of Whitehall horizon-scanning and contingency planning – the rash of trade union militancy and strikes after the Great War in 1919. The Prime Minister, David Lloyd George, approved the making permanent of the *ad hoc* arrangements his Supply and Transport Committee had improvised to keep key services moving.[9] For twenty years thereafter, the Supply and Transport Organisation was the regular Whitehall provider of foresight and contingency planning to cope with strikes that hit what its legal underpinning, the Emergency Powers Act 1920, called 'the essentials of life', which it defined as the 'distribution of food, water, fuel … light … [and] … the means of locomotion'.[10] The Supply and Transport Organisation was the chief instrument which enabled Prime Minister Stanley Baldwin to break the General Strike in May 1926.[11]

It was the Army's man on the Supply and Transport Committee, Winston Churchill,[12] who was the moving spirit behind the creation of the next Whitehall innovation, the Chiefs of Staff Committee with its own horizon-scanning team, the Joint-Planning Committee. Churchill, as Secretary for War and Air, was determined to bring together properly the three chiefs of the armed forces and floated the idea in a debate in the House of Commons on 12 November 1919.[13] A CID inquiry, chaired by Lord Salisbury with the ubiquitous Hankey as its secretary, was required before the Chiefs of Staff Committee came into formal existence in 1923 and it fell to the first-ever Labour government under Ramsay MacDonald to implement the Salisbury Report in 1924.[14] The Chiefs of Staff Committee remains today the regular weekly Monday afternoon meeting of what since 1958 have been the four Chiefs of Staff (the Chief of the Defence Staff, the Chief of the General Staff, the First Sea Lord and the Chief of the Air Staff). In a second burst of institution-building, MacDonald created his Economic Advisory Council in 1929, which he intended to be his economic equivalent of the military Chiefs of Staff, though it was of little use as the economic and financial blizzard engulfed the world after the Great Crash of that year.[15]

It was the Chiefs of Staff Committee itself which spawned the next innovation, the Joint Intelligence Committee, created in June 1936 and until 1957 itself a sub-committee of the Chiefs of Staff Committee, to co-ordinate inter-services intelligence. Hankey, once more, was instrumental in persuading the chiefs to take this step.[16] The JIC did not seriously become a shaper of the British horizon-scanners' craft until the pressure of total war finally gave it the bespoke capacity it needed and which neither the chiefs' joint planners, the Foreign Office nor the individual service intelligence departments wished it to have in the first years of its life, leaving it until the weeks before the outbreak of the Second World War 'a peripheral body'. 'Nor', as the official historian of British intelligence 1939–45, Professor

Sir Harry Hinsley, pointed out, 'did the JIC itself show any initiative in volunteering appreciations on more important questions like the intentions and military thinking of foreign states, partly because there was a dearth of reliable information on such questions and partly because service opinion in Whitehall frowned on speculation'.[17]

Churchill's arrival in No. 10 changed all that when he issued a new directive for the JIC requiring it to 'take the initiative in preparing at any hour of the day or night, as a matter of urgency, papers on any development in the international situation whenever this appears desirable to any member in the light of information that might be received'.[18] Yet not until May 1941 was the JIC's Joint Intelligence Staff created,[19] which rapidly developed into a considerable Whitehall player[20] and can be seen as the lineal begetter of today's Assessments Staff, created in 1968, which works to the JIC in the Cabinet Office.[21]

War is a great examiner and refiner of institutions as well as people. The Second World War was remarkable, too, as a test-bed for *postwar* institution-building and the special kind of horizon-scanning that required. The most vivid and enduringly significant example concentrated on welfare rather than warfare though wartime conditions and enabled the designer of this particular blueprint, the social scientist and administrator Sir William Beveridge, to declare: 'A revolutionary moment in the world's history is a time for revolutions, not for patching'.[22]

Beveridge was not engaged in preparing for the worst – avoiding the worst (a return to the 1930s) or preparing for the best would be a better way of describing his purpose when he seized upon a commission from the wartime coalition government to tidy up existing social insurance provision and turned his inquiry into an extraordinarily comprehensive plan for a postwar transformation designed to tackle and conquer what he called the 'five giants on the road of reconstruction' – 'Want, Disease, Ignorance, Squalor and Idleness'.[23]

Horizon-scanning infused Beveridge's craft because he rightly sensed that unless these 'giants' were hammered simultaneously, the tough shell created by interlocking deprivations would not crack. The Beveridge Report was a public document and attracted great political and press attention from the moment it was published in November 1942 thanks, in part, to the 'People's William' possessing a considerable gift for self-publicity and, in various forms, it sold 635,000 copies, quite extraordinary by any standards let alone those of a government-commissioned document.[24]

Most of the early postwar innovations in horizon-scanning, however, were implemented in intense secrecy. For example, the idea of the 'War Book' was extended to the pound sterling in early 1948 lest the (hugely overvalued against the US dollar) currency needed to be devalued in a fast-moving crisis in those days of fixed exchange rates. At the end of January, a senior Treasury official, Ernest Rowe-Dutton, began the preparation of what he called a 'Sterling War-Book'.[25] By mid-February, a first draft was ready covering who should be told if D (for devaluation) Day were imminent, and in what order, and the kind of technical and administrative readjustments that would be needed. It was real 'need-to-know' country. The Bank of England, understandably, was brought in on the plan but there is nothing in the file to suggest that ministers were told.[26] Work on the 'Sterling War Book' lapsed in the summer of 1948 but it was revived, in something of a panic, in the spring of 1949 when sterling came under pressure. D-Day finally came on 18 September 1949 when the exchange rate of the pound against the dollar fell from $4.05 to $2.80.

But the greatest leap in the imaginative capacities of Whitehall's postwar horizon-scanners was required, as we have seen, on the part of those charged with contemplating a different kind of revolution – the Bomb. Its dreadful potential stretched the craft in several directions and further than anything encountered before.

The potency of the Bomb led Whitehall horizon-scanners to pursue interlocking themes:

- When would the Soviet Union acquire a nuclear capability? How soon and how many bombs would result?[27]
- What those bombs could do to the United Kingdom and its bases overseas.
- The degree to which the civilian population could be protected from

nuclear bombardment and how they could be succoured and the country revived post-attack.

- What a British nuclear deterrent needed to be capable of inflicting on the Soviet Union and its allies.

- From the early 1960s the progress and capability of Soviet anti-ballistic missile defence and its implications for the capability of the UK deterrent.[28]

- How best to prepare and structure the British state to increase the chances of government continuity during and after a nuclear assault (including the command and control of UK nuclear forces).

- The preparation of scenarios for transition-to-war exercises of various kinds.

The Bomb has been a constant horizon-scanning imperative for Whitehall from August 1945 to the present day. For example, when the Joint Intelligence Committee prepared an assessment in the autumn of 2006 for the Official Group on the Future of the Deterrent and Tony Blair's Prime Ministerial Group on the same subject (out of which came the decision to upgrade the Trident system[29]), it looked far further ahead than its normal practice, ffity years, in fact, concentrating on three areas – likely nuclear proliferation; possible developments in anti-submarine warfare; and likely advances in missile defence capabilities.[30]

But the palm for the finest piece of horizon-scanning of the postwar years must go to the *Future Policy Study*, briefly mentioned in chapter 3, which Harold Macmillan commissioned as Prime Minister in great secrecy (only the Foreign Secretary, Selwyn Lloyd, knew about it amongst his ministerial colleagues) in June 1959 shortly before he began the glide-path to his autumn victory in the 'You've Never Had It So Good' election of 1959 on the ticket of peace and prosperity.[31] The *Future Policy Study*'s horizon-scan was a decade forward – to where Britain would be by 1970 on then current policies.

It depicted a Britain evermore dwarfed by the superpowers; increasingly falling behind the EEC 'Six', as they were then, in economic and trade terms; and a country possibly struggling to maintain both a comprehensive welfare state and substantial defence spending. The only thing Macmillan's scanners got seriously wrong was Northern Ireland. In their treatment of Ireland they did not foresee a recrudescence of the 'Troubles'.[32] The final paper was so gloomy that Macmillan pulled it from the intended full Cabinet discussion in February 1960 and took it to a special Cabinet committee instead.[33]

Fifty years on, we desperately need an equivalent of the *Future Policy Study*, which set a still unsurpassed gold standard for width, quality and candour. Though cumulatively, the Foreign Office's Planning Staff, created in 1964, and now called the Policy Unit, has produced fine work. For example, a particular gem, penned by the young diplomat Donald McLaren (or the McLaren of McLaren, to give him his full title) in July 1988 on the future of east–west relations, foresaw the fall of the Berlin Wall.[34]

Ted Heath, as part of his new style of government after winning the 1970 general election, sought to institutionalise an approach to horizon-scanning with his creation of the Central Policy Review Staff, led by the former Head of Research at Shell, Lord Rothschild. From its inception in 1971, reflecting Victor Rothschild's background, it kept a close eye on energy problems, especially the supply of oil, to which we shall return in a moment. More widely it sought to meet ministers' need, most vocally expressed by Willie Whitelaw, to avoid being taken by surprise so often (what Whitelaw actually said was he 'did not want to read about V and G [Vehicle and General, an insurance firm that collapsed in 1972] in the newspapers in his bath'[35]).

Rothschild set up an early warning system (EWS) and attempted to persuade Whitehall departments to share their anxieties about the future. The EWS was a brave stab at horizon-scanning but it was hobbled by two things: the Treasury were highly reluctant to pool information on sensitive economic matters, the exchange rate of sterling in particular; and Heath's unwillingness, given the top secret nature of much of the material, to circulate the EWS reports to all his ministerial colleagues.[36]

As the pace of leaks has grown from the mid-1970s, fear of disclosure has been a considerable problem for the more candid 'what if?' exercises.

In the Heath years anxieties about the security of energy supplies were made still more fraught by the miners' strike of 1972 (the first national one since 1926). Rothschild had, in fact, submitted his first CPRS paper on 'Oil Economics and Supplies' to Heath in September 1971 before the strike began.[37] A refined version of the paper was circulated by Heath to ministers in April 1972 which argued that the country should increasingly rely less on coal and more upon a mix of natural gas and nuclear-powered or oil-fired stations.[38] In May 1973 the CPRS prepared a report for Heath's Cabinet Committee on Economic Strategy on the possible rise in oil prices due to growing scarcity over the next decade possibly to what was then an eye-watering $9 a barrel.[39] Two months later, a Task Force on Oil Supplies, chaired by Lord Carrington, Heath's Defence Secretary, warned the Economic Strategy Committee that a war in the Middle East would have a serious impact on the price of oil though such a war was not thought to be imminent.[40]

It was. On 6 October 1973, Egyptian troops crossed the Suez Canal into the Sinai on the Jewish festival of Yom Kippur and the fourth Arab–Israeli war began. On 16 October, the Organisation of Petroleum Exporting Countries (OPEC) raised the price of oil from $2.90 a barrel to $5.11.[41] In mid-December 1973 they raised it again to $11.65.[42] The price had quadrupled in less than four months. The Carrington contingency and Rothschild's worst-case-by-1985 possibility had met and struck a British economy already reeling from rising commodity prices abroad and growing industrial strife at home.

Each generation of horizon-scanners is shaped by a particular cluster of pacemaker anxieties: Russia and Germany in the early part of the last century; Russia in the 1920s; Germany again in the 1930s; the Soviet Union and the Bomb during the grim forty-year recitative of the Cold War; energy, oil in particular, in the 1970s; jihadi-inspired terrorism from 9/11 on and financial collapses from September 2008 with the cumulative impact of carbon emissions now providing a constant drumbeat, its percussive effect reaching into several other worrying shapes on the horizon.

For example, as George Soros has noted, a future economic shock comparable to that of 2007–08 would, if triggered by a climate change-related event, produce an immense problem for those seeking to put it right.[43] It would reflect decades, if not centuries, of chemical accumulations that could not be remedied either swiftly (if they could be put right at all) or by any of the financial instruments to which individual governments or the G20 resorted at the end of the first decade of the twenty-first century. What Mervyn King, the Governor of the Bank of England, called the 'Panic of 2008', 'because of the almost complete collapse of confidence in financial institutions and the flight of funding that ensued' after the demise of Lehman Brothers in September of that year,[44] would be trumped by a loss of confidence, a surge of anxiety and a level of panic that could scarcely be compared to 2008.

One economist, Professor Lord Stern of Brentford of the London School of Economics, had already produced an analysis and a remedial prescription for the economics of climate change almost exactly two years before the Lehman collapse.[45] Prepared while he was Chief Economic Adviser to the Treasury and written with a style and reach worthy of Beveridge, the Stern Review on *The Economics of Climate Change* scanned the horizon to the period 2030 to 2060 and reckoned that by then there would have been a doubling of pre-Industrial Revolution levels of carbon dioxide in the atmosphere with a 20 per cent probability that the related temperature increase could be over 5°C.

All current Whitehall horizon-scanning that seeks global reach now builds in climate change as both a pacemaker and an omnipresent conditioner of forecasting. For example, the best, in my view, of the regular productions, 'The Global Strategic Trends Programme', run by the Ministry of Defence's Developments, Concepts and Doctrine Centre in London and at the Defence Academy in Shrivenham, treats climate change as one of its three 'Ring Road Issues' (the other two being globalisation and global inequality).[46]

By the end of the last decade the UK government, in horizon-scanning terms (certainly in peacetime), probably had more people at work on a wider canvas than ever before as evidenced by the Future Security and Intelligence Network (FUSION), created by the Government's Chief Scientific Officer, Sir John Beddington, in 2007. Yet the Cabinet Office's first *National Risk Register*, published as the 'Panic of 2008' was really setting in, in its diagram of 'high consequence risks facing the United Kingdom', was completely silent on the financial chaos descending ever more destructively on the UK and the world.[47] If you cast your eye across its range of a dozen anxieties and horrors, nowhere do you find the four horsemen of the financial apocalypse requesting landing permission at Heathrow. In fact, Sir Richard Mottram, former Co-ordinator of Security and Intelligence in the Cabinet Office, has spoken about the UK not engaging in 'own-side' intelligence and how unwelcome a paper on derivatives would have been during his chairmanship of the Joint Intelligence Committee between 2005 and 2007.[48]

Yet the horizon-scanner's craft should blend smartness, and a feel for history enlivened by a sense of the wreckage of predictions past plus an acknowledgement of 'thin wisps' missed. A certain promiscuity of approach is valuable, too, because of the necessary humility this brings. There should be no 'no-go areas'. Horizon-scanning teams should mix insiders and outsiders. The future should not be subject to the Official Secrets Act. It should look for what might be called benign/malign conjunctions. For example, I was very struck by the Shrivenham scanners' assessment of the possibility of clean, abundant and safe nuclear fusion of deuterium and tritium towards the end of their forty-year forward look. Terrific, you might think, without caveat until you realise what it would do to precarious Middle Eastern countries dependent on oil revenues whose value would plummet.[49]

I'll now return briefly to a gap in the Whitehall horizon-scanning machinery which was discussed at a British Academy forum on 15 December 2009, the second of a pair summoned to answer the Queen's question about the financial crisis, when opening a new building at the London School of Economics on 5 November 2008, when she asked: 'If these things were so large, how come everyone missed them?' The first forum resulted in a letter to the Queen from the British Academy signed by myself and Tim Besley, Kuwait Professor of Economics and Political Science at LSE, on the causes and nature of the crisis that had prompted her question, dated 22 July 2009.[50] The second letter, signed once more by Tim Besley and myself on 8 February 2010, examined how the Queen's Crown servants scattered across a host of departments, institutions and agencies might so organise themselves that she would never have to ask such a question again.

As none of the senior Crown servants present at the 15 December 2009 forum had 'volunteered either individually or institutionally' to pull all the scattered horizon-scanning financial and economic material together on a regular basis we finished our letter 'with a modest proposal. If you, Your Majesty, were to ask for a monthly economic and financial horizon-scanning summary from, say, the Cabinet Office, it could hardly be refused. It might take a form comparable to the Joint Intelligence Committee's 'Red Book', which you received each week from 1952 until 2008 when it was abandoned. And, if this were to happen, the spirit of your LSE question would suffuse still more of your crown servants tasked to defend, preserve and enhance the economic well-being of your country.'[51] Sadly, Her Majesty did not take up the suggestion, though there's still time…

There are other, wider problems with the horizon-scanning craft. For example, there is a danger, after a fairly deep immersion into a century or more of the horizon-scanner's trade, of becoming faintly obsessed with the 'thin wisps of tomorrow' and/or growing fatalistic about what can be done about a considerable number of the grimmer contingencies of the kind depicted in the diagram on page 35. Even that great patron of the trade, John Maynard Keynes, was moved to write in September 1931 that 'it is so difficult to predict what is ahead … some of the things which I vaguely apprehend are, like the end of the world, uninsurable risks, and it's useless to worry about them.'[52] Ministers can get like that when confronted, on top of all their instant preoccupations, with less than cheerful material on what might await. Prediction fatigue has afflicted pretty well every set of political customers in Whitehall over the past century, partly because the pictures painted are so rarely jolly.

I am convinced, however, that there is a duty upon governments (and scholars) to *try*, for all the difficulties and the caveats in which horizon-scanning must and will always be embedded. As a historian, I am haunted by what we could and should have picked up in the past in terms of its future significance. Martin Rees, the Astronomer Royal, cited some examples from the 1950s whose life-shaping possibilities were not appreciated at the time in his 2008 Ditchley Foundation Lecture, 'The Next Half Century: A Scientist's Hopes and Fears':

> It was in 1958 that Jack Kilby of Texas Instruments and Robert Noyce of Fairchild Semiconductors built the first integrated circuit – the precursor of today's ubiquitous silicon chips, each containing literally billions of microscopic circuit elements. This was perhaps the most transformative single invention of the past century.
>
> A second technology with huge potential began in Cambridge in the 1950s, when Watson and Crick discovered the bedrock mechanism of heredity – the famous double helix. This discovery launched the science of molecular biology, opening exciting prospects in genomics and synthetic biology.[53]

Martin Rees, perhaps the most thoughtful and careful of the UK's individual horizon-scanners, carries the necessary scepticism with him when he takes to the lectern. Here he is in the shining, gilded Robing Room of the House of Lords in June 2009 delivering the Lord Speaker's Mile End Group Lecture on 'The World in 2050', pointing out that the 'past record of scientific forecasters is dismal. Lord Rutherford averred that nuclear energy was moonshine; Thomas Watson, founder of IBM, thought there might be a world market for five computers; and one of my predecessors as Astronomer Royal said space travel was utter bilge.'[54]

Yet, Lord Rees insisted, we owe it to the generations to come to try:

> We don't know what will be the twenty-first-century-counterparts of the electron, quantum theory, the double helix and the computer – nor where the great innovators of the future will get their formative training and inspiration. But one thing seems clear: the UK's standing depends on sustaining our competitive edge as discoverers and innovators – on ensuring that some of the key ideas of the twenty-first century germinate and – even more – are exploited here in the UK.[55]

And, as the handmaiden to that aspiration, I would add: sustaining in this era of cuts the UK's capacity to strive to sense, find and evaluate the 'thin wisps of tomorrow' and to face up to what those 'wisps' might portend. We owe it to our country, ourselves, our children and our grandchildren, to apply a goodly proportion of our industrial and our collective 'little grey cells' to this most constant and vexing of tasks which, as Braudel wrote, is 'difficult, hazardous and indispensable', to avoid consigning it to what Charles Clarke, the former Home Secretary, calls the ever tempting 'Too Difficult Box',[56] and to concentrate, in particular, upon that terrain John Buchan described at the opening of his classic *The Thirty-Nine Steps* as 'where the incidents defy the probabilities, and march just inside the borders of the possible'[57] while always remembering to cede the last word to Pliny the Elder: 'Only one thing is certain: that nothing is certain.'[58]

6

TASKS AND FLOWS:
THE IMPACT OF THE NATIONAL SECURITY COUNCIL ON BRITISH INTELLIGENCE

The NSC brings together all the key Cabinet ministers, the heads of the armed forces and the heads of the intelligence services. They now see the same information and formally discuss policy far more frequently than has ever been the case in the past outside conditions of war.

WILLIAM HAGUE, FOREIGN AND COMMONWEALTH SECRETARY, ON 'THE ROLE OF SECRET INTELLIGENCE IN FOREIGN POLICY', 16 NOVEMBER 2011.[1]

DELIVERING on-the-record lectures about the most secret places of their domain is something British Foreign Secretaries rarely do. Before 1992 they couldn't do it at all because the existence of the Secret Intelligence Service, MI6, in peacetime had not been avowed until the then Prime Minister, John Major, decided that it should be and named the current chief of SIS as Sir Colin McColl. In his opening paragraph that November afternoon in the FCO's Media Centre, with the three heads of the secret agencies sitting in front of him (Sir John Sawers from SIS; Jonathan Evans from the Security Service, MI5; and Iain Lobban from the Government Communications Headquarters), William Hague acknowledged the singularity of the occasion. 'This', he said, 'is an unusual topic for a Foreign Secretary to discuss in public, but there are important reasons to do so.'[2]

There were, casting one's mind back, 'important reasons' for letting Parliament know about Harold Macmillan's post-Suez decision in 1957 to remove the Joint Intelligence Committee from the purview of the Chiefs of Staff Committee and into the Cabinet Office with a new remit to produce more assessments on political rather than military intelligence.[3] Similarly, there were 'important reasons' for Parliament to know that Harold Wilson in 1968 had agreed that the apex of the British intelligence system would be further enhanced by the creation of a new Assessments Staff to work to it in the Cabinet Office.[4] But Parliament could not be so informed as the JIC did not officially exist in peacetime until the central intelligence machinery was also avowed in 1992.

It was plain early on in the David Cameron premiership that his planned-for innovation in the machinery of government – Britain's first ever National Security Council[5] and the first of his ministerial sub-groups to meet in May 2010[6] – was having an impact on the UK's intelligence agencies and processes at least as important as the 1957 and 1968 developments and, perhaps, even on the scale of 1940–41 when Winston Churchill used the demands of total war to bring the JIC fully and continually into the highest councils of the Second World War machine after an indifferent first five years of its institutional life.[7]

In January 2011, before Operation Ellamy in Libya upped the tempo the following month, the Prime Minister and the Cabinet Secretary, Sir Gus O'Donnell, asked the National Security Adviser, Sir Peter Ricketts, and the chairman of the JIC, Alex Allan, 'to review how the central national security and intelligence machinery and structures can best support the NSC'. The job was carried out by Paul Rimmer, Chief of the Assessments Staff, and Ciaran Martin, then of the Cabinet Office's Intelligence and Security Secretariat.[8]

By the time they had completed the task in summer 2011, Libya had added much experience by providing the first, sustained stress-test to the new national security architecture. David Cameron always planned for the NSC to mutate into a 'War Cabinet' should the need arise and it did so as NSC (L) – 'L' standing for Libya – meeting sixty times at ministerial level, as William Hague revealed in his Intelligence speech, a phenomenally high rate outside conditions of total war. In fact it was sixty-two meetings supported by a genuinely amazing eighty-two meetings of its official, back-up committee, NSC (LO), chaired by Peter Ricketts.[9]

The Rimmer–Martin Report was briefly discussed in the House of Lords during the debate on the 2010/11 annual report from the oversight group of parliamentarians, the Intelligence and Security Committee (ISC), on 12 December 2011. I said in that debate that Rimmer–Martin, in essence, 'recognises the new reality – that the JIC has become partially eclipsed by the work of Mr David Cameron's highly significant innovation on the first day of his premiership when he created the National Security Council. As the National Security Adviser, Sir Peter Ricketts, expressed it during an International Institute of Strategic Studies seminar on 30 November [2011] … the NSC has become "the *über*-customer for the intelligence product", which, he explained, has resulted in a "big change in the landscape of the JIC".[10]

The JIC had, in the words of one insider, 'become slightly backwaterish'. Attendance by some of the 'four star' figures had dropped off, with their deputies turning up on Wednesday afternoons instead.[11] From March to October 2009, the JIC even went down to fortnightly rather than weekly meetings for the first time since its foundation in 1936. But, at a JIC 'away day', in September 2009, it was realised that because of this fortnightly rhythm, discussion of valuable papers from the Assessments Staff had been missed.[12]

Restoration of the weekly cycle, however, did not lead to complete revival. Attendance remained sometimes patchy at what one figure called 'the highest-paid redrafting committee in Whitehall'.[13] So the JIC was not in altogether peak condition in the spring of 2010 when David Cameron entered No. 10 bearing his plan for a National Security Council, though, until the NSC came into being, the JIC had not been surpassed as 'the high table of British intelligence', as its former chairman, the formidable Sir Percy Cradock, used to call it.[14]

Straightaway, the regular NSC weekly meeting on Tuesday mornings right after Cabinet, which David Cameron always chairs if he is in London, ensured that the UK's secret service chiefs spent more time in the company of the Prime Minister and senior ministers than at any period in living Whitehall memory – probably since Churchill's War Cabinet of 1940–45. And the meetings usually begin with a discussion of the paper produced for the occasion by the Cabinet Office's Assessments Staff. The Cameron style is direct but collegiate. He takes pride in having restored collective Cabinet government not least through the NSC process.[15] In my judgement this is partly because he has to deal with Liberal Democrat ministers inside the NSC, partly because it (a) suits his temperament and (b) helps distinguish his style of premiership from that of Tony Blair and Gordon Brown.

NSC (L), the 'War Cabinet' mode, met in COBRA, the Cabinet Office briefing room, with direct communications links across the world to the UK's military commands and diplomatic outposts, sometimes as often as three times a day when Libya was at its height. As one participant put it:

> The PM likes COBRA because he has all the practitioners round the table. He uses it to take decisions and make the machine work. He's very good at spotting when officials slope shoulders. He'll poke and poke at questions ... but he backs off and doesn't brutalise people.[16]

So taken with the NSC style is David Cameron, it is said that he had modelled his post-summer riots Cabinet committee on it.[17]

It was not surprising, therefore, that the NSC soon became felt as the primary pacemaker and task-master of British Intelligence and David Cameron became seen by the intelligence providers as at the more assiduous end of prime ministerial consumers of their product. The JIC will remain the setter of the annual requirements and priorities for the agencies and the Assessments Staff continues to produce the daily 'Highlights of Intelligence' summaries each morning (a Blair innovation) for the Prime Minister and the handful of ministers on the inner intelligence loop.[18] But, as Rimmer–Martin made plain, or rather, David Cameron did in September 2011 when he signed off their report:[19] 'The NSC's priorities should be the lead driver of the JIC agenda following as closely as possible the NSC's agenda and timetable.'

As the report explains, the function will in effect fall to the meeting of the NSC (Officials) on Wednesday morning chaired by the National Security Adviser (Sir Peter Ricketts, 2010–12; Sir Kim Darrock from January 2012):

> NSC (O) is best placed to oversee the tasking of the JIC, in line with its core role of setting strategic direction for the NSC. The NSC (O) should therefore task the JIC. However, the JIC must retain the latitude to provide early warning on issues outside the immediate cycle of the NSC agenda.[20]

This new arrangement has significant implications for the rhythm and *modus operandi* of the Joint Intelligence Committee and its supporting staff.

From January 2012, the JIC has been split into a pair of tiers: an upper and a lower. In the words of Rimmer–Martin:

> The needs of the NSC are best supported by the JIC meeting in two formats, at a Principals and Sub-Principals level. This will better balance high level strategic judgements on NSC priorities with those less immediately before the NSC, of importance to policy Departments or more tactical short term assessments. So senior JIC members should meet monthly as 'JIC Principals' to focus on key NSC issues, judgements and papers. Otherwise the JIC should meet at Sub-Principals level to agree papers in between.[21]

There was a gap in the JIC chairmanship between the end of September 2011 when Alex Allan retired and March 2012 when his successor, Jon Day, former Second Permanent Secretary at the Ministry of Defence, was appointed. It was not clear from Rimmer–Martin whether Jon Day would chair the JIC at both Principals and Sub-Principals levels.

Rimmer–Martin made a number of other recommendations to reflect the tone, pitch and needs of the NSC's and the Prime Minister's ways of working. For example, it suggested:

> The JIC should produce a wider range of tailored intelligence products. The number of full JIC papers should be reduced and replaced by more current briefs and summaries, making them more focussed and more accessible to the Prime Minister/Ministerial readership.[22]

But, perhaps most interestingly of all, Rimmer–Martin built on the fine chapter drafted by the late Peter Freeman, a long-serving analyst at GCHQ, on 'The Nature and Use of Intelligence' for the Butler Report on *Intelligence on Weapons of Mass Destruction* prior to the Iraq War.[23] 'Clearer processes', they wrote,

> should be established to ensure that Ministers receive timely, well-chosen and auditable intelligence reports consistent with the principles set out in Lord Butler's report of 2004. These should also enable everyone handling intelligence for Ministers to understand what sets it apart from other reporting, to understand the range of intelligence products, and to know where to go for training and guidance.[24]

Apart from anything else, this recommendation of Rimmer–Martin suggests that some of the Butler recommendations had still to be fully absorbed in Whitehall seven years later.

The specialness of intelligence, the heightened duty of care in its processing and its uses – for which the JIC had been a crucial keeper of the flame since it came of age in World War II – was what concerned me when first contemplating the new system, and during the December 2011 debate in the House of Lords I voiced concern that some of the key elements of the JIC tradition might fade under the new dispensation. The most crucial and lustrous elements of that tradition emerged from the experience of the JIC during the Second World War …

It was the working assumption that the painters of the intelligence picture would keep firmly separate from those who decide what to do on the basis of it, and that the intelligence-providers and the JIC analysts do not fall into the trap either of advocacy or of telling their customers what they wish to hear, rather than speaking truth unto power.[25]

The JIC might for a bit seem a touch 'backwaterish' but its tradition – much admired by Britain's intelligence allies – should never be allowed to slip towards the margins. Its sustenance should be the shining element in whatever training or guidance the ministerial customers of the intelligence product are given.

Sadly, war cabinetry is a continuing feature of the British way of government and a chunk of scholarly endeavour has been devoted to it.[26] Trollope in his *The Prime Minister* has the Duchess of Omnium observe that if a man (a woman PM was inconceivable to an 1870s author) became premier 'do ever so little and the men who write about history must write about you'.[27] Lady Glencora's dictum is doubly true if your tenure of No. 10 sees the creation and use of a War Cabinet.

So, what was the configuration of David Cameron's Libya-stimulated marque, NSC (L)?

Members:
Prime Minister, David Cameron (chair)
Deputy Prime Minister, Nick Clegg
Foreign Secretary, William Hague
Defence Secretary, Liam Fox
Chancellor of the Exchequer, George Osborne
Secretary of State for International Development, Andrew Mitchell

Home Secretary, Theresa May
Secretary of State for the Environment, Caroline Spelman
Attorney General, Dominic Grieve

In attendance:
Cabinet Secretary, Sir Gus O'Donnell
National Security Adviser, Sir Peter Ricketts
Chief of the Defence Staff, General Sir David Richards
Chief of the Secret Intelligence Service, Sir John Sawers
Director General, Security Service, Jonathan Evans
Director, GCHQ, Iain Lobban
Chief of Defence Intelligence, Air Marshal Chris Nicholls

This team, David Cameron declared on 1 December 2011 when publishing Sir Peter Ricketts's report on its performance, 'proved its worth in ensuring effective co-ordination of this country's contribution throughout the crisis in Libya'.[28]

The Ricketts Report, *Libya Crisis: National Security Adviser's Review of Central Co-ordination and Lessons Learned*,[29] was revealing in several ways: of the intelligence, military and diplomatic input; and of the detailed, often real-time picture technology now paints for those sat around the table in COBRA:

16. The intelligence picture was briefed to Ministers at NSC (L) by the chairman of the JIC or an alternate, supplemented by the Heads of the Agencies. The Joint Intelligence Organisation (JIO) in the Cabinet Office, which is responsible for all-source intelligence assessment, including the production of papers for the Joint Intelligence Committee, produced daily written intelligence summaries and situation reports in addition to formal assessments, drawing on inputs from Defence Intelligence [the Defence Intelligence Staff inside the Ministry of Defence], FCO Research Analysts and the intelligence agencies.

17. Real time military, intelligence and diplomatic assessment of the situation, including from theatre, gave Ministers as clear an understanding as possible of the detailed context in which to take strategic decisions as well as identify areas where further action or advice was required. Once British missions in Benghazi and then Tripoli were established, British representatives participated in Ministerial meetings by secure telephone. The role of the Chief of Defence Intelligence in providing assessment of the military situation was important in bringing HMG's wider intelligence assessment capability to bear directly in NSC (L).[30]

A dilemma lurks here. In war conditions, it is a huge advantage if the real picture is available to decision-takers rapidly, sometimes instantly. But the difficulty of winnowing out the strategic questions from the rush of real-time tactical information confronts today's war cabineteers with a pace and a force unknown to those who, in the past, have wrestled with the strategic–tactical dilemma.[31]

What Peter Ricketts called the 'operating rhythm' of NSC (L) appears to have tried to avoid that dilemma by a cornucopia of meetings. At this point in his report, he describes the position and justifies the abundance of War Cabinet time without indicating whether or not it will be desirable for future operations to be handled this way:

> A notable feature of the conduct of the campaign was the time dedicated to collective Ministerial discussion – 62 meetings of NSC (L) alone. A clear lesson is that the conduct of modern conflicts – which require simultaneous consideration of political, humanitarian and military strands and are conducted in a 24 hour media context – requires Ministers to be abreast of the tactical as well as the strategic issues.[32]

Certainly true – but such a rhythm carries with it the temptation to micro-manage the military campaign and plunge excessively into the detail of operations in the manner of the greatest warrior-politician ever to have presided over a War Cabinet table – Winston Churchill (how he would have adored the picture the technological prowess of COBRA can now provide!).

The Ricketts Report is interesting, too, on the collective Cabinet side of the story with its, for the UK, unusual overlay of coalitionism. NSC (L) was chaired by the Prime Minister at thirty-six of its meetings, with the Deputy Prime Minister, Nick Clegg, and the Foreign Secretary, William Hague, chairing thirteen apiece.[33] 'When neither the Deputy Prime Minister nor the Secretary of State for Energy and Climate Change [Chris Huhne] were able to attend, another Liberal Democrat minister, such as the Chief Secretary to the Treasury [Danny Alexander], was invited in order that both Coalition parties were represented.'[34]

I suspect future historians of British war cabinetry will linger awhile on NSC (L) for a number of reasons: (a) it was the first of the line to be spun out of the National Security Council; (b) they will wonder if it met unnecessarily and undesirably often; and (c) was David Cameron's style too fuelled by the tactical?

Of one of Ricketts's conclusions we can be sure. Of the NSC generally he told his audience at the IISS seminar: 'I do think this one is here to stay.'[35] So do I.

7

A VERY PECULIAR PRACTICE:
WATCHING PRIME MINISTERS

The British Constitution presumes more boldly than any other the good sense and good faith of those who work it.
W. E. GLADSTONE, 1879[1]

THE premiership is the greatest single parcel of concentrated personal power in the country. As a people, to be safe, we must accept the potency of that singular prime ministerial bundle under a kind of sufferance and subject its content and shape to sustained vigilance. As Mr Attlee was reported to have said about the H-bomb – it needs watching.[2] Mr Gladstone, one of the three or four most formidable holders of the job, sensed this overmightiness latent in the premiership in his 1879 musings. And, since his time, a range of factors have placed even more power inside that parcel as we shall see shortly.

Yet rarely does the temporary tenant of 10 Downing Street *feel* powerful. H. H. Asquith, a formidable figure in the pomp of his peacetime premiership (His 'opinions in the prime of his life were cut in bronze ... He sat [in Cabinet] like the great Judge he was,' wrote Winston Churchill in his *Great Contemporaries*[3]), sculpted a nice line, too, on his relative powerlessness in No. 10. 'Power,' he said to a lady who suggested it must be fun to enjoy it, 'power? You may think you are going to get it but you never do.'[4]

Harold Macmillan knew exactly how his fellow Balliol classical scholar felt. Let's eavesdrop on him in mid-February 1963 at a grim time for his premiership (it only had another six months to go, though, of course, he did not know this at the time). He is reflecting on what a terrible thumping he has had since Christmas 1962, mainly from President Charles de Gaulle, who had vetoed in mid-January Britain's first application to join what was then the European Economic Community. Now, after Hugh Gaitskell's tragic early death, Macmillan had to face a formidable new Leader of the Opposition in Harold Wilson, bursting with energy and technocracy and attempting, without a trace of self-irony, to portray himself as the British Jack Kennedy.

Here is the old man brooding at Admiralty House after a weekend at Chequers on his woes on the evening of Sunday 17 February 1963:

> The Gallup Poll has been very bad – 15% against the Party; as much against me. The collapse in Europe; the Polaris problem [would the deal with Kennedy on the replacement for Skybolt hold?[5]]; above all the economic setback and the frightful weather (still snow and frost) and unemployment! [the blizzard had blanketed Britain on Boxing Day night 1962]) have caused a wave of depression in the Party in the H of Commons. This has been fomented by my enemies ... and is reaching quite formidable dimensions, 'Macmillan must go' is the cry. Faced with <u>Wilson</u> (47 or so) we must have a young man (Heath or Maudling) ... Of course, there's something in it ... if things do not improve (particularly the unemployment figures) it will not be easy and the pressure for a 'sacrificial victim' in the person of the Leader (or Priest-King, à la Fraser [sic]) will begin to grow.[6]

That reference to Sir James Frazer's pioneering work of ethnography and social anthropology, *The Golden Bough: A Study in Magic and Religion*, is pure Macmillan in two senses: firstly, it is a perfect illustration of Paul Addison's description of the old man in his late premiership and after as 'a wreck of suffering followed by years of apologias';[7] secondly, it bespeaks his classics learning and intense bookishness, both personal and professional (the family firm had published Frazer's three volumes between 1890 and 1900).

There is a third dimension, too. Because not only does it reflect Macmillan's view of the precariousness of the UK's 'Priest-King', that is, the premiership, it's quite a good metaphor for any Prime Minister made vulnerable by serious trouble. Let Frazer, the founding father of social anthropology not just in Cambridge but in Britain as a whole,[8] tell the story his way. 'Who', Frazer asked,

> does not know Turner's picture of the Golden Bough? The scene, suffused with the golden glow of imagination … is a dream-like vision of the little woodland lake of Nemi … In antiquity this sylvan landscape was the scene of a strange and recurring tragedy. On the northern shore of the lake … stood the sacred grove and sanctuary of … Diana of the Wood … In this sacred grove there grew a certain tree round which at any time of the day, and probably far into the night, a grim figure might be seen to prowl.

Very much shades of the Gordon Brown premiership here.

But this particular early twenty-first century specialist in gloom and suspicion was not alone in having a touch of the grove of Nemi about him (or her, come to that). Frazer again on the grim, prowling figure:

> In his hand he carried a drawn sword, and he kept peering warily about him as if every instant he expected to be set upon by an enemy. He was a priest and a murderer; and the man for whom he looked was sooner or later to murder him and hold the priesthood in his stead. Such was the rule of the sanctuary. A candidate for the priesthood could only succeed to office by slaying the priest, and having slain him, he retained office till he was himself slain by a stronger or a craftier.[9]

Mercifully, it's a long time since we stopped killing our failed politicians.

We have, for the past three-plus centuries, decanted them into the House of Lords instead, an unsung service provided by the second chamber as I pointed out in my maiden speech there in December 2010.[10] Yet there lurks a Nemi-like fear about our Prime Ministers much of the time which is a great sapper of both nervous energy and serenity. How wise Clem Attlee was when he wrote in his post-Downing Street years that

> men who lobby their way forward into leadership are the most likely to be lobbied back out of it. The man who has most control of his followers is the man who shows no fear. And a man cannot be a leader if he is afraid of losing his job.[11]

Yet one suspects that most holders of the premiership *do* fear losing it, their time in No. 10 always being a work-in-progress, not an endeavour completed. Anthony Trollope sensed this powerfully in the 1870s when he had his fictional Prime Minister, the Duke of Omnium, contemplate the imminent break-up of the coalition he headed:

> There was in store for him the tranquillity which he would enjoy as soon as a sense of duty would permit him to seize it. But now the prospect of that happiness had gradually vanished from him. That retirement was no longer a winning-post for him. The poison of place and power and dignity had got into his blood. And as he looked forward he feared rather than sighed for retirement.[12]

As the Duke's wife, Lady Glencora knew, premiership is not a job that brings serenity. As she says to her friend Marie Finn: 'There is a devil that creeps in upon them when their hands are strengthened.'[13] Pincered between Frazer's anthropology and Trollope's psychology, the prime ministership of Britain is a highly stressed location.

Yet the social anthropological approach must always have a place in any attempt to anatomise the UK's 'Priest-King' not least because any understanding of the job requires a functional analysis of what the job entails behind the symbols and rituals of parliamentary, public and media performances of various kinds. These are the sorts of questions I want to examine in this chapter.

What are British Prime Ministers for? How do we assess and calibrate their overall performance? Thoughts on that last question first. I have almost invariably declined to take part in those occasional surveys of political scientists and political historians enquiring of them who were the 'best' and 'worst' of the twentieth-century and twenty-first century premiers. It's an absurd exercise because the hand that history dealt them as they entered Downing Street and the problems that what Macmillan called 'the opposition of events'[14] dumped in their laps during their occupation of No. 10 are so different that you cannot compare like with like.

Just think of the fluctuating factors: size of majority; condition of the domestic and world economy; the state of your own party and that of your political rivals; the happenings and vicissitudes of a world in which you have international or territorial responsibilities that you cannot simply abandon or, even when you have, as in the case of the bulk of the old British Empire, you cannot curb the appetite for global influence, that 'instinct to intervene' which we examined earlier. More prosaic, everyday considerations apply: your physical and mental well-being; the efficiency of your digestive system; the amount of sleep you need of a night; your susceptibility to jet lag; the emotional geography of your domestic arrangements; the level of ideological charge you possess.

Some years ago now, when pondering the sheer do-ability of the job of being Prime Minister, I reckoned in my study of *The Hidden Wiring* of British government and constitution published in 1995 that 'the model of a modern prime minister would be a kind of grotesque composite freak – someone with the dedication to duty of a Peel, the physical energy of a Gladstone, the detachment of a Salisbury, the brains of an Asquith, the balls of a Lloyd George, the word-power of a Churchill, the administrative gifts of an Attlee, the style of a Macmillan, the managerialism of a Heath and the sleep requirements of a Thatcher.' My conclusion? 'Human beings do not come like that.'[15] Nothing in the subsequent conduct of the premiership by Tony Blair, Gordon Brown or David Cameron has caused me to modify that view.

Back to what British Prime Ministers are for. What is it that falls to them that others cannot – or should not – do? Over the years, perhaps in an unconscious tribute to Bismarck's physicist-like approach, as Henry Kissinger put it,[16] of breaking questions up into their elements, I have favoured a functional analysis of the job of being Prime Minister. And, to sustain the physics metaphor a little longer, I have reached the conclusion that premierships are subject to their own version of quantum mechanics – they are things of waves and particles.* The waves are the wider sweeps of events, technological changes, shifts in the global political economy; the particles are the problems and pin-pricks, many unexpected, several of short duration but great absorbers of mental and physical energy while they last, that so often take up so much of a Prime Minister's day.

Truly outstanding Prime Ministers are sensitive to this, and, indeed, need a certain humility in their make-up when it comes to the waves, as Churchill recognised before he acquired the office during a faintly critical passage in his 1937 essay on Asquith: 'Conditions are so variable, episodes so unexpected, experiences so conflicting, that flexibility of judgements and a willingness to assume a somewhat humbler attitude towards external phenomena may well play their part in the equipment of a modern Prime Minister.'[17]

Yet a functional analysis can help bring a touch of predictability, of useful management, to at least part of a Prime Minister's workload as head of government. We still await a formal public job description (though the new *Cabinet Manual* floated in draft in December 2010 and published in October 2011 helps a bit without intending to[18]). So, tiring of the endless debate about individual prime ministerial versus collective Cabinet power, I set about in the mid-1990s during the Major years, to attempt an anatomy of the tasks that fall to a British Prime Minister.

* I am grateful to my friend Dr Graham Farmelo, author of the life of Paul Dirac, who won his Nobel Prize at the age of thirty-one in 1933 for his contribution to quantum mechanics (Graham Farmelo, *The Strangest Man: The Hidden Life of Paul Dirac, Quantum Genius*, Faber, 2009), for outlining a guide to quantum for people like me who are not natural mathematical physicists: 'The laws that describe the world around us break down completely at the atomic level – they don't work. The theory of quantum mechanics can describe the atomic world, using the idea that every sub-atomic thing can be described in terms of either a wave or a particle. The theory of quantum mechanics says how these quanta behave – the most fundamental laws we have.' Dr Farmelo wrote this definition down on a postcard when, without warning, I asked him to describe the essence of quantum in three or four sentences for a curious schoolchild while we were having a drink in the House of Lords on 12 April 2011.

The inspiration for this was an old Cabinet Office file from the late 1940s on the 'Function of the Prime Minister and His Staff, 1947–48'.[19] As far as I can tell, neither Clem Attlee, the Prime Minister of the day, nor any of his successors saw it. The list of functions was drawn up by the machinery of government division in the Treasury, in consultation with the Cabinet Office and Buckingham Palace, in response to a request from the Institute of Public Administration to help with a paper they were to present to a conference in Switzerland convened to compare the functions of chief executives in various western political systems. Once completed, it was placed in the then novel Cabinet Office *Precedent Book*.

The 1947 taxonomy honed the PM's head-of-government functions to twelve:

Prime Minister's functions – 1947

1. Managing the relationship between the Monarch and the government as a whole.
2. Hiring and firing ministers.
3. Chairing the Cabinet and its most important committees.
4. Arranging other 'Cabinet business', i.e. the chairmanships of other committees, their memberships and agendas.
5. Overall control of the Civil Service as First Lord of the Treasury.
6. The allocation of functions between departments; their creation and abolition.
7. Relationships with other heads of government.
8. An especially close involvement in foreign policy and defence matters.
9. Top Civil Service appointments.
10. Top appointments to many institutions of 'a national character'.
11. 'Certain scholastic and ecclesiastical appointments'.
12. The handling of 'precedent and procedure'.

No. 1 was – and remains – the traditional function of the Queen's or the King's First Minister as the constitutional hinge between Monarch and Cabinet which runs unbroken from Robert Walpole (the first of the line though he detested being called Prime Minister[20]) to David Cameron and is made manifest in human terms when both are in London at the weekly audience (these days it's on a Wednesday afternoon once Prime Minister's Questions in the House of Commons are out of the way).

No. 2 was established only in Arthur Balfour's time when he sacked a fistful of the more inflamed protagonists of the great Free Trade–Protection debate in his Cabinet.[21] It has had to be modified a little to fit coalition requirement as we shall see shortly. No. 6 is always a temptation for Prime Ministers in trouble, who find it irresistible to show who is in charge by rebadging departments or shifting their boundaries (nobody is ever fooled by this and it can lead to absurdities such as universities coming under the purview of the Department of Business, Innovation and Skills – a nonsense ministers recognise in private while explaining it will have to await a Cameron second term to be put right[22]). The Ministry of Defence is one of the few departments relatively immune to this as it was created by statute in 1946 and would, therefore, require primary legislation if it were to be dismembered.[23]

Item 10 has a period feel. The word 'quango' had yet to be invented. There was a surge of patronage in the mid and late 1940s as the National Health Service was created and industries nationalised. No. 11 baffled foreigners with an interest in the mysteries of the British constitution* until Gordon Brown ended the practice of the Prime Minister having the final say in which divine for what see was recommended to the Queen for appointment to Anglican dioceses in England. It is odd, when one thinks of it, that the person who rises to the top of the pile in, indispensable though it is, one of the coarsest and nastiest professional competitions should be the chooser of the top brass in an institution in

*I never cease to be amazed by the reach and dazzle of the magic of the British constitution. Perhaps the most bizarre example was divulged to me by my much-loved and greatly missed friend Daphne Park, Lady Park of Monmouth and Broadway. Daphne was one of the truly legendary figures in the Cold War Secret Intelligence Service. She was, as Sir Gerry Warner, the former Deputy Chief of SIS, explained at Daphne's memorial service in the University Church, Oxford on 29 May 2010, in her spell as British Consul in Hanoi at the height of the Vietnam War, 'a window on North Vietnam for both HMG and the Americans. Her reports and despatches were much applauded, especially because she provided unique insights into Soviet thinking – regularly – and Vietnamese – more occasionally. For although Daphne loathed communism … she and the Soviet ambassador got on famously, and met regularly to exchange views' ('Daphne Park 1921–2010', *Memorial Tributes*, Somerville College, Oxford, 2010, pp.24–5.).Daphne over dinner once described to me the special ingredient in that relationship. Her Russian opposite number, like her an intelligence officer serving under diplomatic cover, was fascinated by the intricacies of the British constitution. Daphne would invite him over to dine on scrambled egg and whisky while she captured for him the unwritten beauties of the British way of government.

which, one would hope, matters of the spirit rather than the judgements of Mammon would prevail.

Function No. 12 is the most successfully camouflaged and deceptive in the 1947 dozen. For in a constitution then predominantly unwritten – and proudly so – the person determining the interpretation of 'precedent and procedure', on which the overwhelming corpus of it rested, was in an enormously powerful position. This is what Mr Gladstone was getting at in 1879. For an unscrupulous, unknowing or insensitive Prime Minister either ignorant, uncaring or insouciant about what Sir Sidney Lowe in 1904 called the 'tacit understandings'[24] of the British constitution, this function might be tantamount to acting as judge and jury in their own cause. Yet, I suspect that in the Whitehall of 1947 it would have struck nobody as odd that the single most powerful figure in the land and, therefore, the one who needed the most careful watching, should possess this capability – and not just because of the understated, constitutional traditionalist then resident in 10 Downing Street in the person of Mr Attlee. There were gaps in that 1947 list which were apparent when I sought to update it during the Major years in the mid-1990s. Like the young William Armstrong, who, as head of the Treasury's machinery of government division in 1947, produced the first draft of the list of prime ministerial functions, I sought the help of Whitehall insiders when I took my first stab at the genre.

Even allowing for the late-1940s omissions, I was surprised by the number of mid-1990s functions (up from twelve to thirty-three). Britain's relative power in the world was much diminished in the interim. But the Prime Minister's relative power – as converted into functions – inside his or her governing domain had waxed considerably. And, as an aid to grasping them, I broke the functions down into bundles.

Prime Minister's functions – 1995

Constitutional and Procedural

1. Managing the relationship between government and the Monarch
2. Managing the relationship between government and opposition on a Privy Counsellor basis.

3. Establishing the order of precedence in Cabinet.

4. The establishment and interpretation of procedural guidelines for both ministers and civil servants.

5. Oversight of changes to Civil Service recruitment practices.

6. Classification levels and secrecy procedures for official information.

7. Requesting the Sovereign to grant a dissolution of Parliament.

Appointments

(Made in the name of the Sovereign but chosen by the Prime Minister).

1. Appointment and dismissal of ministers (and final approval of their Parliamentary Private Secretaries and special advisers).

2. Headships of the intelligence and security services.

3. Top appointments to the Home Civil Service and in collaboration with the Foreign Secretary to the Diplomatic Service and in collaboration with the Defence Secretary to the armed forces.

4. Top ecclesiastical appointments plus regius professorships and the Mastership of Trinity College, Cambridge.

5. Top public sector appointments and appointments to royal commissions.

6. Award of peerages and honours (except for those in the gift of the Sovereign).

Conduct of Cabinet and parliamentary business

1. Calling meetings of Cabinet and its committees. Fixing their agenda.

2. The calling of 'Political Cabinets' with no officials present.

3. Deciding issues where Cabinet or Cabinet committees are unable to agree.

4. Granting ministers permission to miss Cabinet meetings or to leave the country.

5. Ultimate responsibility with the Leaders of the Houses for the government's legislative programme and the use of government time in Parliament.

6. Answering questions twice a week in the House of Commons on nearly the whole range of government activities.

Organisational and efficiency questions
1. Organisation and senior staffing of No. 10 and the Cabinet Office.
2. Size of the Cabinet; workload on ministers and the Civil Service; the overall efficiency of government.
3. The overall efficiency of the secret services; their operations and their oversight.
4. The creation, abolition and merger of government departments and executive agencies.
5. Preparation of the 'War Book'.
6. Contingency planning on the civil side with the Home Secretary, e.g. for industrial action that threatens essential services or for counter-terrorism.
7. Overall efficiency of the government's media strategy.

Budgets and market-sensitive decisions
1. Determining, with the Chancellor of the Exchequer, the detailed contents of the Budget. By tradition, the full Cabinet is only apprised of the full contents of the Budget statement the morning before it is delivered.
2. Determining which ministers (in addition to the Chancellor) will be involved and in which fora in the taking of especially market-sensitive economic decisions such as the level of interest rates.

Special foreign and defence functions
1. Relationships with heads of government (e.g. the nuclear and intelligence aspects of the US–UK 'special relationship').
2. Representing the UK at 'summits' of all kinds.
3. With the Defence Secretary, the use of the royal prerogative to deploy Her Majesty's armed forces in action.

4. With the Foreign Secretary, the use of the royal prerogative to sign or annul treaties, recognise or derecognise countries.

5. The launching of a UK nuclear strike (with elaborate and highly secret fallback arrangements in case the Prime Minister and Cabinet are wiped out by a bolt-from-the-blue pre-emptive strike).

First, filling the gaps in the 1947 taxonomy. No. 2 should have been there. This has been taking place since Arthur Balfour, creator of the Committee of Imperial Defence (as we have seen), was invited to brief it, when Leader of the Opposition in 1909 on Britain's vulnerability to a German invasion.[25] Such relationships also take the form of regular briefings on foreign and defence policy and terrorism of various kinds.[26]

No. 3 matters greatly to ministers who live in a status-conscious milieu often made neuralgic by personal insecurities and ancient animosities towards colleagues. Place on the list takes a frequent and practical form. If Minister A wishes to talk to Minister B and Minister B is higher up the order, Minister A has to go and call on him.

No. 6 should have been listed in 1947. Ever since the Committee of Imperial Defence decided during the war scare summer of 1909 that Britain needed a really tough, new Official Secrets Act not just to keep the Kaiser's spies out of the Royal Dockyards but, while they were at it, a second section to stop Crown servants blabbing generally[27] (the Kaiser duly provided another war scare in July 1911 which enabled the Asquith administration to propel the Bill through Parliament with breathtaking speed[28]), the guarding of official information has been a perpetual prime ministerial function.

In 1947, too, the specific function of a Prime Minister requesting the Monarch for a dissolution of Parliament, thereby triggering a general election, should have been made explicit. Prior to 1918, this had been a Cabinet function. But in the circumstances of the November 'coupon' election in the first days of peace, with David Lloyd George the head of a coalition government but not the leader of the largest political party in the House of Commons, the request fell to him[29] and it stayed with Prime

Ministers ever after until the passage of the Fixed-Term Parliaments Act 2011, which requires the Prime Minister to bring the dissolution question to the House of Commons (and to achieve a majority of at least two-thirds of all MPs) if Parliament is to be dissolved short of the five years prescribed by the new statute.[30] In terms of Downing Street–Buckingham Palace relations, honours and peerages should have been inscribed on the 1947 list.

Other late-1940s gaps include:

- Appointing the chiefs/directors general of the intelligence and security agencies.
- Shaping the government's legislative programme.
- Overall efficiency and operations of the secret services (though most of the latter was devolved to the Home Secretary for MI5 and the Foreign Secretary for SIS and GCHQ).
- Preparation of the 'War Book' (the Committee of Imperial Defence had drafted the first of these in 1911 lest war break out with Germany[31]).
- Contingency planning (with the Home Secretary) for industrial action that threatened the essentials of life.
- Media strategy (though Mr Attlee famously took scant interest in this[32]).
- Budget.
- Use of royal prerogative to deploy the armed forces in action outside UK territory.
- Nuclear policy and the development of the UK's atomic bomb.

These missing elements narrow the functional gap between Mr Attlee's No. 10 and John Major's. But the stretching of the premiership between 1947 and 1995 is, nonetheless, evident. The most awesome is the nuclear weapons responsibilities, on which we have already touched (Ted Heath began the practice of writing 'last resort' letters for the submarines – the ultimate 'capital ships'[33] – to modern Prime Ministers what the Dreadnoughts were to Asquith and Lloyd George and more, *much* more).

Some of the most significant stretchings of the premiership were pulled on the parliamentary front. From 1961, following recommendations by the House of Commons Procedure Committee,[34] Harold Macmillan agreed that henceforth Prime Ministers should answer oral questions in the chamber for fifteen minutes every Tuesday and Thursday while the House was sitting. In 1977, following another Procedure Committee report,[35] Jim Callaghan agreed to take questions from right across the policy spectrum. Previously specific ones had been referred to the Secretary of State for the relevant department. Margaret Thatcher turned this requirement into an instrument of intrusion – for finding out what departments were up to in advance of her taking PMQs.[36]

Tony Blair, unilaterally, without consulting the House of Commons, decided at the start of his premiership to take thirty minutes of questions on a Wednesday. The idea was to increase the chances of light prevailing over heat. It failed; but the half-hour, once-a-week on Wednesdays arrangement has endured through the Brown and Cameron premierships. To his credit, after initially resisting the idea, Mr Blair agreed in 2001 to appear twice a year before the House of Commons Liaison Committee, consisting of all the select committee chairs.[37] There is not – and has never been – a bespoke select committee for shadowing and scrutinising the premiership.

By the spring of 2011 it was high time to mount another reconnaissance flight over the prime ministerial functions. The Blair years had seen still more stretching especially on the media front. From the outside, it looked as if the question 'How will this play on the *Today* programme or *Newsnight*?' was attached to the formative stages of pretty well every piece of policy that was eventually to be made public.

On another front, the Prime Minister's hands, too, had slipped off a swathe of the honours system. Since 2000 the selection of independent crossbench peers has been in the hands of a new House of Lords Appointments Commission. The Prime Minister merely acts as a postman conveying the commission's choices to the Queen (this was the route by which I entered the House of Lords in 2010). The Prime Minister, too, is now but a postman who conveys the Church of England's choice of bishops to its Supreme Governor, the Queen.

The coming of coalition in May 2010 has had a considerable effect in diluting, temporarily no doubt, some of the Prime Minister's functions, as the 2011 list indicates. It reflects, too, some important innovations such as the National Security Council (NSC) – or, re-innovations, to be precise, as the NSC is in some ways an updated version of the old Committee of Imperial Defence but with better IT and decision-taking, as opposed to advisory, functions.

The 2011 list was compiled by the author and Dr Andrew Blick, Senior Research Fellow at the Centre for Political and Constitutional Studies at King's College, London, first as evidence to the House of Commons Committee on Political and Constitutional Reform in February 2011,[38] and, in August 2011 in a slightly updated form, for an Institute of Public Policy Research study, *The Hidden Wiring Emerges*,[39] a study of the *Draft Cabinet Manual*[40] published the previous December.

Prime Minister's functions – 2011

Constitutional and procedural

1. Managing the relationship between the government and the Monarch and the Heir to the Throne.
2. Managing the relationship between the government and the opposition on a Privy Counsellor basis.
3. Managing the relationships between UK central government and devolved administrations in Scotland, Wales and Northern Ireland.
4. Establishing order of precedence in Cabinet.
5. Interpretation and content of procedural and conduct guidelines for ministers as outlined in the *Ministerial Code* and the *Draft Cabinet Manual*.
6. Oversight, with the Cabinet Secretary advising, of the *Civil Service Code* as enshrined in the Constitutional Reform and Governance Act 2010.

7. Decisions, as chairman of the Cabinet, with the relevant minister, on whether and when to use the ministerial override on disclosure under Clause 53 of the Freedom of Information Act 2000.

8. Requesting the Sovereign to grant a dissolution of Parliament (until Parliament passed the Fixed-Term Parliaments Act).

9. Authorising the Cabinet Secretary to facilitate negotiations between the political parties in the event of a 'hung' general election result.

10. Managing intra-coalition relationships with the Deputy Prime Minister.

Appointments

(Made in the name of the Sovereign but chosen by the Prime Minister.)

1. Appointment and dismissal of ministers (final approval of their Parliamentary Private Secretaries and special advisers) in consultation with the Deputy Prime Minister for Liberal Democrat appointments and the appointment of the Law Officers.

2. Top appointments to the headships of the Security Service, the Secret Intelligence Service and the Government Communications Headquarters.

3. Top appointments to the Home Civil Service and in collaboration with the Foreign Secretary to the Diplomatic Service and with the Defence Secretary to the armed forces.

4. Top ecclesiastical appointments (although, since Gordon Brown's premierships, the Prime Minister has conveyed the preference of the Church of England's selectors to the Monarch without interference).

5. Residual academic appointments: the Mastership of Trinity College, Cambridge; the Principalship of King's College, London; a small number of regius professorships in Oxford and Cambridge (the First Minister in Edinburgh is responsible for the Scottish regius chairs). Since the Blair premiership the No. 10 practice has been to convey the wishes of the scholarly institutions to the Queen without interference.

6. Top public sector appointments and regulators (with some informal parliamentary oversight).

7. Appointments to committees of inquiry and royal commissions.

8. The award of party political honours.

9. Party political appointments to the House of Lords (independent crossbench peers are selected by the House of Lords Appointments Commission and the Prime Minister conveys the recommendations to the Monarch without interference).

Conduct of Cabinet and parliamentary business

1. Calling meetings of Cabinet and its committees. Fixing their agenda and, in the case of committees, their membership in consultation with the Deputy Prime Minister.

2. The calling of 'Political Cabinets' with no officials present.

3. Deciding issues where Cabinet or its committees are unable to agree.

4. Deciding, with the Deputy Prime Minister, when the Cabinet is allowed an 'opt-out' on collective responsibility and subsequent whipping arrangements in Parliament.

5. Granting ministers permission to miss Cabinet meetings or leave the country.

6. Ultimate responsibility (with the Deputy Prime Minister and the leaders of the House of Commons and the House of Lords) for the government's legislative programme and the use of government time in the chambers of both Houses.

7. Answering questions for thirty minutes on Wednesdays when the House of Commons is sitting on nearly the whole range of government activity.

8. Appearing twice a year to give evidence before the House of Commons Liaison Committee.

Policy, strategy and communications

1. Keeper, with the Deputy Prime Minister, of the coalition's overall political strategy.

2. Oversight of No. 10 communications strategy and work of the Government Communications Network.

3. Pursuit and promulgation of special overarching policies particularly associated with the Prime Minister, e.g. the 'Big Society'.

Organisational and efficiency questions

1. Organisation and staffing of No. 10 and the Cabinet Office (including the Prime Minister's relationship with the Deputy Prime Minister and the two senior Cabinet Office ministers dealing with policy strategy and public service reform).

2. Size of Cabinet, workload on ministers and the Civil Service.

3. The creation and merger of government departments and executive agencies.

Budget and market-sensitive decisions

1. Determining with the Chancellor of the Exchequer, the Deputy Prime Minister and the Chief Secretary of the Treasury the detailed contents of the Budget. By tradition, the full Cabinet is only apprised of the full contents the morning before the Budget statement is delivered.

2. Interest rates are now set by the Monetary Policy Committee and the Bank of England. The Prime Minister and the Chancellor of the Exchequer possess an override under the Bank of England Act 1998 if the 'public interest' requires and 'by extreme economic circumstances' but this has never been used.

National security

1. Chairing the weekly meetings of the National Security Council (which also serves, when needed, as a 'War Cabinet').

2. Oversight of the production and implementation of the national security strategy.

3. Oversight of counter-terrorist policies and arrangements.

4. Overall efficiency of the secret agencies, their operations and

budgets, and oversight and the intelligence assessments process in the Cabinet Office.

5. Preparation of the 'War Book'.

6. Contingency planning to cope with threats to essential services and national health from whatever sources.

7. With the Foreign and Defence Secretaries, the use of the royal prerogative to deploy Her Majesty's forces in action (with the House of Commons, by convention, being consulted if time allows)

8. With the Foreign Secretary, the use of the royal prerogative to ratify or annul treaties, and to recognise or derecognise countries (although in certain circumstances, the House of Commons can block treaty ratification under the Constitutional Reform and Governance Act 2010).

Special personal responsibilities

1. Representing the UK at a range of international meetings and 'summits.'

2. The maintenance of the special intelligence and nuclear relationships with the US President under the terms of the 1946 Communications Agreement, the 1958 Agreement for Co-operation on the Uses of Atomic Energy for Mutual Defence Purposes and the 1963 Polaris Sales Agreement.

3. The decision to shoot down a hijacked aircraft or an unidentified civil aircraft which responds neither to radio contact nor to the signals of RAF interceptor jets, before it reaches a conurbation or a key target on UK territory (plus the appointment of two or three deputies for this purpose).

4. Authorisation of the use of UK nuclear weapons including the preparation of four 'last resort' letters for installation in the inner safes of each Royal Navy Trident submarine and the appointment, on a personal basis rather than the Cabinet's order of precedence, of the 'nuclear deputies', lest the Prime Minister should be out of reach or indisposed during an emergency.

The 2011 taxonomy lists forty-eight functions. The growth area has been national security since the atrocities of 11 September 2001 in the United States and 7 July 2005 in London. The third of the 'special responsibilities' section – authorising the shooting down of what, on the best evidence, appears to be a 'suicide' flight into UK airspace is a particularly vivid and chilling example of this.[41]

Overall, the functional analysis of the post-1945 UK premiership is a story of one-way traffic. An extra job acquired is rarely balanced by a function shed. The setting of interest rates by the Bank of England's Monetary Policy Committee is a rare example. Even here there is an override permitted by the Bank of England Act 1998. But it is highly unlikely to be used. In the event of a clash, it is odds-on that the markets would side with the Bank, rather than with the Prime Minister and the Chancellor of the Exchequer, and the pound would plunge accordingly.

Naturally, the functional analysis of the premiership takes you only so far. It deals essentially with the particles of the job rather than the waves – internal, and, above all, external – by which the incumbent is buffeted. Equally, not all of the functions are exercised anywhere near the bulk of the time (and the Trident submarine on patrol exists to deter, i.e. not to be activated by a premier carrying out his most immeasurably awesome task).

For the individual sitting atop that list of forty-eight it is not a matter, as Winston Churchill once told Parliament, of being 'left in undisputed enjoyment of vast and splendid possessions' (Churchill was as First Lord of the Admiralty presenting the 1914 Naval Estimates a few months before the catastrophe of the Great War and talking of the British Empire).[42] It is a precarious and constantly anxiety-inducing business. Most Prime Ministers, once through their usually brief honeymoons, find themselves wounded and/or haunted by an event (John Major, Black Wednesday, September 1992 and its fall-out; Tony Blair, the Iraq war of March 2003 and its aftermath) or the anticipation of trouble to come.

Even if somehow you get by, there is the problem of the last slaughter either by a Frazer-style rival 'Priest-King' or by the electorate. It is not a job that leads to tranquillity, certainly not while you possess it and rarely once it's all over (all that temporary power; so little permanent legacy). Trollope, as usual, was eloquent on this in *The Duke's Children*, his sequel to *The Prime Minister*. Premiership can often be hellish at the time and yet, retirement can produce atavistic longings for old battlegrounds: 'In truth, they [the Duke and Duchess of Omnium] had both sighed to be back among the war-trumpets. They had both suffered much among the trumpets and yet they longed to return.'[43]

It's a mystery to me why so many people aspire to the premiership; how they come to persuade themselves that their party, their country and the world need their special gifts and insights; those, like Tony Blair, who, as one of his most senior officials observed, 'liked to see policy as a play in which he was the centre of the drama';[44] and, even more, how a few of them continue to feel that humanity still craves their wisdom even after the removal van has called. Being Prime Minister really is a very peculiar practice.

8

POWER AND THE PURSUIT OF INFLUENCE:
WHY STUDY GOVERNMENT AND PARLIAMENT?

To retain respect for laws and sausages, one must not watch them in the making.
REMARK ATTRIBUTED TO PRINCE OTTO VON BISMARCK, UNDATED[1]

BISMARCK was not one of nature's parliamentarians. The first Chancellor of a unified Germany was not built for the mixture of tribalism and compromise or the sheer noise and clutter that make up parliamentary life. He could tolerate politicians as individuals. But, as a breed or a herd, they really disturbed the old Prussian's atoms.

Listen to him in 1863 writing to an old friend, John Motley:

> I never dreamed that in my riper years I would be forced to practise so unworthy a profession as that of parliamentary minister. As an ambassador, although a civil servant, I maintained the feeling that I was a gentleman … As a minister I am a helot. The deputies are not dumb in general; that is not the right expression. Looked at individually these people are in part very shrewd … as soon as they assemble *in corpore*, they are dumb in the mass…[2]

Bismarck had a point, however, about the bumping and grinding that goes with legislating in Parliament as it does with slaughtering and processing of animals in abattoir and meat factory. It is not a business for the fastidious or the faint hearted. Though as someone who became a member of the House of Lords in his riper years, I have to salute the part of Parliament in which I work as almost certainly the most courteous and restrained legislative chamber in the world, though, of course, in the House of Lords there are practitioners who can use both courtesy and understatement as a weapon should the circumstances require.

However, our best guide to the beauties, subtleties and sheer indispensability of parliamentary institutions is not 'blood and iron'[3] Bismarck but another great nineteenth-century figure – journalist and supreme constitutional observer Walter Bagehot, author of that enduring classic *The English Constitution* of 1867.[4] Listen to Bagehot writing six years later:

> Our system though curious and peculiar may be worked safely … if we wish to work it we must study it.[5]

He is describing there not Westminster or Whitehall but the money markets in his great study of the City of London, *Lombard Street*. But Bagehot's words are as wholly transferable to government and Parliament in the early twenty-first century as they were in the mid-nineteenth.

The verb 'work' is interesting and significant. It's the same one W. E. Gladstone used six years after *Lombard Street* appeared in his *Gleanings of Past Years*. The British constitution, the Grand Old Man declared, as we saw earlier, 'presumes more boldly than any other the good sense and good faith of those who work it'.[6] For all the codes and constitutional statutes created over the past quarter of a century, those Bagehotian and Gladstonian prescriptions apply as powerfully as they ever did – just as the senses both of history and of the governing and legislative grains the past has cut along cry out for understanding if we are going to operate our historic constitution – this 'creation of ages', as Disraeli once described the House of Lords[7]– satisfactorily.

Successful operations in Whitehall and Westminster still depend heavily on a sense of both process and convention. For Parliament must be more than a succession of carefully choreographed showdowns between competing parties and interests. It has to serve its country as a kind of permanent royal commission on the constitution. This was illustrated vividly in a House of Lords debate on constitutional change just before the Christmas recess of 2011–12.

It was held to discuss a report from the House of Lords Constitution Committee of October 2011 on *The Process of Constitutional Change*.[8] The committee's chair, Baroness Jay of Paddington, explained that the stimulus for the inquiry was the torrent of substantial constitutional bills the coalition had brought forward in its first eighteen months of life and explained the reasoning for the

> committee's overall recommendation … that, in contrast with existing practice, the United Kingdom needs to adopt a clear and consistent process to make governments accountable for the constitutional changes that they introduce … the process of constitutional change matters because the constitution, even when it is unwritten, is the foundation on which our laws and government are built … We argue that constitutional legislation is qualitatively different from other legislation and should therefore be treated differently.[9]

Unlike the government, which declined to accept that there is a qualitative specialness about constitutional legislation,[10] I agreed with Lady Jay and her committee and cited in support what the constitutional historian-turned-politician Sir Kenneth Pickthorn had said in the House of Commons in 1960 when he declared: 'Procedure is all the constitution the poor Briton has.'[11] Much more of our constitution is written in 2012 than it was in 1960 in bundles of statutes and a growing pile of codes. But the Pickthorn principle still applies in a country whose governing rules are still to a remarkable degree unwritten and for whom, therefore, care in the use of procedure is a prime requirement.

It is plainly difficult to delineate those measures that might be deemed 'constitutional' in the way that the Speaker of the House of Commons denominates those 'Money Bills' with which the House of Lords, since the Parliament Act 1911, has been unable to tamper.[12] Governments, I suggested during the December 2011 debate, cannot be left to do this for themselves.[13] A better way would be a joint Commons–Lords committee created for the purpose as floated by Lord Desai earlier in the same debate.

No constitutional cartography can provide a definitive description of what questions should be inside or outside the boundary, but Sir John Baker, Downing Professor of the Laws of England at the University of Cambridge, had earlier given the Constitution Committee a pretty good map[14] which Baroness Jay summarised as

> any alteration to structure and composition of Parliament; any alteration to powers of Parliament or any transfer of power, as by devolution or international treaty, which would in practice be difficult to reverse; any alteration to the succession to the Crown, or the functions of the monarch; any substantial alteration to the balance of power between Parliament and government; any substantial alteration to the balance of power between central government and local authorities; and any substantial alteration to the liberties of the subject, including the right to habeas corpus and trial by jury.[15]

The government offered one hopeful note in a response to the Lords' Constitutional Committee otherwise dominated by a mood music comparable to what I called 'a long, withdrawing sigh'[16] as if exhausted by the huge constitutional bills they had already put through Parliament. This was the possibility of ministers crafting constitutional impact statements next time they troubled the two Houses of Parliament in this way.[17] It also occurred to me, when the Lords debated the question, that the recommendations of Baroness Jay's committee possessed a 'lesser, if noteworthy, benefit of not having any public expenditure implications that I can see. Virtue is rarely cost free, and we should seize it, cherish it and implement it when we find it.'[18] Parliament, I suspect, will return to this especially if the coalition remains in a state of exhausted torpor on the parliamentary procedural side of constitutional reform.

Any essay in praise of the importance of procedure needs to move across Parliament Square, up Downing Street and into the Cabinet Room. There is no conduct of Cabinet government law in the UK, though we do have a form of words on how Cabinet business should be conducted in various editions of *Questions of Procedure for Ministers* and its successor volumes, *The Ministerial Code*. My former student Amy Baker in her study of *Prime Ministers and the Rule Book*[19] traced them right through from Clem Attlee's first consolidated version of *Questions*, circulated as a Cabinet paper in April 1949 (*Questions* was always a Cabinet document, and, therefore, secret until John Major declassified it in 1992[20]), to Tony Blair's first edition of what he renamed *The Ministerial Code* in May 1997.

The wording was scarcely changed. This is the Attlean vintage of 1949:

> The business of Cabinet consists in the main of –
> (i) Questions of major policy which affect a number of Departments or engage the collective responsibility of the Government.
> (ii) Questions on which there is a conflict of interest between Departments, which has not been resolved.

Here is the Blair version of 1997:

> Cabinet and Ministerial Committee business consists, in the main, of:
> (a) Questions which significantly engage the collective responsibility of the Government, because they raise major issues of policy or because they are of critical importance to the public;
> (b) Questions on which there is an unresolved argument between Departments.[21]

These procedural guidelines existed throughout the two great command premierships of modern times – those of Margaret Thatcher and Tony Blair (but, to be fair to Lady Thatcher, though she often began in Cabinet by declaring the conclusion she wished to be reached, she wanted a really good argument before getting her way, as numerous of her ex-ministers have attested). Procedural guidelines can, in reality, be no more than aspirations if you have a destiny politician in the chair.

To fail to make the importance of being collective your ruling Cabinet norm as Prime Minister is to court disaster – though it can be quite a time coming, as one of Mrs Thatcher's grander ministerial resigners put it privately to me when we were discussing what Tony Blair might be like as PM shortly before he became so. Anthony Eden found this over Suez in 1956,[22] Margaret Thatcher over Europe in 1990[23] and Tony Blair over Iraq in 2003, when his conduct of Cabinet government was strongly criticised by the former Cabinet Secretary Lord Butler of Brockwell and his fellow Privy Counsellors on the 2004 inquiry into *Intelligence on Weapons of Mass Destruction*.[24] In the end, command premierships always finish in tears.

Yet, most political lives end in tears whatever the level at which they are lived – another reason why tyro-politicians need to steep themselves in history before hurling themselves before the electorate. As Enoch Powell famously put it in his 1977 study of Joseph Chamberlain: 'All political lives, unless they are cut off in midstream at a happy juncture, end in failure, because that is the nature of politics and of human affairs.'[25] Interestingly, in a much less well-known quotation over four years before he delivered the April 1968 speech on immigration which brought him notoriety and ended his career as a Conservative frontbencher,[26] Powell, writing about Benjamin Disraeli in the *Sunday Times*, reflected:

> At the end of a lifetime in politics, when a man looks back, he discovers that the things he most opposed have come to pass and that nearly all the objects he set out with are not merely not accomplished, but seem to belong to a different world from the one lives in.[27]

The latter half of that quotation has a general applicability far wider than those who have pursued political lives.

Yet, there are some themes which, however much they mutate according to circumstances and weather-making personalities, sustain a powerful and recognisable DNA generation upon generation (another sustaining argument for a deepish study of government and Parliament).

In my lifetime I would pick out at least four:

1. Britain's place in the world and its enduring great – or greatish – power impulses.
2. Britain and Europe; related to theme one but with special bite because it carries into our sense of who we are wherever we stand on the Europhiliac/Eurosceptic spectrum.
3. The performance of our economy; its mix of private enterprise and public provision and the proportion of gross domestic product devoted to each; its productivity and growth compared to its competitors.
4. Related to theme three, distribution and redistribution of wealth, the desirable levels of equality to be pursued and how best to pursue them.

Each generation has a crack at this quartet. Each generation needs a sense of how and why its predecessor generations came out where they did on these questions before tackling them anew themselves. We have a duty to get inside the skulls and hearts of those who have gone before both to do them justice and to light up our own grey cells and impulses.

To fulfil this task, we must also turn ourselves into our own bespoke version of George Orwell and contemplate the sounds and ingredients of exchange in the practice of parliamentary government as we hear and behold it. For here we find the most indispensable process of all – care and precision in the use of language. In the second paragraph of his classic 1946 essay 'Politics and the English Language', published by the magazine *Horizon* in April of that year,[28] Orwell set out his thesis like this:

> Now, it is clear that the decline of a language must ultimately have political and economic causes: it is not due simply to the bad influence of this or

that writer. But an effect can become a cause, reinforcing the original cause and producing the same effect in an intensified form, and so on indefinitely. A man may take to drink because he feels himself to be a failure, and then fail all the more completely because he drinks. It is rather the same thing that is happening to the English language. It becomes ugly and inaccurate because our thoughts are foolish, but the slovenliness of our language makes it easier for us to have foolish thoughts.[29]

We all fail here. We reach for the cliché or banality or well-rehearsed one-liners more swiftly and readily than we strive for original thought or fresh ways of expressing it. Much of contemporary Whitehall and Westminster, for example, is infected with management consultese as it faces up to the challenges of issues around governance and the need to deliver more with less while always pursuing excellence going forward, to plunge into today's argot as best I can.

Orwell drew up six rules which together, he hoped, might, if applied, reverse the decline evident to him in mid-twentieth-century political language:

(i)   Never use a metaphor, simile or other figure of speech which you are used to seeing in print.

(ii) Never use a long word where a short one will do.

(iii) If it is possible to cut a word out, always cut it out.

(iv) Never use the passive where you can use the active.

(v)   Never use a foreign phrase, a scientific word or a jargon word if you can think of an everyday English equivalent.

(vi) Break any of these rules rather than say anything outright barbarous.[30]

Tough tests, those, and I fail most of them much of the time. But I treat them as a literary equivalent of 'The Sermon on the Mount' – as a set of gold-plated aspirations.

In fact, 'The Sermon on the Mount' is my preferred test for the fads and banalities of various kinds of professional language. For example imagine how 'The Beatitudes' in St Matthew's Gospel, chapter 5, a mere 121 words of caveat-free inspiration which changed the world, would be drafted by today's practitioners in Whitehall as a White Paper.[31] Take verse 5. In White Paper-talk it would sound like this:

> Blessed are the meek: for they shall inherit the earth, always bearing in mind the deficit reduction programme and the government's overriding constraints on public expenditure and only in those special circumstances when the Secretary of State for Work and Pensions, in consultation with the Chancellor of the Exchequer, may, from time to time, permit.

Or let's imagine the Ministry of Defence's redraft of Verse 9:

> Blessed are the peacemakers: for they shall be called the Children of God, provided proper verification procedures are agreed and that nothing is conceded in negotiation that might prejudice the effectiveness of the UK's strategic nuclear force.

Letting the fantasy run on, given the importance of the print and electronic media to the condition of political language, I wonder how my old newspaper, *The Times*, might have reported 'The Sermon on the Mount' had it been around 2,000 years ago:

> **From Our Jerusalem Correspondent.**
> Reports reached Jerusalem last night of an up-country meeting addressed by the political activist and religious fundamentalist Jesus. He shocked his audience, reliable sources suggested, by the stridency of his tone and the austerity of his message.
>
> His opening words set the theme for the whole speech. 'Blessed are the poor in spirit,' he said. 'For theirs is the Kingdom of Heaven.'
>
> It was, witnesses added, an attack entirely directed at the 'haves' rather than the 'have nots', for whom Jesus did not have a critical word. It was

received with rapture by his largely working-class followers perched precariously on the side of a mountain.

A spokesman for the Psephological Research Centre at the Jerusalem Institute of Technology commented: 'This kind of thinking will have little appeal at a general election. Far from offering mortgage or tax relief to the hard-pressed executive and middle classes, Jesus' speech seemed to suggest they should give up everything and follow the scriptures.'

Pontius Pilate's Press Secretary said: 'That bit about "blessed are the persecuted" will go down particularly badly in the Centurions' Mess.'

Quite apart from perhaps unkindly applying the 'Sermon on the Mount' test to politicians and journalists, who have to live in the world as it is, there is a more immediate requirement of political language in the second decade of the twenty-first century.

It now appears that the UK will be facing the prospect of about 1 per cent annual growth as its new norm for the next generation. This is less than half of the average annual growth of the sixty years from my birth to 2008 and the banking crisis of that year plus the fiscal crisis then the sovereign debt crisis which followed. It may be, to use Winston Churchill's *World Crisis* metaphor, that a spell has been broken[32] and that low growth will be the new politico-economic weather-maker.

If it is, those in authority and those who seek to be in authority will have to find a new language spoken in a different tone with which to talk to our people – a language that does not deceive about the reality of what we are facing; yet a language that gives hope, offers shared purpose and does not collapse into the all too familiar vocabulary of political tribalism and mutual scapegoating. Great prizes await the politician or politicians who can do this. But it will be very difficult to emerge from our deeply sound-bitten society.

On a more cheerful note, the final reason for studying power and the pursuit of influence is the sheer fascination and fun of it. There is an Anthony Trollope within all of us sniffing for who's up and who's down, straining to pick up the latest ripple of gossip. How, for example, he would love, were he here, observing the fate of our first coalition government since 1945. Listen to Trollope on a fictional coalition in the 1870s in his great political novel, *The Prime Minister*, as he depicts the Duke of Omnium musing about what faces the government over which he presides:

> When one branch of a coalition has gradually dropped off, the other branch will hardly flourish long. And then the tints of a political coalition are so neutral and unalluring that men will only endure them when they feel that no more pronounced colours are within their reach.[33]

And if there isn't a little Trollope within you, the final impulse for studying the history and unearthing the hidden wiring of the way in which we are governed and the power of government arbitrated and scrutinised is the sheer romance of it all.

The choicest distiller of this is, perhaps unsurprisingly, Winston Churchill. It's March 1917; a particularly grim patch during the Great War. Churchill is in the company of his fellow Liberal MP McCallum Scott, who recorded in his diary what transpired:

> As we were leaving the House last night, he called me into the Commons to take a last look round. All was darkness except a ring of faint light all around under the Gallery. We could dimly see the Table but walls and roof were invisible. 'Look at it,' he said. 'This little place is what makes the difference between us and Germany. It is in virtue of this that we shall muddle through to success and for lack of this Germany's brilliant efficiency leads her to final destruction. This little room is the shrine of the world's liberties.'[34]

Marvellous. Bismarck would never – could never – have understood.

9

THE VIEW FROM A HOGWARTIAN WINDOW:
THE QUESTION OF THE LORDS

The House of Lords is a kind of Valhalla for civilians where they can relive old political battles.
PROFESSOR SIR MICHAEL HOWARD, JULY 2011.[1]

It's a permanent farewell tour in here.
LORD DUBS, FEBRUARY 2012.[2]

I once said, when I was being interviewed for a job in the City of London, that I grew up in a pit village in County Durham where we thought nothing of the House of Lords and even less of the City of London. Now I find myself a member of one and working for the other so, yes, my views have changed.
LORD CUNNINGHAM OF FELLING, EVIDENCE TO THE JOINT COMMITTEE ON THE DRAFT HOUSE OF LORDS REFORM BILL, 30 JANUARY 2012.[3]

ONE of the many jolly aspects of becoming a member of the House of Lords is the Introduction Ceremony. It's not just the terrific kit – the scarlet and the ermine – irresistible to one of nature's peacocks such as myself, it's the choreography of it. One passes through the chamber, finishing with a handshake with the Lord Speaker. In between the oath is sworn and there are the words of the Reading Clerk, Rhodri Walters, when one halts with one's sponsors on the flanks, for the middle section of the constitutional ballet.

Dr Walters receives the Writ of Summons to Parliament from one's hand and then he recites the Warrant from the Queen. However many the Introductions in which he has participated, Rhodri has an actor's modulation and timing. The passage I particularly enjoyed was 'that he may have hold and possess a seat place and voice in the Parliaments and Public Assemblies and Councils of Us Our heirs and successors within Our United Kingdom amongst the Barons'.

Finding myself 'amongst the Barons' in November 2010 was especially fascinating for a constitutional historian because coalition plans for Lords reform were in the air. It was a bit like entering a wonderfully gilded laboratory to become a tiny particle in a very big moving part of the British constitution, whose composition and laws of motion might be about to mutate dramatically – I use the word 'might' deliberately because, by the time I crossed the line, the country had been waiting for almost a century for the fulfilment of the preamble to the Parliament Act 1911, which curbed the Lords' powers while leaving its composition intact.

That preamble, in a passage inserted at the insistence of Sir Edward Grey, Foreign Secretary in Asquith's Liberal Cabinet and a keen Lords reformer, famously declares:

> Whereas it is intended to substitute for the House of Lords as it at present exists a second chamber constituted on a popular instead of a hereditary basis, but such a substitution cannot immediately be brought into operation.[4]

When I entered the Lords we were still waiting, though the Coalition Agreement, entitled *Freedom Fairness Responsibility: Our Programme for Government*,[5] drawn up over five days in May 2010 by the Conservatives and the Liberal Democrats, promised in its section on 'Political Reform' to 'establish a committee to bring forward proposals for a wholly or mainly elected upper chamber on the basis of proportional representation'.[6]

Their individual election manifestos had both promised change. The Conservatives' so-called *Invitation to Join a Government* said:

> We will work to build a consensus for a mainly-elected second chamber to replace the current House of Lords, recognising that an efficient and effective second chamber should play an important role in our democracy and requires both legitimacy and public confidence.[7]

The Liberal Democrats' *Change That Works for You* pledged to

> replace the House of Lords with a fully-elected second chamber with considerably fewer members than the current House.[8]

Labour's *A Future Fair for All* stated:

> We will ensure that the hereditary principle is removed from the House of Lords. Further democratic reform to create a fully elected second chamber will then be achieved in stages. At the end of the next Parliament one third of the House of Lords will be elected; a further one third will be elected at the general election after that ... We will consult widely on these proposals, and on an open-list proportional representation electoral system for the second chamber, before putting them to the people in a referendum.[9]

So in May 2010 Sir Edward Grey's wish looked, on the face of it, to be about to be fulfilled albeit in a phased way.

But the pure, elect-the-lot position of his Liberal Democrat successors faced two instant problems even when those Lib Dems found themselves, to general amazement (including mine), possessing the deputy premiership and a light scattering of Cabinet seats. The Conservatives immediately squirted in a douche of watering down with that Coalition Agreement's undertaking to 'bring forward proposals for a wholly or mainly elected upper chamber'. And David Cameron let it be known, in what might be called shallow privacy, both before and after the general election, that, if he had secured an overall Conservative majority in his own right, Lords reform would be something for his third term.[10] And when Nick Clegg declared in the first of the cross-party meetings he chaired to draw up proposals that 'of course' it had to be wholly elected and 'of course' all the Church of England bishops had to go, it was made plain to him that there was nothing 'of course' about those two declarations of intent.[11]

Nick Clegg should have known that it would not be simple to practise invasive and decisive surgery on the Lords. Its history since the ink dried on the 1911 Act had been a kind of constitutional Bermuda Triangle. Many plans, some proposed by considerable figures, had disappeared into it never to reappear (see timeline below). The one outstanding success was Harold Macmillan's Life Peerages Act of 1958, which had, cumulatively, transformed the chamber, filling it with the 'respected revisers' for whom Walter Bagehot had called in 1867 if the Upper House was not to 'atrophy' and 'decline'.[12] This somehow seemed lost on Nick Clegg in his 'young Lochinvar out of Sheffield' mode,[13] as when he told Jon Snow on *Channel 4 News* in April 2011, ahead of the publication of his proposals the following month, that our political system 'is past its sell-by date' and that shortly he would be introducing a plan to 'gently cajole [the House of Lords] from the nineteenth into the twenty-first century'.[14]

Lords reform has its equivalent of the Kondratiev wave in the realm of economics and business cycles[15] or, to put it more graphically, it is a case, in Aldous Huxley's phrase, of 'routine punctuated by orgies'.[16] Roy Jenkins, whose elegant pen in the early 1950s turned to recreating the great Commons–Lords crisis of 1909–11 triggered by David Lloyd George's 'People's Budget'[17] in his *Mr Balfour's Poodle*, was writing in one of the quiescent phases even though the Parliament Act 1949 (which reduced the Lords' power to delay legislation from the two years established in 1911 to one) was still fresh on the parliamentary page. Reflecting on the Grey-inspired opening to the 1911 Act, he wrote:

> The preamble of the first Parliament Act has entered upon its fifth decade
> of non-fulfilment. Nor is it easy to see the conditions for an agreed

reform arising in the future [though all-party agreement had been close in 1947–48[18]]. In a broad sense the positions of 1910 are still occupied by the contending parties in the state [*Mr Balfour's Poodle* was published in 1954].

The right, attracted by instinct and tradition to the existing hereditary house [the Life Peerages Act was still four years away when Jenkins wrote that], contemplates a change only because its attachment to a powerful second chamber is still stronger. The left, distrustful of the existing archaicism but interested above all in the supremacy of the Commons, sees the relationship between the two Houses, rather than the composition of the second, as the dominant issue and is unwilling to accept a reform which might increase the prestige of an Upper House still essentially conservative.

'This', concluded Jenkins, with a characteristic ironic flourish, 'is a deadlock which the nation has survived for some years, and the continuance of which it may face with a degree of equanimity.'[19]

In the quiescent phases of the Lordly equivalent of the Kondratiev cycle – when the question of the Lords scarcely flickers (though it is never entirely dormant) – one could be forgiven for seeing its 800-year history (or longer, if you take the Saxon Witenagemot as its initial institutional DNA, as Enoch Powell did in his 1967 study, *The House of Lords in the Middle Ages*[20]) as the creation of a formidable resistance movement to change with but one caesura to break the chain back to Edward the Confessor. This was Cromwell's eleven-year Protectorate, which temporarily abolished the Lords. In this context, to succeed where Grey, Asquith and Lloyd George failed would be a real scalp for any leader who can claim lineal descent from the Liberal heyday.

But, once again, that would be to ignore 1911, 1949, the beginning of the life peerages and the admission of women in 1958 and the removal of the right to sit from all but ninety-two of the hereditaries by the House of Lords Act 1999. Mr Clegg and his group were not dealing with the people or the powers Asquith, Lloyd George and Grey faced in 1909–11. For the most potent illustration of this, the prime example is that of the meritocratic gene grafted on to the ancient DNA by the Life Peerages Act 1958, which set in train a wholly beneficial mutation that continues to this day. The impact of the 1958 statute demonstrated the British gift for absorbing rising and broadening elements of society inside the welcoming membrane of ancient institutions and usages.

This was beautifully exhibited in that delightful vignette played out before the Joint Committee on the Draft House of Lords Reform Bill in January 2012 from which I quoted at the head of this chapter. Jack Cunningham told me that in High Heworth, the pit village that nurtured him,

> there was the mine, the National Union of Mineworkers, the Labour Party and the Co-op. The miners thought 'nowt' of the House of Lords. Many years later, after Jarrow Grammar School and Durham University, I found myself a member of the House of Lords and an adviser to the City of London Corporation![21]

In his evidence to the Joint Committee, Jack Cunningham said he had 'learnt a lot more about the House of Lords, as people generally do on entering it'. He explained that he wanted to see reforms along the lines proposed by David Steel's House of Lords Reform Bill. 'However,' he continued,

> I have respect for the House of Lords. My great mentor, the late Lord Callaghan, once said to me just before I took my seat: 'Remember, if you stand up to make a speech, three, four or five of the world's experts on the subject will be sitting listening to you, so you had better be careful what you say.' That was, as ever, sound advice from him.

Jack concluded by telling Malcolm Wicks, the Labour MP and former minister who had asked him had he changed his mind: 'So, yes, I have respect and affection for the House of Lords but I am not a supporter of the status quo.'[22]

Jack's mentor, Jim Callaghan, was one of many Prime Ministers whose energies had been dissipated by the question of the Lords, in his case when Jim was Home Secretary in the late 1960s. He later wrote that the experience of trying and failing to put the Parliament (No. 2) Bill through the Commons in 1968–69 'vaccinated' him 'against enthusiasm for legislation on constitutional reform'.[23] The swiftest glance at the Lords reform timeline compiled by my friend and former student Dr Andrew Blick shows on just how many twentieth- and twenty-first-century prime ministerial watches the matter has arisen: Asquith, Lloyd George, Attlee, Churchill, Macmillan, Blair, Brown and Cameron.

House of Lords Reform: a timeline to May 2010

1671	House of Commons passes resolution 'that in all aids given to the King by the Commons, the rate or tax ought not to be altered by the Lords'.
1678	Commons passes resolution 'that all aids and supplies, and aids to His Majesty in Parliament, are the sole gift of the Commons; and all bills for granting of any such aids and supplies ought to begin with the Commons; and that it is the undoubted and sole right of the Commons to direct, limit and appoint in such bills, the ends, purposes, considerations, conditions, limitations and qualifications of such grants, which ought not to be changed or altered by the House of Lords'.
1702	House of Lords passes resolution against 'tacking' extraneous matter to Bills of aids and supplies, thus recognising that it is not entitled to amend the Bills to remove the additional material. The right to reject such Bills outright is, however, retained by the Lords until 1911.
19th century	Conservatives become the numerically dominant group within the Lords.
1871	Bankruptcy Disqualification Act prevents bankrupts from sitting and voting in the House of Lords.

1876 and 1887	Appellate Jurisdiction Act grants four Lords of Appeal in Ordinary seats in the House for life.
1886 and 1888	Resolutions condemning the hereditary right to a seat in the legislature are debated in the Commons but not carried.
1893	House of Lords defeats W. E. Gladstone's second Home Rule Bill.
1906:	Liberals elected with overwhelming Commons majority, with radical social programme.
1907	Lord Newton, a Conservative peer, introduces a Bill to end the automatic right of hereditary peers to sit in the Lords. It is withdrawn and a select committee chaired by the Earl of Rosebery, the former Liberal Prime Minister, is appointed to consider Lords reform. It reports in 1908 with recommendations along the lines of Lord Newton's Bill for a House of about 400 members, mostly representatives of the hereditary peerage elected for the life of one parliament by all members of their order, along with hereditary peers having seats by virtue of their qualifications (e.g. ex-Cabinet ministers), as well as a limited number of life peers. No action was taken on the report.
1909	Lords reject Liberal Chancellor of the Exchequer David Lloyd George's so-called 'People's Budget'. The Budget is eventually passed the following year after a general election fought on the issue in January 1910.
1910	Liberals retain office following elections in January and December of this year, but in both instances they are dependent on Irish Nationalists for a Commons majority. The Conservative majority in the Lords is determined to block the Nationalist objective of home rule. The Liberal government lays resolutions in the Commons on the restriction of the powers of the Lords, later included in the Parliament Bill. The Lords also approve resolutions proposing reform, particularly of composition, and

advocating a 'strong and efficient' second chamber. A conference of Liberals and Conservatives fails to reach agreement on the powers of a second chamber.

1911   Marquess of Lansdowne, the Leader of the Opposition in the Lords, introduces a Bill to make the House of Lords consist of mainly indirectly elected members. It is dropped when the government continues with its Bill to deal only with the powers of the Lords (though the introductory text noted the intention to introduce popular composition in the future – and to readdress the issue of powers at the same time). The *Parliament Act 1911* is passed following the threat to the Lords to create Liberal peers *en masse*. The Act means that Money Bills could be passed without the consent of the Lords; and while the Lords retains its veto on Bills extending the life of a parliament (which was reduced from seven to five years by the Bill), all other bills could receive Royal Assent without the consent of the Lords if passed by the Commons in three successive sessions (effectively about two years), other than Bills introduced in the Lords, which the Lords could still veto.

1914   *Welsh Church Act* and *Government of Ireland Act* enabled using *Parliament Act 1911* following rejections by the Lords.

1918   Conference of fifteen members of each House set up under Viscount Bryce in 1918. In 1918 it proposes that the second chamber be an examining and revising chamber, creating minimal legislative delay, initiating less controversial Bills and discussing policy. 246 members would be indirectly elected by regional groups of MPs; 81 members would be chosen by a Joint Standing Committee of both Houses (of the latter group, all would be hereditary peers or bishops at first, reducing eventually to thirty hereditaries and bishops and fifty-one others). Law Lords would sit *ex officio*. There would be twelve-year terms, with one-third retiring every four years. The Lords would have full powers on

	non-financial legislation. Differences between the two Houses would be resolved by a 'Free Conference Committee' of up to thirty members from each House. No action is taken on the Bryce Report, which appears during wartime.
1920, 1921, 1922	King's Speeches refer to House of Lords reform.
1922	Following the establishment of a Cabinet committee to consider reform, it concludes that the Bryce proposals would not be acceptable to the Commons or the public. In 1922, the coalition government proposes 350 members either directly or indirectly elected; hereditary peers elected by their own; members nominated by the Crown, with the number set by statute; proposals on finance similar to those put forward by Bryce; the Parliament Act to apply to all other legislation except measures altering the constitution of the House of Lords. These proposals come to nothing.
1927	Proposals similar to those of 1922 brought forward following recommendations of a Cabinet committee, but are dropped following resistance in the Commons.
1929, 1933, 1935	Private members' Bills proposing various reforms introduced by Conservative peers but not taken up by the government.
1945	Labour government elected with radical reform programme. Salisbury-Addison agreement established that the Lords would not resist Bills enacting commitments that had been included in the Labour manifesto.
1947–48	Labour government introduces a Bill to ensure passage of Bills in the fourth session of the Parliament, dealing only with the powers of the Lords. Following pressure from Conservatives and Liberals, the Bill is adjourned and there are talks between party leaders, discussing not only powers but also composition. Agreement is reached on key principles: the Lords as a complementary, not rival House; no permanent majority for one party; heredity not by itself sufficient

to guarantee membership; women should be permitted membership. The talks break down in April 1948 over the period for which the second chamber could impose delay on legislation and the Lords rejected the Parliament Bill.

1949	*Parliament Act 1949* enacted using the *Parliament Act 1911* following rejections by the Lords. The effect is to reduce the delaying powers of the Lords from three to two sessions (in practice, from about two years to one year).
1951	Conservative general election manifesto promises to reconvene an all-party conference on Lords reform.
1953	Viscount Simon introduces a Life Peers Bill and the Conservative government invites the leaders of the Liberal and Labour parties to talks, but Clement Attlee, the Labour leader, declines to participate and the talks do not take place.
1958	House of Lords standing orders amended to enable Lords to obtain leave of absence, in response to criticism of 'backwoodsmen'.
1958	*Life Peerages Act 1958* enables the Crown to create as peers men and – for the first time – women who could sit and vote in the Lords whose peerages expired on their deaths.
1960–61	'Stansgate case' sees Anthony Wedgwood Benn disqualified from the Commons against his will when he succeeds to the Viscountcy of Stansgate.
1962	Parliamentary Joint Committee considers issue highlighted by the Stansgate case as to whether hereditary peeresses could sit in the Lords.
1963	*Peerage Act 1963* enables hereditary peerages to be disclaimed for life; hereditary peeresses to be admitted to the House, along with all Scottish peers (the system of Scottish representative peers is abolished).
1966	Labour general election manifesto promises further protection of measures passed in the Commons from 'frustration' in the Lords.

1967	Queen's Speech promises legislation to reduce powers of Lords and remove hereditary basis.
1967–68	Inter-party talks reach substantial agreement over reform to composition and powers of the Lords. Talks are broken off when the Lords vote down sanctions against Rhodesia. The opposition parties are consequently not formally committed to the proposals, but the Labour government presses on. In November 1968, a White Paper proposes a two-tier House with 230 voting, created peers; and non-voting members. Succession would no longer entail the right to a seat in the House. Existing hereditaries would be non-voting members, or could be created life peers. The government would have a small majority in the House. The delaying power would be reduced to about six months in duration. The Lords would be able to require the Commons to reconsider secondary legislation, but not to reject it altogether. These proposals are eventually dropped after meeting with considerable cross-party resistance in the House of Commons where committee stage has to be taken on the floor of the House.
1969	Parliament (No. 2) Bill dropped.
1978	Labour Party National Executive Committee issues a paper suggesting that abolition is the preferable option for the Lords. A Conservative committee chaired by Lord Home of the Hirsel proposes a chamber in which two-thirds of members would ultimately be elected and one-third appointed.
1983	First hereditary peerages created since 1964 are conferred on William Whitelaw and George Thomas. Labour Party general election manifesto proposes abolition of the Lords.
1991	*War Crimes Act 1991* enacted under Parliament Act following rejections by the Lords.
1992:	Labour Party general election manifesto advocates reform rather than abolition of the Lords.

1996:   Tony Blair, the Labour leader, proposes a two-stage reform: the removal of hereditary peers followed by alteration of composition and powers.

1997:   Labour Party general election manifesto proposes removal of hereditaries as first stage of reform.

1998:   Queen's Speech refers to legislation to remove automatic right of hereditaries to sit and vote in the Lords as the first stage of a reform process. On 2 December it is announced that an agreement has been reached between the Labour government and Lord Cranborne, Conservative leader in the Lords, that ninety-two hereditary peers could remain until second stage of reform.

1999:   Government publishes a White Paper, *Modernising Parliament: Reforming the House of Lords*, and establishes a Royal Commission on the Lords chaired by Lord Wakeham, a Conservative peer. House of Lords Act provides for removal of all but ninety-two hereditary peers, most of whom would be elected from their own party groups. *European Parliamentary Elections Act 1999* enacted under the Parliament Acts following rejection by the Lords.

2000:   Royal Commission on Reform of the House of Lords reports in January with proposals including that a significant minority of second chamber members be elected. In May the non-statutory House of Lords Appointments Commission is established, nominating independent crossbench members and vetting on propriety grounds recommendations put forward by political parties. *Sexual Offences (Amendment) Act 2000* enacted under the Parliament Acts following rejections by the Lords.

2001:   Labour Party general election manifesto pledges to implement the conclusions of the Royal Commission. In November, the government publishes a White Paper, *The House of Lords: Completing the Reform*, proposing the removal of the remaining hereditary peers, and a majority appointed House of Lords.

2002:   Joint Committee on House of Lords Reform established in May. Its first report recommends votes on a number of options on composition should take place in both Houses.

2003:   In February, there is a series of votes on different options for composition; none receives a majority in the Commons, while the Lords votes in favour of a wholly appointed second chamber.

2004:   *Hunting Act 2004* enacted under the Parliament Acts following rejections by the Lords. Legal appeal against the validity of this Act is made, with the claim that the *Parliament Act 1949* is invalid because it was enacted under the *Parliament Act 1911*, which contained the implication that it could not be used to enact alterations to itself that were not approved by the Lords.

2005:   Law Lords reject appeal against the *Hunting Act 2004*, deciding that the *Parliament Act 1949* is valid. In their judgements, a majority of the Law Lords express the view that an attempt to remove the Lords veto over bills which extend the life of a parliament using the Parliament Acts would not be lawful. The *Constitutional Reform Act 2005* provides for the removal of the Law Lords from the House of Lords to a UK Supreme Court.

2006:   Labour government establishes a parliamentary Joint Committee to investigate the possibility of codifying the conventions governing the relationship between the two Houses, accepting the principle of Commons primacy. It offers definitions of how it sees the conventions governing the relationship between the two Houses as having developed, but cautions against detailed, enforceable definitions being introduced. Queen's Speech includes a commitment to attempt to build a consensus on Lords reform.

2007:	White Paper, *The House of Lords: Reform*, is published. In a debate on the document in March the Commons votes for two options – 80 per cent elected and 100 per cent elected. The House of Lords votes for 100 per cent appointed. A cross-party group on Lords reform is established.
2008:	Labour government publishes White Paper arising from cross-party talks, *An Elected Second Chamber: Further Reform of the House of Lords*. Its proposals include: an 80 per cent or 100 per cent elected second chamber; various options for the electoral system to be used; single renewable terms of 12–15 years; a significant reduction in the size of the House; and primacy for the Commons to be retained.
2009:	Limited reform measures included in the Constitutional Renewal and Governance Bill, including allowing the expulsion of members of the Lords. They are not included in the Bill as passed in 2010. The Supreme Court becomes operational, replacing the Appellate Committee of the House of Lords as the highest court in the UK.
2010:	Labour and Liberal Democrat general election manifestos contain pledges to wholly elected Lords; Conservatives commit to largely elected Lords.

This litany of a history suggests that in the constellation of constitutional and political reform, the question of the Lords has an astronomy all its own. Sometimes it dazzles and dominates (as in 1909–11); sometimes it frustrates (1968–69). Occasionally significant change is effected (1911, 1949, 1958) before the question fades for a political generation or two. But over the past decade and a half, since Labour's return to office in 1997, the sightings have been more frequent and have already produced one big shift – the removal of all but ninety-two of the hereditary peers under the House of Lords Act 1999.

Like any British political historian, I had long carried a certain idea of the House of Lords in my head (including the suspended sentence contained in the preamble to the 1911 Act) and knew its possible reform was part of the recitative of UK politics for a century plus. But not until I joined up, acquired an office in a turret and took in the view from a Hogwartian window (my grandsons, Joe and Jack Cromby, call the great Gothic edifice 'Hogwarts') did certain flavours and pulses emerge including the extent of the anthropological and behavioural difference between the Lords and the Commons. For example, the weather in the House of Commons is generally made by people who look for things to fall out over whereas the House of Lords contains quite an infusion of people who look for matters to agree about whenever possible. One House encourages a flaunting, grandstanding style of speech-making and question-asking; the other a more consensual, contemplative, conversational approach. The Commons culture favours carnivores; the Lords breeds herbivores. The Commons conducts its business amidst a near-continuous hubbub. The Lords almost always listens in courteous silence. At moments of high passion the Commons roars; the Lords mutters.

However, the very future of the House of Lords itself naturally has a capacity to disturb their Lordships' atoms that is all its own. Before joining I knew well enough that the question of the Lords was a great, if spasmodic, absorber of parliamentary time and political energy with a latent, if ever lurking, potential for surging back into life during the quieter interims. And within days of being introduced into the House in November 2010, I felt the pulse of the emotions it can arouse when I delivered my maiden speech during the second reading debate of David Steel's House of Lords Reform Bill on 3 December of that year.[24]

But not until I served on the Joint Committee on the Draft House of Lords Reform Bill in 2011–12 did I fully appreciate how truly sodden the question was – dripping with complications and awash with unintended consequences – or why so many who have plunged into the reform pool have emerged chilled to the bone, more than a little disorientated and often resolved on only one thing – never to dive back in. This is partly due to the depth and murk of the mixture of water in that pool. What streams had gone into its making when the Conservative–Liberal Democrat coalition draft Bill was being worked over by the Joint Committee? The chart produced by the House of Lords Library in February 2012 shows how the waters divided.

Composition of The House of Lords (as at 1 February 2012)

Party	Life Peers	Excepted Hereditary Peers*	Bishops	Total
Conservative	170	48		218
Labour	235	4		239
Liberal Democrat	87	4		91
Crossbench	154	32		186
Bishops			25	25†
Other**	27	2		29
Total	673	90	25	788

Note: This table excludes 22 members who are on leave of absence, three who are suspended, 13 disqualified as senior members of the judiciary and one disqualified as an MEP.

By type	Men	Women	Total
Archbishops and bishops	25	0	25
Life peers under the Appellate Jurisdiction Act 1876	22	1	23
Life peers under the Life Peerages Act 1958	509	178	687
Peers under the House of Lords Act 1999	90	2	92
Total	646	181	827

* Made up of 74 peers elected by parties and groups, 15 peers elected by the whole House and one royal office-holder (The Earl Marshal). The second royal office-holder (the Lord Great Chamberlain), and one peer elected by the Crossbench peers, are currently on leave of absence.

† One bishop's place was vacant.

** These are:

Other political parties:

L. Bannside: DUP	L. Maginnis of Drumglass: UUP
L. Browne of Belmont: DUP	L. Morrow: DUP
L. Elis-Thomas: Plaid Cymru	B. Paisley of St George's: DUP
L. Empey: UUP	L. Pearson of Rannoch: UKIP
L. Laird: UUP	L. Rogan: UUP

L. Rooker: Labour Independent	L. Wigley: Plaid Cymru
L. Stevens of Ludgate: Conservative Independent	L. Willoughby de Broke: UKIP

Non-affiliated Members:

L. Archer of Weston-Super-Mare	L. Paul
L. Bhatia	L. Roper: Principal Deputy Chairman of Committees
L. Black of Crossharbour	L. Smith of Finsbury
L. Brabazon of Tara: Chairman of Committees	L. Truscott
L. Collins of Mapesbury	L. Watson of Invergowrie
B. D'Souza: Lord Speaker	B. Young of Old Scone
L. Jacobs	Source: House of Lords Library.
L. Kalms	

A constitutional hydrologist would start by separating out the two most ancient feeder streams:

- Blood. The hereditary peers. Down in number to ninety-two following the House of Lords Act 1999. Replenished by by-elections when one dies. None but the British political genius could have engineered an outcome whereby the only elected members of the House of Lords are the hereditary peers.
- Piety. There remain two archbishops and twenty-four bishops of the established Church of England. The pair of archbishops, Canterbury and York, are there *ex officio* as are the bishops of London, Durham and Winchester. The others come in on the basis of seniority and leave the Lords on retirement from their sees. Former Archbishops of Canterbury return as independent crossbench life peers.

The largest contributor to the House of Lords pool is a veritable torrent of:

- Political appointees chosen by their party leaders. Within that cataract, however, are experienced figures with substantial, non-political professional careers behind them who sit alongside the former

Cabinet ministers and ex-MPs. In this way, several overlap with the more modest flow of

- Independent crossbench peers who are appointed more for what they know rather than what they believe. I am one of these and came in via the House of Lords Appointments Commission, which, since it began to operate in 2000, has sent fifty-nine crossbenchers into the Lords[25] at a rate of four to five a year.

The commission operates independently of ministers though it relies on government departments, Her Majesty's Revenue and Customs, the Secret Intelligence Service and the Security Service for papers on candidates. At the final stage of the process:

> The Commission makes recommendations to Her Majesty the Queen, via the Prime Minister, on non-party-political life peerages. The Prime Minister has undertaken to pass the Commission's recommendations directly to the Queen and will only intervene in the most exceptional cases.[26]

'Most exceptional cases' means security and, so far, there have been no interventions by the three Prime Ministers (Tony Blair, Gordon Brown and David Cameron) under whom the system has operated.[27]

This mixture of human flaws has a certain Gormenghast quality. But the chamber so created is, nonetheless, a thing of utility if not rationality.

The coalition's draft Bill would replace this blending of ancient and modern streams with a waterway dominated by a wave of elections with a second chamber, perhaps renamed the Senate, of 300, 80 per cent of whose members would be elected by some form of proportional representation and 20 per cent found by the House of Lords Appointments Commission, which would itself be put on a statutory basis.[28] In the final paragraph of their joint 'Foreword' to the White Paper, David Cameron and Nick Clegg said:

We look forward to the report from the Joint Committee which we will consider with great care. We are both strongly persuaded that this is a unique opportunity for our country to instil greater democracy into our institutions and are fully committed to holding the first elections to the reformed House of Lords in 2015.[29]

The Fixed-Term Parliaments Bill had yet to become law when the two party leaders wrote that but they were anticipating its passage in seeking the first tranche of elected members of the new second chamber entering in May 2015.

The 'opportunity', as Cameron and Clegg saw it, may have been 'unique' but the problems the draft Bill threw up were not. Indeed, they were very familiar and explained why the search for the 'consensus' on Lords reform, for which the Conservative Party called in its 2010 general election manifesto, was bound to be seriously stretching; to be candid, impossible. Because an unholy trinity of factors comes into play each time the question of the Lords goes on heat:

- powers
- functions
- composition

In a rational world, they would be seen as a triple helix crucial to the effective refashioning of a reformed chamber or the creation of an entirely new one. Yet history has shown British policy-makers and second chamber redesigners to be generally averse to this trinitarian approach.

The 1911 and 1949 Parliament Acts were about Lords' powers in relation to the House of Commons. The Life Peerages Act 1958 and the House of Lords Act 1999 concentrated upon composition. The Parliament (No. 2) Bill 1968 looked at both powers and compositions but was brought down in flames in the House of Commons by those most skilful of parliamentary fighter pilots, Enoch Powell[30] and Michael Foot,[31] before it reached the Lords.

The draft Bill of 2011 outlined dramatic and fundamental changes in composition but, in my view, deluded itself that powers would thereby be unaffected. 'The Government believes', the accompanying White Paper declared,

> that the powers of the second chamber and, in particular, the way in which they are exercised should not be extended and the primacy of the House of Commons should be preserved. The present balance between the two Houses ... serves the legislative process well, and gives the second chamber the opportunity to make a substantive contribution while not at the same time undermining the relationship between the Government and the House of Commons.[32]

When the House of Lords debated the White Paper and draft Bill on 21 June 2011, I argued: 'It is the question of powers that is the fault line into which this draft Bill will sink.'[33]

Alerted by Andrew Blick to the often forgotten second paragraph of the famous preamble to the Parliament Act 1911, it was on the question of powers that I concentrated that day. The key 1911 paragraph reads like this:

> And whereas provision will require hereafter to be made by Parliament in a measure effecting such substitution [of an elected House for a hereditary one] for limiting and defining the powers of the new second chamber, but it is expedient to make such provision as in this Act appears for restricting the existing powers of the House of Lords.[34]

I went on to say: 'The key verbs are "limiting" and "defining". In other words, Asquith, Lloyd George and Grey acknowledged that a popularly chosen second chamber required a statutory limitation of its powers – that, without a redefinition of the relative powers of the two Houses, the dangerous prospect of duelling chambers would arise.'[35]

That remained my belief throughout all the sessions of the Joint Committee on the draft Bill between July 2011 and March 2012. In fact, clause 2 of the draft Bill enshrining the no-changes-in-powers conviction of the coalition turned out to be friendless amongst those who gave oral evidence to the Committee apart from Nick Clegg and his Conservative junior minister, Mark Harper.

I had an interesting exchange with Mark Harper on clause 2 when he first came to see the committee on 10 October 2011:

HENNESSY: Minister, if there is a consensus in embryo on this extraordinary Bill about this subject that has distracted people for over a century, it is, perhaps, that history teaches one thing and one thing only, which is that to try to take composition without powers is almost certainly fatal – it is certainly undesirable. As you know we had a historical session[36]... I think that it strongly emerged from that that it is delusory to split the two. The idea that composition changes will not affect powers is central to the Bill, but do you really think, in all honesty, having sat at the feet of the great Vernon Bogdanor all those years [Mark Harper as an undergraduate at Brasenose College, Oxford was taught by Professor Vernon Bogdanor] and knowing the history as well as we do, that that argument is sustainable?

HARPER: There are two things. This has come up in the debates in your House and in the House of Commons when we were discussing the proposals. It is, of course, the case that when you change composition you will to some extent change the relationship between the two Houses. The relationship between the two Houses has changed already. It changed when the hereditary peers were excluded and it has changed since the general election last year – now that the Liberal Democrats are part of the coalition government, they no longer have the role that they had in the last parliament as the swing voters, which is a role that, in my observation, the crossbenchers have taken on. I do not think that the government's position is that there will be no change whatever in the relationship between the houses, but the statutory underpinning in the Parliament Acts means that the House of Commons remains the primary chamber.[37]

The Government's mixed signals on powers – no change; but there will be evolution – was evident from day one when the White Paper and draft Bill were published.

In my diary for Tuesday 17 May 2011 I wrote:

The big day. Everybody – wherever they stand – is dissatisfied with the White Paper and draft bill. Hywel Francis [Labour MP for Aberavon] told me as I was going in to hear Tom Strathclyde that Clegg had faced extraordinary hostility in the Commons when he made his statement.[38] Tom S seemed to contradict himself on powers (I'll chapter and verse this once I have the Hansard).[39]

I did so the following day, noting in my diary that:

Tom Strathclyde is engaged in what strikes me as a remarkable display of signals intelligence.

Listen to him during Questions on Monday in reply to Lord Kakkar:

We would decide the issue of a free vote when we come to a final conclusion about what would appear in a Bill, *if any*, and when it would be presented to Parliament [my italics].[40]

And yesterday he seemed to be putting out conflicting signals on the unchanged powers of the new chamber which is, for me, the greatest single fault line fissuring the White Paper and draft Bill:

There is a rationale for an elected House: it is to give legislators in this House the authority of the people who would elect them, to make the peers of this House stronger and to make this House more assertive when it has that authority and the mandate of the people.[41]

A few paragraphs later Tom said this:

It is an important assumption that underlies the White Paper that the powers of the existing House should not be changed if it were to be elected or partly elected.[42]

A few minutes later in reply to John Wakeham, Tom said:

I have long believed that giving this House an electoral mandate would make it stronger, more independent of party and more assertive.[43]

The H of C [House of Commons] seems in no doubt about the calculus of power being seriously altered by an elected body at the southern end of the Palace of Westminster … The glorious Maurice Peston, who told me yesterday my views on Lords reform were 'complete bollocks', came up with a wonderful definition of the motive power of the H of L when I introduced him to two naval friends coming in for coffee (Gerry Northwood and Andy Aspden):

The House of Lords runs on gossip and the exchange of symptoms.[44]

That deserves its place in Anthony Jay's next *Oxford Dictionary of Political Quotations*.

Once the Joint Committee began to scroll through its witnesses, clause 2, the relative powers section, of the Bill was like a tethered goat to be savaged whatever the wider views of its attackers on the question of Lords reform. Here is a flavour of the criticisms:

Peter Riddell, Institute for Government (now its Director), author of Parliament under Blair.[45]

I think the current Bill is defective. Clause 2 is the major flaw in the Bill because all it does is state, 'Because we believe it to be so, it will be so'. I think that is completely fallacious because the actual statutory limitations are pretty limited – the absolute bar on amending designated finance Bills and the one year suspensory veto – but beyond that it is custom and practice…[46]

Lord Adonis, former Labour Secretary of State for Transport, author of *Parliament Today*.[47]

Clearly an absurd proposition. An elected second chamber would clearly be more powerful and much more forthright, which is part of the reason why I support having an elected second chamber.[48]

Lord Cunningham of Felling, former Labour Cabinet minister and Chairman of the Joint Committee on Conventions 2005–6.[49]

In clause 2 of the Bill, which, trying to be kind, I can only describe as disingenuous, there are a number of naïve propositions. It is almost like someone walking off a cliff-edge in the dark. It suggests that all these things can happen – that profound changes can take place but nothing else will be changed.[50]

Yet if the legislation were to be taken back by the coalition and clause 2 as first drafted abandoned in recognition that from the first breaths drawn by the first members of the first elected tranche of new second chamberites the relationship between Commons and Lords *would* change, two alternatives are possible; one a free market, the other a dirigiste solution.

The free market approach would be to get the first swathe of elected senators in and see what happens. Would the new chamber act more assertively? Would there be a sequence of showdowns with the Commons in cases of serious disagreement? Would the Parliament Acts 1911 and 1949 be deployed more frequently by the government of the day, as Mark Harper suggested in reply to a question from Lord Trimble, Conservative peer and former Leader of the Ulster Unionists:

Because of the way the system works at the moment, you [Lord Trimble] are quite right that the House of Lords has often exercised a self-denying ordinance. But that is also the reason why the Commons has not needed to use the legislative underpinning more frequently. The whole reason why we do not have frequent use of the Parliament Act is exactly that the House of Lords and the House of Commons have a relationship which has developed. It seems to me that, if you change that relationship, the House of Commons may have to exercise the use of the Parliament Acts more frequently and you will have the Houses testing each other. That relationship will then settle down and a new set of conventions will develop, but legislative underpinning is still there.[51]

But the question arises: will the Parliament Acts of 1911 and 1949 still apply to a second chamber containing elected members? When those statutes were passed, the House of Lords was a wholly hereditary chamber apart from the Law Lords (who were life peers) and the bishops (who were there only as long as they occupied their sees). At the very least, with elected senators in place, the continuing bite of the Parliament Acts would be open to challenge.

So the dirigiste option would be to replace the existing delusional clause 2 in the draft Bill with one that recognises the new circumstances and legislates for statutory arrangements for both retaining the primacy of the House of Commons and constructing mechanisms for resolving disputes between Commons and Senate. There would, however, be an immediate consequence of this second course. The judiciary would undoubtedly be drawn in not just on the terrain covered by the Parliament Acts but across the wide swathe of what were once the conventions and self-denying ordinances that prevented the two Houses from paralysing both each other and successive governments' legislative programmes.

It would be very difficult to judge-proof such legislation by framing a clause which said that they should keep their hands off relationships between the two chambers. When I asked the Clerk of the House of Commons, Robert Rodgers, about this, he replied: 'I do not think the courts like all-purpose ousters. '[52] And both Mr Rodgers and his opposite number in the House of Lords, David Beamish, the Clerk of the Parliaments, pointed out that if the judiciary were to become involved, the courts would 'have to look at parliamentary materials to come to a decision' and 'that will drive a coach and horses through Article 9 of the

Bill of Rights 1688', as Robert Rodgers put it.[53] Article 9, for those who have not read the Bill of Rights recently, declares

> That the Freedome of Speech and Debates or Proceedings in Parlyament ought not to be impeached or questioned in any Court or Place out of Parlyament.[54]

The unearthing of ancient, but still valid, usages such as the Bill of Rights might be immensely frustrating for would-be modernisers who, no doubt, see it as a byzantine displacement activity for the traditionalist and the nerdy. But, as George Steiner wrote in his *My Unwritten Books*, 'in thought, in the arts, precedent can both inspire and lame.'[55] So it can, too, in the life of politics, government and institutions including, I think, the question of the Lords. For the possibilities of incremental, organic reform are nowhere near exhausted.

The Joint Committee was convened to discuss the draft Bill placed before it rather than the reforms which some of its members might wish had been brought forward instead. But in its session with Baroness Hayman, the former, indeed the first, Lord Speaker, an organic alternative was put forward as a series of steps which, she suggested, might be taken before the question of elections to a second chamber was tackled.

Lady Hayman did this by presenting the committee on 16 January 2012 with what amounted to an oral Green Paper. Her 'gravest concern, whatever my views on the proposals in the White Paper and the Bill, is that out of this will come not an elected House but a messy debate that ends up with no progress whatever and what I consider to be a House of Lords that is not improving its performance as a parliamentary chamber because we are not making any incremental progress.'[56] I agree very strongly with this. Since the passage of the House of Lords Act 1999, a kind of planning blight has crept over the chamber where nothing has grown in the shadow of the big shift to come in the direction of a wholly or largely elected House, or, as Lady Hayman put it, 'trying to do everything often ends up in doing nothing.'[57]

What she was seeking was 'some of the areas where it is possible to build if not unanimity then consensus, which in a sense would clear away the undergrowth for resolution of an issue that … is fundamental and deeply divisive: whether election would destabilise the relationship between the two Houses in a way that was detrimental to Parliament as a whole'.[58]

What were the ingredients of the Hayman Plan, as one might call it?

- Reducing the size of the House of Lords by introducing a retirement system.
- Phasing out the hereditary element.
- Ending the link between honours and peerages.
- Time-limiting appointments to the House of Lords.
- Reaching agreement on the balance between party political peers and independent peers.
- Placing the House of Lords Appointments Commission on a statutory basis.

Lady Hayman said these changes could be implemented over a five- to ten-year period: 'If we did those things and cleared that undergrowth, the issue of whether what you gain in democratic legitimacy from election outweighs what you lose in terms of experience and expertise could be considered, as well as focusing democratic accountability in one place – the clarity that we have at the moment … That is an issue which could be put in a referendum.'[59]

Lady Hayman's pathway to reform was very similar to that outlined by Peter Riddell in his evidence to the Joint Committee on 24 October 2011.[60] I share their views. Getting down to a streamlined House of Lords of 500 members by 2020 plus, as Andrew Adonis suggested in his evidence, making better use of the combined expertise of their Lordships through more overarching select committees[61] is the organic reform Parliament should go for. Such a plan may seem like a call for 'a better yesterday' (as Ralf Dahrendorf, himself a life peer who moved from the Liberal Democrat to the crossbenches, rather unkindly described the SDP of the 1980s[62]), but, in my judgement, it's all the better for that.

I agree with Lady Hayman, too, about the need to put the question of the Lords to a referendum once what she describes as clearing the undergrowth is complete – a kind of 'better yesterday' versus 'new dawn' poll perhaps to coincide with the 2020 election (if the five-year cycle prescribed by the Fixed-Term Parliaments Act 2011 is not revised by fresh legislation in the meantime).

Nick Clegg is not keen on a referendum. He told the House of Lords Select Committee on the Constitution on 1 February 2012 that the coalition was not proposing to abolish the House of Lords:

> It is not about putting to the British people the question of whether we should move to a unicameral system. If one were to do that, there would be a very good case for putting it to a referendum. I also happen to think that there are some political realities here. This has been debated for over 100 years now. In the previous general election all parties, for the first time, had clear manifesto commitments to move towards reform of the House of Lords. I do not share the view that it requires a referendum.[63]

Nick Clegg's reply was in response to a reminder about a previous Lords Constitution Committee report on the use of referendums published in 2010.

In that document the Constitution Committee had declared:

> Notwithstanding our view that there are significant drawbacks to the use of referendums, we acknowledge arguments that, if referendums are to be used, they are most appropriately used in relation to fundamental constitutional issues. We do not believe it is possible to provide a precise definition of what constitutes a 'fundamental constitutional issue'. Nonetheless, we would consider to fall within this definition any proposals:

- To abolish the Monarchy;
- To leave the European Union;
- For any of the nations of the UK to secede from the Union;
- To abolish either House of Parliament;
- To change the electoral system for the House of Commons;
- To adopt a written constitution; and
- To change the UK's system of currency.[64]

In my view the proposals in the coalition's draft Bill *are* abolitionist. It may be abolition of the existing House in stages but abolition it is. Theirs is an engineering solution to the question of the Lords – to decommission the existing chamber over ten years, 2015–25, and to replace it with a new structure built to a completely new design which may or may not be called a Senate. The coalition's is a mechanical, demolish-and-rebuild proposal, not an organic, incremental approach to reform. They are proposing to construct the parliamentary equivalent of a new town rather than to refurbish an old city centre that has been centuries in the making and reshaping.

It is impossible to forecast the likely result of a referendum if the coalition were to persist, the Lords to resist, the government to use the Parliament Acts (of which more in a moment) and the referendum to take place at the same time as the May 2015 general election. The two most recent polls on Lords-related public opinion in Ian Cruse's House of Lords Library paper, *Public Attitudes Towards the House of Lords and House of Lords Reform*,[65] show a strong preference for a largely or wholly elected second chamber and also considerable support for retaining an element of members chosen for their professional or academic expertise.

October 2010: Angus Reid – House of Lords Reform

In October 2010 Angus Reid published the results of a survey of 2,004 individuals on House of Lords reform, in which it tested a number of different propositions:

Now, we'd like to ask you some questions about the House of Lords. Which of these statements comes closest to your own point of view?

- The UK does not need a House of Lords, all
  legislation should be reviewed and authorised
  by the House of Commons   30%
- The UK needs a House of Lords, but the
  people should be allowed to take part in the
  process to choose Lords   40%
- The UK needs a House of Lords, and the current
  guidelines that call for appointed Lords should
  not be modified   9%
- Not sure   21%

Would you support or oppose holding a nationwide referendum to decide the future of the House of Lords?

- Support   66%
- Oppose   11%
- Not sure   23%

As you may know, several proposals have been made to reform the House of Lords. Do you support or oppose each of these ideas? Allowing the people to directly elect their Lords

- Support   58%
- Oppose   15%
- Not sure   28%

Abolishing the House of Lords altogether

- Support   30%
- Oppose   39%
- Not sure   31%

When do you expect the people will be able to directly elect the members of the House of Lords?

- In the next two years   10%
- Three to five years from now   29%
- Six to ten years from now   21%
- More than ten years from now   14%
- Never   26%

September/October 2011: Unlock Democracy

As part of its submission to the Joint Committee on the Draft House of Lords Reform Bill, Unlock Democracy included the results of an online survey it had carried out between 14 September and 5 October 2011, in which online respondents were asked a series of questions about House of Lords reform. The survey was not carried out by a polling company and it is not clear whether sampling was used.

1. The government has proposed that the reformed second chamber should be either fully or 80% elected. Do you think it should be…

- Fully elected   2300   57.69%
- 80% elected, 20% appointed   1192   29.90%
- Other   495   12.42%
- Total number of responses   3987

2. If some members of the second chamber are to be appointed, what types of people would be acceptable?

- Anglican bishops   385   10.64%
- Representatives of all faiths   1263   34.89%
- Specially appointed government ministers   401   11.08%
- People appointed by political parties   425   11.74%
- People appointed by an independent body   2970   82.04%
  for their professional/academic expertise
- Representatives of professional bodies   3190   88.12%
  (e.g. British Medical Association, Royal

College of Nursing)

- Representatives of trade unions   1745   48.20%
- Members of the public randomly selected   1269   35.06%
  from the electoral roll
- Other   361   9.97%
- Total number of responses   3620

3. MPs are currently elected for up to 5 years at a time. This is usually longer for elected second chambers and the government has proposed they should be elected for 15-year terms. How long do you think members of the second chamber should be elected for?

- 15 years   356   9.21%
- 10 years   1529   39.55%
- Less than 10 years   1981   51.24%
- Total number of responses   3866

4. Should elected members of the second chamber be able to stand for re-election?

- Yes   2998   76.46%
- No   923   23.54%
- Total number of responses   3921

5. The government is considering using the two voting systems to elect the second chamber: the single transferable vote (STV), in which voters can rank any or all candidates in order of preference; or open lists, in which voters put an 'X' beside the candidate they most prefer. Both systems are broadly proportional, STV offers more choice and ensures that more votes will count. It is also better for independent candidates. However, the open list system is significantly simpler to vote in. Which system would you prefer?

- Single Transferable Vote   3169   86.33%
- Open lists   502   13.67%
- Total number of responses   3671

6. *The current House of Lords can delay government legislation by up to a year. However, the House of Lords rarely exercises this right, and has only used it four times in the past 60 years. Most experts agree that a wholly or mainly elected second chamber is likely to want to use this power more frequently. Should the powers of the second chamber be changed to reflect this?*

•	No, the current rules should stay	1734	44.61%
•	Yes, the current rules should change	2153	55.39%
•	Total number of responses	3887	

7. *Which of the following proposals to alter the second chamber's existing powers to delay legislation would you find acceptable (tick all that apply)?*

•	Reduce the amount of time the second chamber can delay legislation by	781	21.34%
•	Allow the House of Commons to overrule the second chamber if two-thirds of MPs vote to do so	2085	56.98%
•	Only allow the House of Lords to block legislation on more than one occasion if two-thirds of its members vote to do so	1388	37.93%
•	Require both chambers to set up a joint committee to work out a compromise if the second chamber rejects the legislation a second time	2690	73.52%
•	Total number of responses	3659	

There are two impulses at work here. As a senior figure involved in Lords affairs put it, it's as if 'the public want elected experts which is the one thing they cannot have'.[66]

As I confessed earlier, I have a hopeless record as a political forecaster. Trying to sort out the shards of the past is quite stretching enough for me, and, naturally, I'm hugely error prone when it comes to looking back as well as peering forward. And I am writing this portion of the chapter in mid-March 2012 just as the Joint Committee is drafting its report on the government's proposals. The firm indications are that a House of Lords Bill of some kind will have a prominent place in the May 2012 Queen's Speech. There are plentiful signs, too, that opposition in the Lords itself will be considerable and prolonged if that Bill is based on the draft legislation.[67]

The big question is whether in the event of the Lords voting down the government's bill twice, the coalition would reach for the Parliament Acts to force it through. And could their use of the Parliament Acts be challenged in the courts if they did? The Joint Committee asked for the opinion of the Attorney General, Dominic Grieve, on this and were refused,[68] perhaps because he had yet to write one (a suspicion on my part; not a fact). So the last piece of Law Officer's advice on the matter we have dates from the Thatcher years, 1981, in a file declassified by the Cabinet Office in January 2012. It was provided for a sub-group of the Cabinet's Home and Social Affairs Committee on the House of Lords, known as H (HL) in the Cabinet committee lexicon.

A memorandum of 29 January 1981 presented to the Cabinet committee by its chairman, the Home Secretary, Willie Whitelaw, took a wide look over the constitutional landscape. The exercise was stimulated in part by the possibility that a future Labour government might be elected with an abolitionist paragraph in its manifesto. Labour duly did bring forth such a paragraph in its 1983 election manifesto, *The New Hope for Britain*, which declared:

> We shall … take action to abolish the undemocratic House of Lords as quickly as possible and, as an interim measure, introduce a Bill in the first session of parliament to remove its legislative powers – with the exception of those which relate to the life of a parliament.[69]

Labour failed miserably at the polls. Mrs Thatcher returned with a majority of 144 seats.[70]

But it remains interesting that her first government should have spent time anticipating an abolitionist election. The Whitelaw memorandum of 29 January 1981 is also significant because it contains within it the most recent externally available internal Whitehall opinion on the legality of using the Parliament Acts to drive through a Bill abolishing the House of Lords (this would have been fed in by the then Attorney General, Sir Michael Havers, who sat on the Cabinet committee).

Under the heading 'Methods of abolition', the Whitelaw memorandum stated:

> Abolition of the House of Lords, or diminution of its powers, without the consent of its present members might be pursued by an 'abolitionist' Administration commanding a sufficient House of Commons majority in either of two possible ways –
>
> i. under the terms of the Parliament Acts (Parliament Act 1911, as amended by Parliament Act 1949) by legislation passed by the House of Commons in two successive sessions; or
> ii. by the creation of a sufficient number of 'abolitionist' Peers to ensure that there would be a majority in the House of Lords for a bill to abolish that House or to diminish its powers. If these new Peers were created during the session when an 'abolition' bill was first passed by the House of Commons, this method could avoid the delay involved in the use of the Parliament Acts procedure.
>
> It should perhaps also be noted that a severe diminution of the present powers of the House of Lords (e.g. if the delaying power were reduced to, say, one month from the date of receipt of a bill) could be tantamount to abolition.[71]

The members of H (HL), meeting in Conference Room A (the one which contains George III's throne and the old, tiny Cabinet Table inside the more modern furniture of the Cabinet Office) on the morning of

3 February 1981 were helpfully provided with relevant extracts from the Parliament Acts 1911 and 1949. It might be useful to reproduce here the statutory material Willie Whitelaw's colleagues were given not least because the Parliament Acts might be used to force the coalition's Bill through the Lords before the general election of 2015.

Extracts from Parliament Act 1911

An Act to make provision with respect to the powers of the House of Lords in relation to those of the House of Commons, and to limit the duration of Parliament.

[18 August 1911]

Whereas it is expedient that provision should be made for regulating the relations between the two Houses of Parliament.

And whereas it is intended to substitute for the House of Lords as it at present exists a Second Chamber constituted on a popular instead of hereditary basis, but such substitution cannot be immediately brought into operation.

And whereas provision will require hereafter to be made by Parliament in a measure of effecting such substitution for limiting and defining the powers of the new Second Chamber, but it is expedient to make such provision as in this Act appears for restricting the existing powers of the House of Lords.

Be it therefore enacted by the King's most Excellent Majesty, by and with the advice and consent of the Lords Spiritual and Temporal, and Commons, in this present Parliament assembled, and by the authority of the same, as follows

Powers of House of Lords as to Money Bills

1. – (1) If a Money Bill, having been passed by the House of Commons, and sent up to the House of Lords at least one month before the end of the session, is not passed by the House of Lords without amendment within one month after it is so sent to that House, the

Bill shall, unless the House of Commons direct to the contrary, be presented to His Majesty and become an Act of Parliament on the Royal Assent being signified, notwithstanding that the House of Lords have not consented to the Bill.

Restriction of the powers of the House of Lords as to Bills other than Money Bills

(2) A Money Bill means a Public Bill which in the opinion of the Speaker of the House of Commons contains only provisions dealing with all or any of the following subjects, namely, the imposition, repeal, remission, alteration or regulation of taxation; the imposition for the payment of debt or other financial purposes of charges on the Consolidated Fund or on the money provided by Parliament, or the variation or repeal of any such charges; supply; the appropriation, receipt, custody, issue or audit of accounts of public money; the raising or guarantee of any loan or the repayment thereof; or subordinate matters identical to those subjects or any of them. In this submission the expressions 'taxation', 'public money', and 'loan' respectively do not include any taxation, money, or loan raised by local authorities or bodies for local purposes.

(3) There shall be endorsed on every Money Bill when it is sent up to the House of Lords and when it is presented to His Majesty for assent the certificate of the Speaker of the House of Commons signed by him that it is a Money Bill. Before giving his certificate, the Speaker shall consult, if practicable, two members to be appointed from the Chairmen's Panel at the beginning of each session by the Committee of Selection.

2. – (1) If any Public Bill (other than a Money Bill or a Bill containing any provision to extend the maximum duration of Parliament beyond five years) is passed by the House of Commons in three successive sessions (whether of the same Parliament or not), and, having been sent up to the House of Lords at least one month before the end of the session, is rejected by the House of Lords in each of those sessions, that Bill shall, on its rejection for the third time by the House of Lords, unless the House of Commons direct to the contrary, be presented to His Majesty and become an Act of Parliament on the Royal Assent being signified thereto, notwithstanding that the House of Lords have not consented to the Bill. Provided that this provision shall not take effect unless two years have elapsed between the date of the second reading in the first of those sessions of the Bill in the House of Commons and the date on which it passes the House of Commons in the third of those sessions.

(2) When a Bill is presented to His Majesty for assent in pursuance of the provisions of this section, there shall be endorsed on the Bill the certificate of the Speaker of the House of Commons signed by him that the provisions of this section have been duly complied with.

(3) A Bill shall be deemed to be the same Bill as a former Bill sent up to the House of Lords in the preceding session if, when it is sent up to the House of Lords, it is identical with the former Bill or contains only such alterations as are certified by the Speaker of the House of Commons to be necessary owing to the time which has elapsed since the date of the former Bill, or to represent any amendments which have been made by the House

of Lords in the former Bill in the preceding sessions, and any amendments which are certified by the Speaker to have been made by the House of Lords in the third session and agreed to by the House of Commons shall be inserted in the Bill as presented for Royal Assent in pursuance of this section:

Provided that the House of Commons may, if they think fit, on the passage of such a Bill through the House in the second or third session, suggest any further amendments without inserting the amendments in the Bill, and any such suggested amendments shall be considered by the House of Lords, and if agreed to by that House, shall be treated as amendments made by the House of Lords and agreed to by the House of Commons; but the exercise of this power by the House of Commons shall not affect the operation of this section in the event of the Bill being rejected by the House of Lords.

Extracts from Parliament Act 1949

An Act to amend the Parliament Act, 1911

[16 December 1949]

Be it enacted by the King's most Excellent Majesty, by and with the advice and consent of the Commons, in this present Parliament assembled, in accordance with the provisions of the Parliament Act, 1911, and by authority of the same, as follows:–

1. The Parliament Act, 1911, shall have effect, and shall be deemed to have had effect from the beginning of the session in which the Bill for this Act originated (save as regards that Bill itself), as if –

Substitution of references to two sessions and one year for references to three sessions and two years respectively 1 & 2 Geo. 5

(a) there had been substituted in subsections (1) and (4) of section two thereof, for the words 'in three successive sessions', 'for the third time', 'in the third of those sessions', 'in the third session', and 'in the second or third session' respectively, the words 'in two successive sessions', 'for the second time', 'in the second of those sessions', 'in the second session', and, 'in the second session' respectively; and

(b) there had been substituted in subsection (1) of the said section two, for the words 'two years have elapsed' the words 'one year has elapsed':

Provided that, if a Bill has been rejected for the second time by the House of Lords before the signification of the Royal Assent to the Bill for this Act, whether such rejection was in the same session as that in which the Royal Assent to the Bill for this Act was signified or in an earlier session, the requirement of the said section two that a Bill is to be presented to His Majesty on its rejection for a second time by the House of Lords shall have effect in relation to the Bill rejected as a requirement that it is to be presented to His Majesty as soon as the Royal Assent to the Bill rejected may be signified in the session in which the Royal Assent to the Bill for this Act was signified.

The Whitelaw memorandum touched next on those Bills to which the Parliament Acts did not – and still do not – apply:

- any bill proposing to extend the maximum duration of a Parliament beyond five years
- public bills 'starting their life in the Lords'.

The memorandum then made plain that

> The Parliament Acts do not, however, contain provision to exclude from
> this procedure bills proposing either the abolition of the House of Lords
> or reductions in its powers. Thus the Parliament Act of 1949 amending
> that of 1911 was enacted without the consent of the Lords.* Historically,
> the omission of any provision excluding 'abolition' Bills from the scope
> of the 1911 Act may derive from the fact that as its preamble indicates, it
> was enacted in anticipation of a reformed second chamber. Entrenchment
> of the existing House would have appeared inappropriate in this context.[72]

The memorandum then sets out the procedure that will apply if a
great Parliament Act showdown occurs in the Parliament of 2010–15:

> Prima facie, therefore, any bill to abolish the House of Lords, or to
> reduce its powers significantly, could become law under the procedures
> laid down in section 2 of the Parliament Act, 1911, as amended. If any
> such bill were passed by the Commons, but rejected by the Lords, it
> could become law without the Peers' consent provided that it had been
> passed by the Commons in two successive sessions, and sent up to the
> Lords at least one month before the end of these sessions, and provided
> that one year had elapsed between the date of the second reading in the
> Commons in the first session and the date on which the bill passed
> the Commons in the second session.[73]

The Whitelaw paper noted that any attempt to create a unicameral
Parliament at Westminster 'would seem certain to provoke a constitutional
conflict … [and that] … the political and constitutional repercussions of
a conflict on such a fundamental issue cannot be foreseen'. The coalition's
proposals are not unicameralist, fundamental though they are. But the
next paragraph of the Whitelaw memorandum on likely resistance has a
certain application to current prospects in 2012–15:

---

* A body of academic legal opinion takes the view that the 1949 Act is not within the scope of the 1911 Act and is
accordingly invalid.

Account would also need to be taken of the risk that in such extreme circumstances [of Lords abolition] the House of Lords, or at least, some of its members, would seek to disrupt the Government's entire parliamentary programme over a prolonged period. There could, for example, be substantial scope for delay in the fabrication of unnecessary amendments and in various forms of prevarication short of 'rejection', and the members of the then opposition in the Commons might support such tactics.[74]

There would, I think, be danger for the Lords, however, in certain forms of behaviour if such conduct struck the general public as self-serving, undignified or extreme. It would increase the chances of any referendum being clothed in Peers versus the People raiment by those who sought abolition/replacement.

As for the applicability of the Parliament Acts to the coalition's proposals, the evidence to the Joint Committee from Lord Goldsmith QC, Attorney General 2001–07, and the crossbench peer Lord Pannick QC corroborated that contained in the Whitelaw memorandum of 1981. Lord Goldsmith argued that 'the issue was, I believe, resolved by the decision of the House of Lords in R (Jackson and others) *v.* the Attorney General [2005] UK HL 56' – the legal challenge to the use of the Parliament Act 1949 to secure the passage of the Hunting Act 2004.[75] In preparing his evidence, which was based on his Birkenhead Lecture delivered at Grays Inn on 17 October 2011, Lord Pannick had examined the parliamentary debates which preceded the passage of the Parliament Act 1911. It was plain from these, Lord Pannick wrote,

that the 1911 Act was intended to allow the House of Commons to enact legislation without the consent of the House of Lords on fundamental constitutional issues, including reform of the House of Lords. Winston Churchill, the Home Secretary, made the point very clearly during the committee stage of the Parliament Bill. The passage of the Bill was, he said, 'an indispensable preliminary to the discussion of any grave questions in regard to the constitution of the second chamber'. This was, he insisted, for a very good reason: 'It is obvious that we could not embark upon discussion on equal terms while the last word rests with the House of Lords.'[76]

'There can be no doubt', Lord Pannick concluded, 'that the 1911 Bill was presented to Parliament, and the relevant amendments were rejected, on the basis that clause 2 (1) would apply even to fundamental constitutional issues, including reform of the House of Lords.'[77] So, in my view the Parliament Acts *can* be applied to a coalition Bill. The question is, in the last resort, *would* they be? On the current question of the Lords, I had expected in late 2011 that the first weeks of 2012 would see a retreat from the draft Bill once the Cabinet contemplated (a) which Bills would fail to reach the Queen's Speech of May 2012 in order to free up the huge amount of time the Lords legislation would absorb in both Houses (as a first order constitutional Bill all its stages will have to be taken on the floor of the House of Commons and the coalition may have insufficient votes on the question to timetable (i.e. guillotine) the Bill in the Commons), and (b) the prospect of losing a substantial proportion of those Bills that did make it into the Queen's Speech if a considerable number of their Lordships turned themselves into a resistance movement.

I was quite wrong. In January 2012, Nick Clegg insisted the Bill go ahead in 'the Quad' (the meeting of Cameron, Clegg, George Osborne, the Chancellor of the Exchequer, and Danny Alexander, Chief Secretary to the Treasury, where coalition difficulties are tackled), inside the formal coalition committee of the Cabinet designed to resolve disputes between the coalition partners as well as full Cabinet.[78] In Conservative circles it became known in February that Clegg's bargaining power was boosted by the Conservatives' need for Liberal Democrat support to get the boundary changes through Parliament which flowed from the reduction of Commons seats from 650 to 600 under the Parliamentary Constituencies and Voting Act 2011 and which were widely thought to increase the chances of a Conservative general election victory, and the press, too, picked this up.[79] As one seasoned Conservative put it, this 'placed David Cameron in a hole'.[80] Agreeing to proceed towards a largely elected second chamber in January 2012 may or may not prove to have been a strategic error on David Cameron's part. There was an interesting exchange on this at the end of February 2012 between two Conservative figures when the Cabinet Office Minister, Oliver Letwin, gave evidence to the strategy inquiry conducted by the House of Commons Public Administration Committee chaired by Bernard Jenkin.

JENKIN: Why do you think abolition of the existing House of Lords is an urgent and strategic priority against the present economic crisis and other challenges the government are facing, given the ability this legislation might have to paralyse the whole government?

LETWIN: If we thought it was urgent, we would have introduced it at an earlier stage in the Parliament.

JENKIN: So it's not urgent?

LETWIN: What we thought was most urgent we began by doing: for example, deficit reduction we thought was urgent. However, we think it is important. There are many things that are important that are not as urgent as some things that are urgent. We think it is important to reform the House of Lords, because we think it is important for the sake of achieving the very first of my goals here – a free and democratic society – that governments and the executive should be continuously held in check by the legislature, and we think that the House of Lords is more likely to be able to hold the government properly to account and to check the power of the executive effectively if it contains a healthy, democratic element. So that is precisely part of achieving our strategic goals, and that is why it was set out from the beginning in the coalition agreement.

JENKIN: The Prime Minister used to say it might be a third-term priority.

LETWIN: The Prime Minister, indeed, took a view in the Conservative Party manifesto that we would work towards a 'consensus'. That was the word in the Conservative Party manifesto. When we came into coalition, we made an agreement with our counterparts in the coalition to advance this activity as an important part of creating a more effective check on the executive, wrote it in the coalition agreement and are now implementing it. I do not think you could choose a better case of the government being clear minded about their strategy.[81]

'Clearmindedness' is not exactly the first word that comes to mind when contemplating the history of Lords reform over the past century. Though, as I write, the Joint Committee is striving for just that as it races towards its end of March 2012 deadline sitting for many, sloggy hours in Committee Room 4A of the Palace of Westminster. The question of the Lords carries abundant freight. Sitting on the Joint Committee one could often feel the weight of the débris of the past.

In fact, almost all the fragments of thought, evidence and possibility that passed through Committee Room 4A had been touched by previous hands and the arguments worn smooth by repetition. Our task was as much archaeology as futurology. The problem, which we could not solve any more than those who had gone before, was arranging those fragments in such a way as to prove a consensual path to reform.

Yet each time the particles are thrown once more into the political air, there are fascinations – not least the frisson of possibility, which horrifies some and excites others, that, this time, a hugely significant and irreversible shift will take place. Though as I put my pen down, somehow I hear Sir Edward Grey emit a hollow laugh.

10

THE POWER AND THE STORY:
POLICY-MAKERS AND HISTORIANS

Study history, study history. In history lie all the secrets of statecraft.
WINSTON CHURCHILL TO AN AMERICAN SCHOOLBOY,
CORONATION WEEK, 1953.[1]

WINSTON Churchill adored history. He read it, wrote it, lived it. History made him and he reciprocated by making history himself. On grand and romantic occasions it consumed him and unleashed his intoxication with words. He conceived of his country and its institutions historically. He was fully conscious and self-aware about this. In a powerfully autobiographical paragraph – thinly camouflaged as an essay on Lord Rosebery, formerly and very briefly Liberal Prime Minister in 1894–95 – Churchill wrote of his old friend:

> His life was set in an atmosphere of tradition. The past stood ever at his elbow and was the counsellor upon whom he most relied. He seemed to be attended by Learning and History, and to carry into current events an air of ancient majesty. His voice was melodious and deep, and often, when listening, one felt in living contact with the centuries which are gone, and perceived the long continuity of our island tale.[2]

Apart from the deep and melodious voice, that is Churchill on Churchill. I must admit, I suffer from a mild version of past-at-the-elbowism myself.

Churchill made his remark about history and statecraft to James Humes, then at Stowe School on an English-Speaking Union scholarship, at a reception before a Commonwealth Parliamentary Association lunch on 27 May 1953. 'Churchill's mind', wrote his official biographer, Sir Martin Gilbert, 'was full of memories – he had served as a soldier in the armies of Queen Victoria, and had written in his histories about the first Queen Elizabeth and Queen Anne.'[3]

The new, young Queen was present at the CPA lunch. Churchill was besotted by her. As his Principal Private Secretary, Jock Colville, later wrote: 'He was an old man whose passions were spent, but there is no doubt that at a respectful distance he fell in love with the Queen.'[4] That lunchtime, her propinquity launched him into a great paean of praise for the magical, unwritten beauties of the history-honed British constitution. 'In our island', rumbled that unmistakable voice,

> by trial and error, and by perseverance across the centuries, we have found out a very good plan. Here it is: the Queen can do no wrong. But advisers can be changed as often as the people like to use their rights for that purpose. A great battle is lost – Parliament turns out the government. A great battle is won – crowds cheer the Queen. We have found this a very commanding and durable doctrine. What goes wrong passes away with the politicians responsible. What goes right is laid on the altar of our united Commonwealth and Empire.[5]

As Paul Addison wrote of him: 'To Churchill the past was alive and Whig history was true'[6] (on the Whig front, Churchill was an avid reader of Macaulay and won a prize at Harrow for reciting his *Lays of Ancient Rome* from memory[7]).

For Churchill, every thought, every action, was refracted through the prism of history. He saw, too, his personal biography as unfolding history and was determined to write his own version of it to increase the chances that posterity would see him as he saw himself, as John Ramsden illustrated so vividly in his *Man of the Century*.[8]

Churchill was not alone in this. In a successor political generation that heard for itself the old lion's final roars in the House of Commons across the decade after the war, Roy Jenkins is perhaps the outstanding literary-political figure who held high office (Home Secretary twice, 1965–67, 1974–76; Chancellor of the Exchequer once, 1967–70). During his time as, by his own account, a not very successful cryptographer at Bletchley Park, when the work slackened as the Second World War approached its end, Captain Jenkins found himself in a remote room with not enough to do. 'There', he wrote,

> no one disturbed me with work or anything else for days on end (night shifts had happily been abandoned). I settled down to read the 'tombstone' volumes which then formed the core of English modern political biography … I read all day, apart from getting up for a few minutes every one and half hours or so and playing a ball game with arcane rules of my own devising against a wall of my solitary room.

This faintly eccentric finale to Jenkins's military service paid great dividends for the ball-bouncing bibliophile and for the genre of British political biography, as Jenkins wrote in his highly polished memoir, *A Life at the Centre*: 'This immersion course transformed my knowledge and interest in the lives and careers of British political figures of the previous hundred years.'[9]

Roy Jenkins, whom I admired, always struck me as measuring himself almost daily against his own political hero, Henry Asquith, who formed the subject of his second and much acclaimed foray into political biography[10] (the first had been an interim study of Clem Attlee in 1948[11]). The fit with Asquith was striking – Home Secretary, Chancellor of the Exchequer and, in retirement, Chancellor of the University of Oxford. Though the apogee of No. 10 Downing Street between Whitehall and the ceremonial headship of his ancient *alma mater* (sadly, I think) eluded Roy Jenkins. A connoisseur's sense of the history of the job would have undoubtedly have burnished a Jenkins premiership. He did his best, at one stage removed, as a mentor to Tony Blair. Mr Blair once confided in Lord Jenkins his 'regret that he read Law and not History at Oxford' and that he had 'become a considerable addict of political biography'.[12]

As Oxford's Chancellor, Lord Jenkins prepared a lecture posing and answering the question 'Should Politicians Know History?' On balance, he thought they should provided theirs was 'a reasonably detached study of history' and not a version arising from 'living in its shadow with an obsessive concentration' for, Jenkins continued, '[no] communities are more difficult to bring together – Northern Ireland, Cyprus – than those where the contemplation of ancient wrongs is a way of life.' Jenkins's final answer to his own question was cautious for one who thought historically so naturally. He turned out to be somewhere between Henry Ford's 'History is Bunk' (which the great motor magnate declared in the witness box during his libel suit against the *Chicago Tribune* in 1916[13]) and Cicero's rather earlier judgement that 'to be ignorant of what happened before you were born is to remain a child always'.[14]

Lord Jenkins, with that gift he possessed for grandeur and treating fellow political practitioners past and present as curiosities and specimens, summed up by giving his

> vote in favour of history rather than Henry Ford's dictum upon it, but I do so with suitable caution and reservation. What I really believe is that those with curiosity, whatever their educational and occupational backgrounds, are bound to have an interest in and acquire some knowledge about the past; and that those without it are likely to be dull fellows and uncomprehending rulers.[15]

Jenkins lines up, therefore, with Einstein's dictum 'never lose a holy curiosity'.

Jenkins the political lepidopterist was especially interesting in the distinction he drew between a pair of vividly marked butterflies – Winston

Churchill and Harold Macmillan, neither of whom were entirely at ease as Conservatives even though this was the political colouring they wore when in No. 10. Macmillan, wrote Jenkins,

> had little of Churchill's command over written English ... But his knowledge was at least as great as Churchill's, and covered a wider span. He knew Greek and Roman history in a way that Churchill, whose interests were always concentrated on the past 300 years, never did. Harold Macmillan may not have been a great writer of history, but his most characteristic speeches moved easily from the Peloponnesian War to the Battle of the Somme.[16]

What Macmillan himself called the interplay between the 'gownsman' and the 'swordsman'[17] – the classical scholar and the Grenadier Guardsman – was bravely and poignantly illustrated on 15 September 1916 between Delville Wood and Guillemont when German machine gunners struck Macmillan in his left thigh and pelvis. For ten hours he lay in a shell hole until rescued by his company sergeant major dozing in and out of consciousness. When conscious he fished out a copy of Aeschylus in the original Greek from his battledress and read to himself.[18]

His time as a young man in the Great War – rivalled only by his encounter with mass unemployment as MP for Stockton-on-Tees in the interwar years – was what shaped Macmillan in all the senior ministerial posts he held. These experiences – Greats at Balliol, service in the trenches with the Grenadiers, walking the deprived back streets of 1920s and 1930s Stockton – made the political weather system in which Macmillan lived and operated as Prime Minister.

On one occasion – the most critical of his premiership, and, for those of us breathing in autumn 1962, the most perilous of our collective lives – the Cuban missile crisis, Macmillan's recent historical reading influenced his conduct of events as it did President Jack Kennedy's in Washington. They had both been absorbing the then new study, *The Guns of August* by Barbara Tuchman,[19] of the great powers falling into total war in 1914 through a combination of inadvertence and the rigidities of their mobilisation plans. Macmillan, 'profoundly affected'[20] by Mrs Tuchman's analysis, pressed his caution on General Lauris Norstad, the outgoing NATO Supreme Allied Commander Europe, at a dinner in No. 10 on 22 October 1962 ('I said that "mobilisation" had sometimes caused war,' he recorded in his diary[21]). On the fraught Saturday 27 October, the day before Khrushchev backed down and agreed to remove the Soviet missiles from Cuba, Macmillan told the Chief of the Air Staff, Sir Thomas Pike, to bring the V-bombers (then the carriers of the UK's nuclear deterrent) to alert condition 3 (that is, fifteen minutes' readiness) but to avoid overt preparations.[22] They remained at alert condition 3 until Guy Fawkes Day, 5 November.[23]

Recollecting that extraordinary crisis which was unanticipated by western intelligence (though a Joint Intelligence Committee assessment had outlined a comparable scenario in 1957[24]), one can be profoundly grateful for that combination of reading habit and temperament which governed the thinking of both Kennedy and Macmillan as they contemplated the missiles of October. It reminds me of Cardinal Fleury, adviser to the King of France in the early eighteenth century, declaring, rather loftily it has to be said, that 'a man of mediocre status needs very little history; those who play some part in public affairs need a great deal more; and a Prince cannot have too much.'[25]

Roy Jenkins, however, was right to be careful about placing too much weight on history as *the* key ingredient of statecraft. Parallels are never exact. As Mark Twain famously said: 'History does not repeat itself but sometimes it rhymes.'[26] And the Soviet Empire, which placed its bets on history possessing 'scientific' laws about the relationship between capital and labour that guaranteed the eventual triumph of its system, ended in dissolution in 1989–91 as nearly all imperiums (so far) have.

History, in short, is a plentiful bringer of context and background to the current preoccupations of policy-makers. It is an antidote to an oversimplified or self-serving, partisanship-distorted view of the past. It decreases the chances of previous generations of policy-makers who grappled with comparable questions and difficulties having their views parodied and their efforts patronised. Current ministers and officials can always benefit from timelines which help explain how the dilemmas or choices they face have, to adapt a phrase of Churchill's, scored the pages of history[27] in transit to their desks.

But history is not the carrier of special insights with great predictive power. It is a horizon-scanner's aid not a crystal ball. The very best it can offer is Braudel's thin wisps of tomorrow.[28] To freight the historian's craft with excessive, unfulfillable expectations is to risk bringing what history can offer into disbelief and disrepute.

How much could a chief historical adviser offer a Whitehall department? Such figures, as we have seen, were recommended by the former Secretary of the Cabinet, Lord Butler of Brockwell, at a Royal College of Defence Studies seminar on 'What's Wrong with Government?' in April 2011.[29] Firstly, when an issue went live, providing a swiftly produced and easily digestible road map of how this particular policy area reached where it is now can only add value. An obvious example before the next Strategic Defence and Security Review, due in 2015, would be a summary of the previous eleven since the end of World War II. This, apart from anything else, would enhance reality and boost humility on the part of the next set of reviewers as well as acting as an antidote to hubris.

Secondly, though no chief historical adviser could offer omniscience however steeped they are in the subject areas institutionalised by the department that employs them, they should know the range of scholars, books and papers that, between them, do carry that knowledge which can be provided in aid of the ministry concerned in an *ad hoc* but quick and timely manner.[30]

Thirdly, history is sadly replete with the consequences that can follow if on big, urgent and anxiety-inducing matters such as wars (Suez 1956 and Iraq 2003 come to mind) procedural corners are cut.[31] The chief historical adviser, like all the Queen's Crown servants, would possess a prime duty of 'speaking truth unto power'. There would be no point keeping a scholar in the attic if he or she failed so to speak.

What we also need is a sustaining stream of official histories. In 2008, the former Permanent Secretary to the Northern Ireland Office, Sir Joe Pilling, recommended just this in a report for the Cabinet Office.[32] Sadly, since that year, the strain on the public finances has prevented forward commissioning of new ones, though a way is being found to produce one on the history of civil nuclear power to fill a huge gap at a time when a new wave of civil nuclear power stations is planned for 2018 onwards.[33] Official histories are particularly valuable – for policy-makers, Parliament and the reading public alike – when they cover the most secret parts of the state where substantial parts of the archive will be retained way beyond any Thirty- or Twenty-Year Rule.

In the 1970s, for example, this applied to the early years of UK nuclear weapons policy. Margaret Gowing and Lorna Arnold went a very long way towards filling that gap in 1974.[34] More recently Christopher Andrew and Keith Jeffery did the same for the Security Service (this an 'authorised' rather than an official history) and the Secret Intelligence Service respectively in 2009 and 2010.[35] Sir Lawrence Freedman's two-volume official history of the Falklands War, published in 2005, was another example.[36]

There is the Whitehall equivalent of a patron saint of official histories who died in 1968. He was Sir Edward Bridges, Secretary of the War Cabinet during World War II. In late 1941, at one of the bleakest moments of the war, Bridges decided to commission a series of both civil and military histories of the conflict. Professor Sir Keith Hancock was asked to edit them. He never forgot his first meeting with Bridges, another classical gownsman and swordsman (he won an MC during the Great War). 'Was there', Hancock wrote later,

> any use or point, I asked him, in starting to write the history of the war before we had won it? He replied that I would find ways of making myself useful in short term but I must also think in long term of the continuity of the state and the advantage of funding our wartime experience for future use.[37]

I am a Bridges man. He believed in history; so do I. He believed history is an aid to the continuity of the state; so do I. He believed in nurturing a collective memory; so do I. History is also, to use another favourite Edwards Bridges word, fun,[38] unlike the product of the management consultants whom Whitehall employs in battalions.

Finally to extend Churchill's line about Joe Chamberlain in his *Great Contemporaries*, yesterday's history is a powerful shaper of today's political weather.[39] It is to the good if current policy-makers are sensitive to that. The power really does need the story. For, as the great historian of the waning of the Middle Ages, Johann Huizinga, put it ,'historical thinking has altered our very blood'[40] even if some policy-makers are more aware of it than others.

A current practitioner whose blood history has most certainly infiltrated is the Foreign Secretary, William Hague, author of acclaimed biographies of William Pitt the Younger[41] and William Wilberforce.[42] Central to his great speech of September 2011 on restoring the Foreign and Commonwealth Office to 'its rightful role at the heart of government' was the need to turn history into a weapon of diplomacy. He set out to do this by 'cultivating and retaining knowledge throughout the institution', firstly by 'bringing the work of FCO historians back into the consideration and formulation of policy along with the academic vigour that our research analysts bring, including regular seminars to learn from history' and secondly by creating a 'Locarno Group' [presumably because they will meet in one of the Locarno Rooms] of former members of the Diplomatic Service to act as 'an additional source of advice to ministers on foreign policy'.[43] A few days after his Locarno Room threnody about the indispensability of history, Mr Hague was asked a so-called 'quickfire' question by Rachel Sylvester and Alice Thomson as part of a long interview in *The Times*. 'Historian or Politician?' they asked. 'I enjoy cycling between them – at the moment politician,' he replied.[44]

That September morning, William Hague had a horror story to tell about his taking up the office of Foreign Secretary in May 2010:

> As a historian and a politician I was surprised and indeed shocked upon
> my arrival here by the sight of the vast expanse of empty wooden shelves

where once the 60,000 books, pamphlets, reports and manuscripts of the historic Foreign Office Library were housed here in this building.

The library, part of which was rescued by King's College, London, 'embodied', Mr Hague went on,

> 500 years of British and world history; of our experiences of exploration, diplomacy, war, peacekeeping and the forging of treaties; of our role in the abolition of the slave trade and the creation of the Commonwealth. It contained unique historical documents such as the 1692 Charter of Massachusetts, many of them annotated by officials.

Lord Granville, Gladstone's Foreign Secretary, William Hague said, had regarded the FO Library as 'the pivot on which the whole machinery of the Foreign Office turned'.[45]

William Hague, by far in my judgement the best and funniest performer in the Coalition, finished his restoration-of-history peroration with a passage that was pure northern music hall (at which he excels). 'It is ironic', he said,

> that the only object to survive the gutting of the Library is a 100-year-old 20-foot stuffed anaconda known as Albert, who remains suspended over the empty bookshelves,* while the books from the period when such an unusual foreign gift found its way into the Foreign Office have been dismantled around it, and can never be reassembled.

'To my mind', the Foreign Secretary concluded, 'the fate of the FCO Library is emblematic of a gradual hollowing out of the qualities that made the FCO one of our great institutions.'[46] Three cheers for Albert the Anaconda. And three cheers for William the Foreign Secretary. When it comes to history and statecraft, Mr Hague is a true Churchillian.

---

* Listening to Mr Hague at this point reminded me irresistibly of Stanley Holloway's monologue about 'Albert and the Lion'.

11

PAPER TRAIL:
BECOMING AN ITEM IN THE ARCHIVE

… Mr Peter Hennessey [sic] – the Prime Minister [Jim Callaghan] conclud-
ed that no special action should be taken to identify the source of Mr Hennes-
sey's information, that his irritating articles would have to be endured, but
that it would be prudent to keep a close eye on the situation to see if it proved
possible to identify his source.
KENNETH STOWE, PRINCIPAL PRIVATE SECRETARY TO THE PRIME
MINISTER, TO SIR IAN BANCROFT, HEAD OF THE HOME CIVIL SERVICE,
13 SEPTEMBER 1978.[1]

ON 16 August 2011, BBC Radio 4 broadcast a documentary, *One Hundred Years of Secrecy*, which my producer Rob Shepherd and I had put together to mark the high speed passage through Parliament a century earlier of the Official Secrets Act 1911 in the middle of a war scare precipitated by the Kaiser putting a warship, the *Panther*, into the Moroccan port of Agadir the previous month.[2] Rob and I traced the history of the statute's notorious catch-all, section 2, which potentially criminalised the divulging of any information an official was not specifically authorised to release.

The Franks Report of 1972 noted that about 2,000 separate charges could be brought under section 2 and recommended that it should be pensioned off and replaced by a new Official Secrets Act immensely narrower in scope and directed at those areas of official information where confidentiality could be justified.[3] Not until 1989 was such a substitution effected after Douglas Hurd, as Home Secretary, had finally managed to persuade a reluctant Mrs Thatcher this was the sensible way to proceed, that, as Lord Hurd put it to me in the summer of 2011, 'you had to have something which worked and it inevitably would have a narrower scope.' 'That', he explained, 'was the argument which prevailed with her.'[4]

The BBC Radio 4 centenary programme contained the following exchange between myself and Lady Thatcher's ever-direct and forceful former Downing Street Press Secretary, Sir Bernard Ingham.

INGHAM: You spent a lot of your time talking and, may I say, buttering up civil servants.

HENNESSY: Thank you, Bernard.

INGHAM: And I was astonished how much they were prepared to say but not to me. I mean the sheer hypocrisy of the whole blessed thing is revealed by your relationship with them, if I may say so. I mean they wouldn't say what they said to you to me.

HENNESSY: Oh, I see. I was the recipient of their confidences and you weren't about how they felt?

INGHAM: Oh yes, oh yes.

HENNESSY: Well, everybody has to talk to somebody, Bernard.

INGHAM: Why didn't they talk to me?

HENNESSY: Maybe the beauty of your personality was lost on them.

INGHAM: No, no, it wasn't the beauty of my personality. They were playing their own games. So much for the Official Secrets Act.[5]

At the time, I knew that Bernard Ingham (of whom I have grown fond), released a certain amount of heat when my name was mentioned. But not until our interview for the secrets programme recorded in July 2011 did I realise quite what it was that had so upset him and plainly continued to do so.

It was a piece of recently declassified archive, which I showed Sir Bernard before we began our conversation, which lit the blue touch paper that summer morning in the BBC's Millbank studios – a 1980 file from the No. 10 papers dealing with leaks. In January that year, at the suggestion of Sir Ian Bancroft, Head of the Home Civil Service, Mrs Thatcher had commissioned an inquiry into the phenomenon.

Bancroft, with the Cabinet Secretary, Sir Robert Armstrong, and the Permanent Secretary to the Home Office, Sir Brian Cubbon, had been considering, as he expressed it to Clive Whitmore, Mrs Thatcher's Principal Private Secretary, 'the case for commissioning a study of unauthorised disclosures of information to the press'. Bancroft, a man of wit and charm whom I liked greatly, reckoned that

the growth of so called investigative journalism and the proliferation of lobbies and pressure groups which can readily command the attention of the media has created a climate which I suspect positively encourages disclosure by an individual who holds strong personal convictions on an issue currently under consideration with central Government and who sees a way of furthering the cause he supports without being detected. These misguided people represent I suspect a much more serious threat to the security of Government documents than those who are motivated by extremist political views.[6]

'The Prime Minister', Whitmore told Bancroft, 'has no great hope that such a study will produce anything of value but, even so, she agrees with you that the attempt is worth making.'[7]

Sir Nicholas Morrison, former Permanent Secretary at the Scottish Office, was recalled to the colours to carry out the task. His report was ready by July. Sir Nick saw no plots and recommended tightening up procedures generally ('not particularly far-reaching', was how Mrs Thatcher put it to her Home Secretary, Willie Whitelaw[8]).

Her press secretary, Sir Bernard, however, plainly thought the Morrison Report feeble. On 21 July 1980, he dashed off a minute to Michael Pattison, one of Mrs Thatcher's private secretaries. 'I have read the Leak Inquiry report', said Sir Bernard, 'and would merely like, at this stage, to comment on one aspect referred to in Para 6.'

The author there states:

I have found no evidence at all of any kind of subversive plot or any connecting link indicating a continuing common source or sources for the leaks.

Bernard suggested to Michael Pattison that

you may care to consider that:

- prima facie there is a continuing common source or sources of leaks to Peter Hennessy of The Times, most notably on CCU [Civil Contingencies Unit] and D-Notice matters.

Bernard went on to name Keith Harper and Richard Norton-Taylor of the *Guardian* and Michael Edwards of the *Daily Mail* as other recipients of regular leaks.[9]

The Civil Contingencies Unit, forerunner of today's Civil Contingencies Secretariat, was located in the Cabinet Office and prepared plans for coping with industrial disputes in sixteen key industries.[10] The D-Notice system (now known as the DA system) involved advisory notices from the Ministry of Defence on sensitive defence and intelligence matters, overseen by a joint press–Whitehall committee – an arrangement involving voluntary self-censorship by the press.[11]

Given the obligation to keep one's helpers secret unto the grave – theirs and mine – unless they 'out' themselves in the meantime, I can confirm Bernard Ingham's use of the plural 'sources' and Nick Morrison's conclusion that neither 'subversion' nor 'plot' was involved either in my pieces for *The Times* or inside the book *States of Emergency*, which Keith Jeffery and I co-authored, that appeared in 1983.[12]

For a historian, it's a strange feeling to find oneself part of the national archive, one's old preoccupations frozen in the stacks at Kew. It produces a mixed reaction – makes one feel a bit old to be an item released under the Thirty-Year Rule; and to think of all the distraction that one's pieces caused people who had quite enough to worry about without such pinpricks. I felt that particularly strongly about Jim Callaghan and his irritation at my open government crusade in the late 1970s.

I can understand the sensitivities aroused in Whitehall in the late 1970s, with trade union power at its height, the Labour government majority-less in the House of Commons and growing stress within the Labour movement, by my desire to anatomise the contingency plans for what amounted to strike-breaking. It was a concern that ran through into the early months of the Thatcher government as *The Times* printed my articles as a series in November 1979, when the paper reappeared after nearly a year's shutdown due to a dispute with the print unions about the introduction of new technology.[13]

I'm sad, too, that my much-admired friend Sir John Hunt, the Cabinet Secretary, thought the draft articles I sent the Ministry of Defence on Jim Callaghan's highly secret deliberations on Polaris replacement in 1978–79 were such a danger to the state (on nuclear weapons matters I would voluntarily let Whitehall see such pieces in draft lest the Russians learnt things they should not know about the UK's nuclear weapons programme). The articles did not run as written as *The Times* did not resume publication in time for the May 1979 general election, though a single story did appear in the one edition of the paper the management was able to print in Germany.

In the middle of the general election campaign, John Hunt minuted Ken Stowe in No. 10 that his 'first instinct' had been to approach informally

Sir Denis Hamilton, Editor-in-Chief of Times Newspapers, and William Rees-Mogg, Editor of *The Times* and my boss, to try and persuade them not to publish. But, Hunt concluded,

> we could not plead national security [indicating that my reason for showing MOD the pieces was met]: and the Labour Party Manifesto itself talks about the desirability of 'full and informed debate' on the matter.[14] I think the only argument could be made that this is a thoroughly irresponsible article and that if it is published consideration would have to be given to instructing Departments to cease to have any dealings with Mr Hennessy.[15]

Next to this, Jim Callaghan scribbled: 'No. We should not try to stop publication.'[16] No approach was made to *The Times* though I was aware of the mother-and-father of the leak inquiry John Hunt recommended be carried out in the Ministry of Defence, the Foreign and Commonwealth Office and the Treasury,[17] which later took place and turned out to be fruitless.[18]

My private view then – as now – was that I wished the UK to remain a nuclear weapons state. I was keen, however, on the internal debate within Whitehall feeding into the wider public discussion a country like ours must have when the nuclear question goes live (as it is again in 2012).

Away from nuclear matters, on the wider front of more open government, however, I must confess that it's fun – and a touch gratifying – to know one had a tiny, walk-on part in the greater, longer drama of Britain getting out, bit by bit, of the corset of excessive secrecy the Edwardians' anxieties had imposed on us for so long in the form of section 2 of the Official Secrets Act 1911 (of which more in a moment). In fact, initially, as a young, would-be (though unannounced) Whitehall correspondent of *The Times*, the instinctive reaction of No. 10 to my early efforts paid dividends.

In the summer of 1974 I left the *Times Higher Education Supplement*, where I had worked since December 1972 with the excellent Brian MacArthur, a natural trainer of young journalists, for the Night Desk of *The Times*. *The Times*' Home Editor, Charlie Douglas-Home, suggested I work up an area not routinely covered by the paper during the gaps between the arrivals of the rivals' first editions and any late-breaking stories the Night Desk would have to cover.

I decided to take a crack at Whitehall. It had long fascinated me, thanks to reading Anthony Sampson's anatomies and Samuel Brittan's *Steering the Economy*.[19] I'd already had a stab at it on the *THES* with a profile of the still relatively new Civil Service College[20] and, more recently, I had set about preparing a profile of Sir Kenneth Berrill pegged to his move from being Chief Economic Adviser to the Treasury to the directorship of the Central Policy Review Staff, the Cabinet Office's think tank.[21]

I had known Ken as chairman of the University Grants Committee during my *THES* spell, and, over lunch, told him I was interested in reporting Whitehall more generally and gave him an idea of areas I might look at. The efficient Ken alerted his friend Sir Douglas Allen, Head of the Home Civil Service, even before his profile appeared in the paper. I enter the files when the sympathetic Douglas Allen briefs No. 10 on me and my intentions in a minute sent on 7 November 1974 to Robert Armstrong, then Principal Private Secretary to Harold Wilson, who had returned to No. 10 the previous March.

Allen told Armstrong that the Civil Service Department (CSD)

gathered two or three months ago that Mr Peter Hennessy might be approaching senior civil servants in order to gather material for a series of articles in the Times. The topics in which he was reportedly interested were:

a. Main trends since Fulton [the report on the Civil Service from a committee chaired by Lord Fulton published in 1968[22]]
b. Special Advisers [then a relatively new phenomenon].
c. Dispersal of the civil service [to Scotland, Wales and the Regions].
d. The rules on senior civil servants moving out into industry and commerce.[23]

Allen explained to Armstrong that the CSD planned to consult the Prime Minister when the first approach was made to senior officials. This had yet to happen. In fact, I was still reading my way into the subject over those long hours on the Night Desk though I had been in touch with some senior figures about possible briefings. I had, however, asked the Oxford politics don Lord Crowther-Hunt, an influential figure on the Fulton Committee and now a Minister of State in the Cabinet Office, for an interview. It was this, the file shows, that triggered Allen's approach to No. 10.

Douglas Allen thought I should be helped within certain ground rules – matters 'of political and public controversy' should be avoided and there was to be no whiff of 'classified matters'.[24] This did not find favour inside No. 10. Robert Armstrong discussed the Allen minute with Joe Haines, Wilson's Press Secretary, and he briefed the Prime Minister accordingly on 8 November 1974.

> I have discussed this with Mr Haines. We do not think that it is necessary to object to Mr Hennessy seeing Lord Crowther-Hunt (now a Minister) [in fact, the interview never took place]. But we think that senior civil servants should not be given permission to grant interviews to Mr Hennessy. The political implications of many of the matters which he would want to discuss are such that it would be better for civil servants not to be involved.

Joe Haines remarks that this is reminiscent of Anthony Howard's project as a Whitehall correspondent of the *Sunday Times* in 1965, which was firmly sat on at the time.[25] On this Harold Wilson has written

> I certainly agree <u>no</u> civil servants. But why any interview at all – it seems to be 'The Times'. Say no. HW.[26]

The second sentence is a touch baffling. Presumably Wilson was ruling out a Crowther-Hunt interview but as for 'it seems to be "The Times"', we'll never know what he was getting at.

As a result Robert Armstrong on 13 November 1974 sent the memo to Douglas Allen which did me an enormous service (as I shall explain in a moment). It read:

SIR DOUGLAS ALLEN

ARTICLES IN THE TIMES ON THE CIVIL SERVICE

Thank you for your minute of 7 November, which I have shown to the Prime Minister.

He would prefer no assistance to be given to Mr Hennessy by Ministers or civil servants. There should in any case be no interviews with civil servants; and he would much prefer that Lord Crowther-Hunt should find it necessary to decline the request or an interview.

R. T. ARMSTRONG.[27]

It was the contents of this memo that were leaked to me by two people who rang *The Times'* Night Desk on the late afternoon/early evening of, I think, Thursday 5 December 1974 (one gave his name; the other did not). As I recalled later:

Pride mingled with panic. I was new to the game. Official Secrets Act and D-notices were still a matter of awe to me. Charlie Douglas-Home had been the paper's Defence Correspondent. He would know what to do. Charlie was somewhat taken aback – why had Wilson done it? I told him I had found an area to write about Whitehall. No. 10 had found out before my boss did and clearly did not like it. Charlie said it was magnificent and that I should hit them.[28]

So I did. First by writing a kind of innocent-boy letter to Joe Haines.

There turns out to have been a nice symmetry here. When Robert Armstrong and I relived this episode for *One Hundred Years of Secrecy* nearly thirty-seven years later, he said: 'Harold was rather old-fashioned. I think there was a sense of outrage that a young whippersnapper on *The Times* should be put on to this sort of thing.'[29] (I was twenty-seven at the time.)

I despatched my letter on 8 December 1974 affecting shock (some of which *was* genuine). It is beautifully preserved in the No. 10 file now at Kew:

Dear Mr Haines,

Three months ago I began to prepare a feature article on the civil service for *The Times* and subsequently approached a number of ministers and civil servants seeking 'off-the-record' interviews with them on a variety of topics.

Last week I discovered from two sources that a memorandum had been sent, both to the civil servants I had approached and to others, indicating that the Prime Minister would prefer that I be given no assistance in this enterprise.

Needless to say, I have no way of verifying the existence of such a memorandum. But one of those whom I had initially approached and found agreeable to participating in an interview, has since made his excuses.

I must confess to being puzzled by the matter and would be most grateful if you could offer any clarification.

Yours sincerely,

Peter Hennessy,

Home News Reporter, *The Times*.[30]

On 12 December 1974 Joe Haines forwarded my letter to Robert Armstrong with a handwritten note attached:

Mr Armstrong

Any comments?

You will notice that the phrase 'prefer no assistance' is almost identical to the one used in your memo to Douglas Allen.

Joe [31]

Armstrong replied to Haines the following day:

As you say, the gist of my minute of 13 November to Douglas Allen must have been conveyed to civil servants in other Departments and reported by one of them to Mr Hennessy.[32]

The Armstrong memo plainly had done the rounds widely across Whitehall. This, for me, was like winning the jackpot. I hadn't written a word of my planned pieces in *The Times* and the policy-making strands of the senior Civil Service were alerted to my intentions from the highest level, and plainly some of them felt I was more sinned against than sinning. Harold Wilson did me a great service. He was the No. 1 recruiter of my network of helpers, which seven years later was to so enrage Bernard Ingham.

In the meantime, Robert Armstrong suggested to Joe Haines the line he might like to take with me:

> Presumably your reply should be to the effect that civil servants are required to obtain the permission of the Heads of their Departments to give interviews to journalists; that the Head of the Civil Service was consulted by the Heads of a number of Departments, and thought it right in turn to consult the Prime Minister; and that the Prime Minister, while not of course wishing to comment or stand in the way of his proposals, did not think it appropriate that civil servants should grant interviews to him for this purpose.[33]

Silkily done.

In fact, Joe Haines sent me quite an amiable, almost chatty letter on 17 December 1974:

> Dear Mr Hennessy,
>
> I am sorry not to have replied to your letter of 8 December earlier, but we have had a fairly hectic time of late.
>
> As you know, civil servants are required to obtain the permission of the Heads of their Departments before giving interviews to journalists. Clearly a number of consultations would then take place. It would not be our practice to disclose what form those consultations would take, or to confirm or deny what has been said to you. Ministers, of course, are free to talk to you if you wish, and I would have thought that on

the question of special advisers, for example, the Lord President of the Council [Ted Short] would be able to help you more than anyone else. This is my personal thought – I have not suggested it to him or to anyone in his office.

Yours sincerely,

Joe Haines[34]

Joe later became a good friend. As did Ken Stowe, John Hunt, Robert Armstrong and Jim Callaghan (though, in Jim's case, not before the mid- to late 1980s).

Jim, like Harold Wilson, was a traditionalist in Civil Service matters. He did not like it one bit when he discovered in July 1978 that Permanent Secretaries, including the Cabinet Secretary, John Hunt, would occasionally have lunch with me. Ken Stowe had alerted him that 'senior officials were taking lunches off Hennessey [*sic*] in a casual way'.[35] Jim writes on the memo:

The civil service has obviously been very free and easy with their acceptance of hospitality. It shall stop.[36]

Some stopped. Some didn't. Others resumed lunching later.

It was a particular leak – not one of mine – that goaded Jim Callaghan into wider action on the Official Secrets Act front. After Frank Field, Director of the Child Poverty Action Group and later Labour MP for Birkenhead, disclosed in the magazine *New Society* in June 1976 confidential Cabinet documents about the government's discussion on the possible abandonment of its plans to introduce child benefit,[37] Callaghan decided that what was wanted was a new streamlined Official Secrets Act to replace the discredited section 2 of the 1911 statute. Douglas Allen had conducted a leak inquiry[38] and failed to find those to whom Mr Field refers to this day as 'deep throat ... or deep throats' (his helpers are alive but they still do not wish to emerge).[39]

The political journalists were briefed by No. 10 (I was there during a brief spell as Lobby Correspondent of the *Financial Times* in 1976) that this was to be a liberalising measure. I suspected not and rang Dr Bernard Donoughue, Jim Callaghan's Senior Policy Adviser in No. 10. Bernard, as he recorded in his diary, gave me the killer phrase (which I used non-attributably) which vividly illustrated that this was not so.

His entry for Friday 30 July 1976 records:

> 10.30 we had a Cabinet committee on the Franks Report on Official Secrets. The PM was quite open that he wants 'reform' in order to tighten the law and make it more effective. Jenkins [Home Secretary] wanted something more liberal than Franks, and quoted my (original) phrase about replacing the blunderbuss with the Armalite rifle (which I gave to Peter Hennessy of the *FT* and now keeps cropping up everywhere).[40]

Callaghan commissioned a special Cabinet committee, GEN 29, to work up a new law to replace section 2. It came to nothing. He had no majority and ministers feared any attempt to legislate would lead to freedom of information clauses being tacked onto the measure in a House of Commons Callaghan's whips could not entirely control and Jim was definitely not an FOI man.

As we have seen, not until 1989 did Douglas Hurd, as Home Secretary, pilot through the Commons a slimmed-down Official Secrets Act along Franks lines. Freedom of information won statutory form in 2000 but did not become operational until January 2005. And since 1992, thanks to John Major, we have the list of ministerial Cabinet committees regularly published by the Cabinet Office.[41]

Whitehall is no longer the stone-clad citadel it once was for journalists trying to write about it, though, sadly, only a few do nowadays on a regular basis. This greater routine openness is all to the good. But do I envy today's Whitehall reporters? Not entirely. It was fun penetrating the hard old target – made you raise your game. And, thanks to the great tradition of Whitehall record-keeping in the paper days (I have serious worries about the electronic data era), the National Archives and the Thirty-Year Rule (due to come down to twenty a year at a time from January 2013), there is a heap of deferred gratification lying around at Kew.

Have I a favourite piece in the pile? If I do it's Merlyn Rees writing to Jim Callaghan on 2 September 1977 after I had partially penetrated GEN 29, the Cabinet committee on reform of the Official Secrets Act which he, Rees, chaired. The gentle Merlyn had succeeded the polished Jenkins when Roy departed for the Presidency of the European Commission the previous year. 'I expect', wrote Rees to Callaghan,

> you have seen two recent articles in The Times about the discussions we have been having amongst ourselves on the content of the new legislation to replace Section 2 of the Official Secrets Act 1911, and on the form and timing of our next move. Hennessy seems to be very well informed about our discussions, so well informed that he must have been briefed by somebody who has been involved in the discussions or has had access to the relevant minutes. I doubt whether this is sufficiently damaging to warrant a full-scale leak inquiry but it seems to me to create needless political embarrassment for us all, and certainly for you and me as the Minister who will be responsible for legislation on this subject, and who will have to defend it in Parliament and at Party Conference whatever decisions we reach. I should like to suggest to my colleagues that any further briefing of the media to be left to me in consultation, of course, with you.[42]

Wonderful. Such agony inspired by the Cabinet committee on secrecy and openness being written about in the press. The irony of it seemed lost on Jim and Merlyn. That memo was worth waiting thirty years for.

The most recent leak inquiry file of mine – or, rather, Whitehall's – dating from mid-July 1980 to February 1981 was declassified in January 2012. Once again the subject was contingency planning for disputes that struck at the essentials of life and the question was the desirability or not of using volunteer labour as strike-breakers. Once more my good friend and now esteemed colleague on the crossbenches of the House of Lords, Robert Armstrong, was involved as Cabinet Secretary as was the Prime Minister, Margaret Thatcher, wielding her famous blue pen and revealing her penchant for underlining:

Confidential.

MR WHITMORE [Prime Minister's Principal Private Secretary] Brigadier Bishop [Secretary of the Civil Contingencies Unit] in the Cabinet Office received a telephone call this morning from Mr Peter Hennessy of The Times, to inform him that The Times would carry an article on Tuesday 18th November about the Civil Contingencies Unit's plans for 'the coming winter of discontent'. In this article Mr Hennessy would 'name names'.

2. Brigadier Bishop made no comment.
3. I suppose that this means that there has been a leak to The Times of the CCU note, circulated to the Ministerial Committee on Economic Strategy, of the current state of planning for possible emergencies this winter.
4. We shall have to wait to see the article. But Peter Hennessy has taken an interest extending now over two years in the emergency planning organisation, and obviously had some source of information with access to CCU papers. When we see what the article actually says, we shall have to consider whether there should be some kind of leak investigation. But one can say in advance that this is unlikely to be a very profitable area for investigation: inevitably CCU papers have too wide a circulation among and within Departments to hold much hope of being able to discover whether and where we have a mole.*
5. I am sending a copy of this minute to the Home Secretary's [Willie Whitelaw's] Private Secretary.

RTA

---

* John Le Carré's *Tinker Tailor Soldier Spy* had been televised to great acclaim on BBC1 during 1979 and Gerald the Mole had led to the common usage of the word 'mole' within Whitehall and by the press (John Le Carré, *Tinker Tailor Soldier Spy* (Hodder, 1974)).

ROBERT ARMSTRONG
14 November, 1980.[43]

Clive Whitmore added his comment for Mrs Thatcher:

<u>Prime Minister</u>
Mr Hennessy's articles about the CCU have not only named names in
the past but have come complete with photographs of one or two of the
senior officials involved.
CAW
14 xi.

To the Armstrong minute and Whitmore comment Mrs Thatcher
added:

Then <u>reduce</u> CCU papers <u>circulation</u>
MT

It was my article on 19 November 1980 ('Cabinet split on use of
civilian volunteers during stoppages'[44]) which actually triggered the
leak inquiry as captured in another three-way exchange between
Armstrong, Whitmore and Mrs Thatcher (complete with her
underlinings):

<u>MR WHITMORE</u>
Thank you for your minute of 18th November about Mr Peter Hennessy's
article in that day's Times about the Civil Contingencies Unit.

2. That day's article was <u>no more than gossip column stuff</u> about
    Brigadier Bishop, and as such did not seem to me to justify a leak
    inquiry.
3. I take a very different view of <u>today's article</u>, which reports
    Ministerial disagreements <u>about the use of volunteers in</u>

emergencies. This follows earlier articles by Mr Hennessy on 17th and 18th July.

4. The source document for the leak on 17th July was one of the Department of the Environment's <u>MINIS returns</u> [MINIS was the DOE's Management Information System for Ministers, pioneered by Michael Heseltine as its Secretary of State] ... It seems that the leak continues – <u>though not necessarily through that channel</u>; and I have come to the conclusion that we should now formally investigate it.

5. I am proposing accordingly to Sir Ian Bancroft [Head of the Home Civil Service]. I have spoken to him informally and I understand that he is likely to agree. I hope that the Prime Minister will agree that Ministers should be included within the scope of the inquiry.

As the No. 10 record-reviewer has noted here when he examined the file on 13 September 2011:

Paragraph 6 deleted and retained under Section 3(4) [of the Public Records Act, 1958].

I suspect it referred to Robert Armstrong telling Clive Whitmore that Willie Whitelaw would be asked to sign a Home Office Warrant to authorise the tapping of my home telephone number in Walthamstow for the duration of the leak inquiry.

RTA
(Robert Armstrong)
19th November 1980

<u>Prime Minister,</u>
Agree that Ministers should come within the scope of the inquiry?
CAW
20 xi

Yes

MT.[45]

Robert Armstrong launched the leak inquiry formally on 20 November 1980 and appointed Denis Payne of the Cabinet Office to conduct it with the Cabinet Office's Establishment Officer, John Stevens. The Attorney General's Office was kept informed, in case the police were to be involved (they weren't).

Unusually, the leak inquiry form sent to those with access to the information I had divulged is included in the file (I'd not seen one before).

> The attached article by Peter Hennessy from the Times of 19 November 1980 appears to reflect knowledge of matters considered at a meeting of the Civil Contingencies Unit on 30 October 1980: moreover it appears that this knowledge could not have been gained solely from unauthorised access to the memorandum there considered (CCU (80) 19), or from the minutes of the meeting (CCU (80) 9th meeting)
>
> It has been decided in this case to conduct full enquiries under the inter-departmental leak procedure, and you are asked to be good enough to answer the questions below and to return this sheet to J W STEVENS as soon as possible
>
> Will you please say whether you have ever met or spoken to Peter Hennessy
>
> YES/NO
>
> If you have:-
> (i) When did you last see or speak to him? ....
> ....
> (ii) What did you talk about?...
> ....
> ....

(iii) Have you ever talked with him at any time about the Civil Contingencies Unit or any civil contingency matter? ....

....

....

Did you have access to either the memorandum considered at the meeting on 30 October or to the minutes?
YES/NO

Did you communicate any information about the Civil Contingencies Unit or any civil contingency matter to anyone else

YES/NO

If so, please say to whom

....

Signature   ....
Name   ....(in block capitals)
Date   ....

If you need any further information before completing this sheet, please ring J W STEVENS on 233 8238.

CONFIDENTIAL

(A revised version of the inter-departmental leak inquiry procedure was amongst the papers declassified in January 2012.)[46]
Payne and Stevens finally reported on 9 February 1981.

5.   The results obtained from the questionnaire and from supplementary questioning are now available. Of the officials who completed the questionnaire 27 had met or spoken to Hennessy at some time. Of

those, 4 had had contact with him around the time of the article but none had discussed CCU matters with him.

6. The inquiries have produced no lead to the identity of the culprit or culprits, and there is no likelihood of success if we attempt to continue the investigation. Hennessy and his editor are aware that enquiries were made, and it is possible that his contacts among officials will have taken note and will be more cautious in future. It is worth noting that in addition to the normal opportunities open to a Times journalist, Hennessy has opportunities to make new contacts when he lectures at the Civil Service College at Sunningdale.[47]

On 10 February 1981 in a letter to Ian Bancroft, Robert Armstrong concurs with the Payne–Stevens judgement: 'I believe that the matter has been taken as far as it usefully can be, and that no good purpose would be served by continuing with the investigation.'[48]

There is a charming twist at the end of the final letter in the file when Bancroft writes to Armstrong on 19 February 1981:

I am grateful for the effort which has been put into this and agree that there is no point in pursuing the enquiries further. However in the light of the last paragraph of the report, I have discussed with Brian Gilmore, the Principal of the College, whether it might be feasible to cut down the opportunities which the College provides for Peter Hennessy. There is, of course, no suggestion that these courses are the source of any of the leaks and it would, I believe, be wrong to try and freeze him out altogether; apart from anything else Hennessy is one of the few journalists who are also good lecturers [very kind!]. But Brian Gilmore will take discreet steps to ensure that Hennessy gets no more than his share of invitations, without arousing suspicion.[49]

The admirable Brian Gilmore, who was an excellent Principal of the Civil Service College, took steps so subtle that I didn't notice the slightest diminution of the flow of invitations to speak. What gentlemen they all were – the discreet charm of the British leak inquiry. It was a treat to do business with them, as it was to revisit that file with Robert Armstrong during a House of Lords debate on freedom of information, archives and the new Twenty-Year Rule for declassifications on 17 January 2012. I had sent a photocopy of it to Robert and told their Lordships that it had 'brought a frisson of amusement to both of us – a kind of bond between us after all these years'.[50]

Robert, now Lord Armstrong of Ilminster, responded in kind. He told the House he was

> glad to be contributing to this short debate initiated by my noble friend and former adversary Lord Hennessy of Nympsfield. I say 'former adversary' because when he was Whitehall correspondent of *The Times* and I was the Principal Private Secretary at 10 Downing Street, I was required by my political masters to see that Whitehall did all it could to frustrate his knavish tricks, designed to extract information about the working of government which government would have preferred not to disclose. He collected nuggets of information with indefatigable diligence, like Squirrel Nutkin collected nuts, but, unlike Squirrel Nutkin, he always knew where he had stored his nuggets and where to find them when he needed them.
>
> Now that the noble Lord is no longer a mischievous journalist but a learned professor, and I am a mandarin long since put out to grass, we are firm friends. I can acknowledge that, though he did not win them all, he did win more than we could have wished, and that much of what he succeeded in extracting was relatively harmless if occasionally a little embarrassing.[51]

After the debate we both reflected on how utterly unforeseeable it was in 1981 that we would work together on the crossbenches in the House of Lords thirty years on.

Finding one's own spoor, however thinly spread, in the great archive at Kew is such a pleasure that it verges on a vice. The story of Whitehall and official secrecy is the Ealing comedy that was never made. Though Rob Shepherd and I, with the help of the indispensable Sir Bernard Ingham and others, certainly gave it our best shot in *One Hundred Years of Secrecy* in the summer of 2011.

12

CONCLUSION

THE TAXI DRIVER
AND BERTRAND RUSSELL:
WHAT'S IT ALL ABOUT? THE ROAD TO 2052

*Sir, – my husband, T. S. Eliot, loved to recount how late one evening he
stopped a taxi. As he got in, the driver said: 'You're T. S. Eliot.' When asked
how he knew, he replied: 'Ah, I've got an eye for a celebrity. Only the other
evening I picked up Bertrand Russell, and I said to him: "Well, Lord Russell,
what's it all about", and, do you know, he couldn't tell me.'*
VALERIE ELIOT, LETTER TO *THE TIMES*, 8 FEBRUARY 1970.

THE desire to decode one's own times – to answer that culturally attuned
taxi driver's question – is present, I suspect, to some degree in all of us.
Plainly it's powerful in me and has provided much of what professional
drive I possess. The files, the diaries, the memoirs, the visits to once top
secret sites – together they give you a substantial, though never complete,
codebook with which to do it – contemporary history as a series of
retrospective signals intelligence breakthroughs. But answering the taxi

driver's question to Bertrand Russell is the truly stretching part. I've covered but a small fistful of the running themes and questions of postwar Britain in *Distilling the Frenzy* and it is those I shall concentrate upon in my attempt to meet the cabbie's cry.

Britain's place in the world is a very pronounced thread running through these pages. A contemporary British historian of the 2050s coming across this collection may conclude that such a preoccupation on my part amounts to an emotional overhang engineered by growing up in the recent shadow of World War II and living through both the mushroom cloud-silhouetted Cold War and the shedding of the great bulk of Britain's territorial empire overseas; the whole representing an example, perhaps, of an incomplete psychological adjustment to one's country's reduced circumstances of being haunted by 'the noble ghosts of Britain's past', as the former Pakistani Foreign Minister, Yaqub Khan, once put it to his British counterpart, Geoffrey Howe, Lord Howe of Aberavon.[1] After all it's a very long time – July 1914 to be precise – since the UK was last, as Plutarch said of Rome, 'an anchor to the floating world'.[2] And within the first five days of August 1914 that anchor chain had snapped and re-forging it proved beyond the Brits ever after.

I would have two answers to that judgement if it were to be made in 2052 (albeit from the grave unless I live to be 105). First that the political leaderships who found themselves in office in the pair of generations immediately younger than mine were similarly afflicted. I am sure Tony Blair's 'muscular liberalism' (a phrase first coined by Michael Howard in his 2008 edition of *War and the Liberal Conscience*[3] which he later came to regret[4]) as flexed in Iraq in 2003 and David Cameron's intervention in Libya in 2011 are, in part, illustrations of the old 'itch after the amputation'. Tony Blair's Chicago speech on 22 April 1999 on the obligations of the international community[5] and David Cameron's assertion in the October 2010 National Security Strategy that there would be no shrinkage of British influence in the world[6] attest to that, as does William Hague's a 'nation that is purely reactive in foreign policy is in decline' speech of September 2011.[7] As for Nick Clegg, generally thought to be at the herbivorous end of the British political spectrum and a great critic of what he regards as our more atavistic ways (not least, as we have seen, the survival of an unelected second chamber), he was as eloquent as anyone about Britain's place in the world after the shock of David Cameron's vetoing a new European Union-wide treaty at the Brussels 'save the euro' summit of 9 December 2011. In the immediate aftermath of the Prime Minister's action, Mr Clegg plainly saw it as a first step on a possible long march of British withdrawal from the European Communities: 'I think a Britain which leaves the EU will be considered to be irrelevant by Washington and will be considered a pygmy in the world when I want us to stand tall and lead in the world,' he said.[8]

Blair's, Cameron's, Hague's, Clegg's and, in a minuscule way, my own positions might strike the contemporary British historian of 2052 as an absurd mixture of atavism and optimism. But it is perfectly possible that such impulses will exist in the 2050s though, no doubt, they will take a different form from those of late twentieth- and early twenty-first-century Britain unless prolonged economic setback or stagnation forces us to abandon what Douglas Hurd, Lord Hurd of Westwell, called the playing fields of intervention and influence.

Even so there may be mid-twenty first century consolations – cultural or individual examples of British creativity and specialness – to compensate for a UK (as opposed to a shared European) permanent seat on the United Nations Security Council. The Union Jack may finally be erased from the Bomb – though I doubt that unless a President of the United States sets his or her hand to the task and rescinds the 1958 Mutual Agreement and the 1963 Polaris Sales Agreement. The same applies to the UK's global reach as an intelligence player should an American President abandon the 1946 Communications Agreement. The armed services generally could be reduced to a residual force for shared peacekeeping in the world under multilateral colours. Heaven forbid that they should be needed for peacekeeping at home.

Despite my shaky record as a forecaster, I reckon the generally shared appetite for Britain to be a touch special and an accomplished swayer in the world will not be but a faded memory in two generations' time in the 2050s.

It has to do with our Archimedean side. What do I mean? Geoffrey Howe, former Chancellor of the Exchequer and Foreign Secretary, is the one to explain as a great quoter of Archimedes. Geoffrey's version, usually cited in support of Britain's continued membership of the European Union,[9] is:

Give me a place on which to stand and I shall move the world.

The *Oxford Dictionary of Quotations* version is

Give me but one firm spot on which to stand, and I will move the earth.[10]

To Lord Howe some attribute the notion of the UK being able to 'punch above its weight in the world'. More commonly it is cited from a speech of Douglas Hurd's at Chatham House, the Royal Institute of International Affairs, on 3 February 1993.[11] Foreign Office insiders, however, might well award the palm to Lord Hannay of Chiswick, Sir David Hannay as he was at the time, in a widely circulated despatch from the United Nations to Douglas Hurd as Foreign Secretary in early 1991 shortly after arriving in New York as the UK's representative on the Security Council. David Hannay wrote of Britain and France, Douglas Hurd's instinctive interveners, as 'both boxing a bit above their weight, which demands a good deal of ingenuity and fleetness of foot if it is to be done successfully'.[12]

The Hannay caveat is very important. For as Lord Waldegrave of North Hill, William Waldegrave, has pointed out, 'If you punch above your weight you place yourself in danger of being knocked out.'[13] To my mind, that inner and outer circle of international and domestic threats described on page 35 are not only inseparable, as post-9/11 international and home-grown terrorism has so plainly illustrated, but are quite enough to cope with without looking for more things to do in the world.

For all the potential horrors and threats on the road to 2052, I remain optimistic about the UK. Why? For a start I am as certain as I can be about anything that we will endure as a parliamentary democracy and an open society. Our politics will remain a tussle between individual and collective impulses. Our BBC will endure as the hourly, daily, weekly transmitter of institutionalised grizzling between the factions, the parties, the media, the commentariat and the general public. The irreversible explosion of the means of communication will, I suspect, amplify the ferment rather than transcend it.

The years left to me on the road to 2052 will have their shocks for myself as for everyone else. This was true on the road from 1947 to 2012. What most surprised me, in the regrettable sense of that verb, about the life of my own country in my own times as a stay-behind groupie of the late 1950s and early 1960s? High on the list are periodic episodes that have assaulted my deeply ingrained assumption of Britain as a natural possessor of a high level of social peace. To be sure in the 1950s there were Teddy Boys and rising crime rates generally after 1955, their ascent seeming to coincide with the increasing bloom of affluence. Certainly by the late 1960s a level of industrial unrest was accruing that had not been seen since the 1920s.

But the real shock was the disturbances first in Brixton, later Southall and Toxteth, in the spring and summer of 1981. Riots on one's own soil still have a particularly searing capacity to tear at the living social tissues of your society. I felt this particularly powerfully in April 1981 when Brixton erupted on an afternoon and evening of the most perfect spring weather. Nothing had been encountered like it on the UK mainland since 1919. The very strong racial element and the deep antagonism towards the police, captured not just in the contemporary media coverage but in the Scarman Report of November 1981,[14] worried me greatly about the longer-term prospects for the internal stability of the UK and that model of Beveridgite-Keynesian policies for economic and social amelioration that I had absorbed almost as a birthright since coming into life as part of what was called 'the postwar bulge' before somebody, I don't know who, described us as the 'baby boomers'.

Each time it has happened – in different places and for a variety of reasons in fluctuating combinations – serious internal disorder has retained its power to shock; Broadwater Farm, Tottenham 1985; the northern cities, Bradford especially, in 2001; the four days of rioting and looting across London and in Liverpool, Salford and Manchester, Nottingham, Wolverhampton and Birmingham in August 2011. It is very difficult, I find, to be detached as a historian of one's own society. When it bleeds, you bleed.

The jihadi-related attacks on London on 7 July 2005 and the Provisional IRA's bombs on the mainland over twenty years produced a rending and an anxiety of their own and are in no way to be diminished compared to the rioting. But their roots were different as were and are the methods used by the authorities to deal with them. Perhaps the special ingredient of the riots for 'my age' is the feeling that in the years of our maturity we should have been, in our various ways, co-creators of a very different society in which educational opportunity, the expectation of health, the levels of productivity and economic growth and the distribution of the resultant wealth should have coalesced in a society enjoying a betterment in both collective and individual terms never experienced before, not least in terms of wealth per head (we are over three times richer than in 1945 in terms of GDP per capita, though inequalities have widened over the past thirty years[15]).

In the days following the riots of early August 2011, two members of the stretched edition of 'my age' caught the feeling on which I have touched. Jonathan Sacks, the Chief Rabbi (born in 1948, educated at a grammar school in Finchley), said: 'There can be no doubt that something in our moral ecology has gone astray ... There are moments in the history of any civilisation when it catches a glimpse of the state of its soul.'[6] Historians usually have a problem with such things as souls (though I happen not to).

The second, the novelist and critic Howard Jacobson (born 1942, educated at a grammar school in Manchester), declared: 'Those looters are criminals all right – but they are *our* criminals, trashing left and right what we, left and right, have trashed already.' 'Of course', he went on, 'we know damn well where they came from – they came from places from which most of us have averted our eyes, hoping they would stay there, praying that their brutalism would be expended on one another...'[17]

Howard Jacobson's *mea culpa*-ism concentrated on the recent past. 'These', he wrote, 'have been a disgusting few years. That form of looting known as corporate larceny continues to rage unchecked. Economic scavengers bring the world to the brink of ruin. We don't need the discrepancy between rich and poor laid out in percentages, we see the brute fact of it with our own eyes in the shops and on the roads and in the restaurants of our richest cities.'[18]

For me, the shock of 1981 was even greater. As Michael Heseltine, Environment Secretary and the minister responsible for inner cities, put it in the title of a paper he prepared for Mrs Thatcher in July that year after the Toxteth disturbances in Liverpool, 'It Took a Riot' before we realised just what a combination of economic and social ills were afflicting many of our urban areas.[19]

I'm still intrigued by why I was so shocked. I suspect that for all the bumping and grinding of the 1970s – its industrial disputes, its 'winters of discontent', its relative economic decline, widespread de-industrialisation and rising unemployment, its rapid turnover of governments and Prime Ministers – I was still running on the rhythm of my own feel for the engines of postwar consensus. This was of a British New Deal (though neither Clem Attlee nor his ministers called it that).

What were those engines? A mixed economy–welfare state design along Keynesian and Beveridgite principles which, generation upon generation, would describe an increasingly virtuous circle encompassing a healthier, better-educated people with an increasingly skilled, productive and largely fully employed workforce shaped by a set of leaderships across industry, commerce, finance, politics and public service increasingly recruited from wider social circles on the basis of merit rather than the socio-economic status of the loins that had brought them into this world.

It was hard to sustain that mental model from the mid-1970s and my version was already battered before the riots of 1981 dealt it such a blow and, bit by bit thereafter, as the 1980s moved through the ruinous miners' strike of 1983–84 and the two major political parties increasingly polarised, I came to realise that the very special bloom of that postwar promise into which I was born and which through its welfare and education provisions had made me a member of a special and privileged generation (Mr Attlee's children, as I conceive of us) was gone. Education and its allied 'ism' – meritocracy – seemed the shining key to our individual and collective well-beings. Mine was the generation for whom Beethoven became our composer-in-residence for having said, when asked if the 'van' in his name meant he was an aristocrat, 'I'm a brain-owner not a landowner.'[20] The ladder from primary school to top-of-the-rung university was ours to climb. Not until much, much later did I realise that free, taxpayer-funded higher education was unsustainable. This I should have appreciated in 1992, the year I became a full-time university teacher and the proportion of the age group going into higher education passed 30 per cent (it was about 7.5 per cent when I joined the scarlet colours of St John's College, Cambridge in 1966[21]). But full realisation only came in 2009–10.

Perhaps it was a mixture of complacency, altruism and selfishness that made me cling to that model of the postwar settlement which had gifted such a cornucopia of free opportunity and well-being in the 1940s, 1950s and 1960s. I expected the state, the educational system, the British and the world economies to leave me in contented possession of these bounties which I was so sure for so long would be even more lustrous for the generations to come inside the UK, including those arriving in successive waves of immigration from what we then called the 'New Commonwealth' once they had been touched, depending on their age, by full employment or our schools, colleges and universities. The only factor that could, I thought, wreck these interlocking benign cycles was the Cold War, whose benign end I did not foresee, tipping into World War III.

Looking back this was my version of Winston Churchill's speech in the House of Commons in March 1914 on the Naval Estimates, which I quoted earlier, asking only 'to be left in undisputed enjoyment of vast and splendid possessions.'[22] To be frank, I've been in search of a surrogate model ever since. And, given the advantages enjoyed by 'My Age', I'm haunted, in terms of legacy to the coming generations, by the fact that, as the former diplomat my friend Sir Jeremy Greenstock put it, 'we have left them an awful lot to do.'[23]

That said, history as autobiography cannot be a kind of personal National Audit Office to be deployed in balancing the pluses and minuses of the developments unfolding over an individual's lifetime. How, for example, can you trade off the transformations in medical treatments against the erosion of civil peace in 1981 or 2011, or the coarsening of everyday life in an urban area, with serious deprivations or even the false glitter of celebritocracy (what the incomparable Sir Roy Strong calls 'the golden age of trashocracy'[24]) ? To be sure, there are paradoxes. Over my first fifteen to twenty years of life, the great concern was to get more and better food into us. Gradually, the anxiety switched to growing obesity.[25]

There is, however, one huge exception where a collective audit is possible. I was born and I shall die a son of the Cold War. I was also born and shall die a child of the postwar welfare state. These were and remain, to borrow a metaphor from Johan Huizinga's classic study of *The Waning of the Middle Ages*, the 'two poles of the mind' I carry in my head.[26] It was, Huizinga again, as if I lived in a 'mixed smell of blood and roses'[27] – the thought of the unimaginable slaughter of a Third World War amidst the increasingly golden provision of rising standards of physical and intellectual life.

Its ending without global conflict and nuclear exchange remains the single greatest shared boon of my lifetime. If I had come into the world in March 1945 instead of March 1947 I would be a man blessed by two priceless bounties if the defeat of the Axis powers was added to the demise of the Soviet bloc.

I would add a third great slice of good fortune. To have lived and breathed in these islands, to have absorbed the ways we pursue our scholarship, arrange our politics, carry out our administration of both government and justice, exchange our gossip, deploy our humour – for all their imperfections and irritations – comes very close, especially when the joys of family are mixed in, to winning the lottery (or, as 'my age' would say, the pools) in life. This is why it is impossible for me 'to evaporate myself off from my country', as an old friend from the secret world, who can't do it either, likes to put it. It is a persistent compulsion, almost part of what IQ researchers call 'crystallised intelligence ... the crystallised fruits of our previous intellectual endeavours'.[28] This, in the end, is why writing the history of one's own country in one's own times is such a pleasurable and self-energising if ultimately unrealisable pursuit in the sense of completeness.

Why unrealisable? It's not just the books one will never write (in my case, a history of gossip and rumour as influencers of politics and government). It's also, as George Steiner wrote in the tantalising studies he called *My Unwritten Books*, 'remembrance is never more than a flashbulb'[29] for all the cryogenic tricks we bring to thawing out the history frozen in the archives. And as Owen Chadwick put it: 'All historical events are in part mysterious.'[30] Therefore, if you accept Warwick's assertion in Shakespeare's *Henry IV Part 2* that 'there is a history in all men's lives',[31] we who have lived, hovered over and written about our own histories will remain more than a touch mysterious to ourselves let alone those who kindly read or listen to our autobiographical fragments. My friend Alan Judd, the historian and novelist, caught this very well in his spy thriller *Uncommon Enemy* when his lead character Charles Thoroughgood reflects on being struck by the limited part played by facts in the sense of an individual past. 'Facts were like longitude on a map, measurements of temporal relativity, evoking but not containing the myriad associations, tones, colours, remarks, incidents, feelings that formed the patchwork brocade of life. It was they that drenched and infused the memory that was the person.'[32]

Yet for all the fickleness of memory and the historical residue we fail to pick up in our attempts to reconstruct the past, the frenzy is never entirely distilled or the curiosity slaked. Nor will it be on the Road to 2052 unless that 'crystallised intelligence', the sacred curiosity of T. S. Eliot's cabbie, doesn't just fade but is lost for ever.

NOTES

INTRODUCTION

1. J. M. Keynes, *The General Theory of Employment, Interest and Money* (Macmillan, 1936), p.383.
2. *Life*, 2 May 1955.
3. John Wood (ed.), *A Nation Not Afraid: The Thinking of Enoch Powell,* (Batsford, 1965), p.136. The lecture was delivered on 13 November 1964.
4. Ibid., p.137.
5. Conversation with Sir Mark Allen, 4 February 2012.
6. Benjamin Disraeli, *Sybil, or the Two Nations* (Oxford World's Classics edn, 2008), pp. 14–15.
7. Rex Collings (ed.), *Reflections of a Statesman: The Writings and Speeches of Enoch Powell,* (Bellew, 1991), pp.373–9. The speech was delivered to the West Midlands Area Conservative Political Centre on 20 April 1968.
8. The broadcast script is reproduced in Peter Hennessy, *Muddling Through: Power, Politics and the Quality of Government in Postwar Britain,* (Gollancz, 1996), pp.16–33.
9. Peter Hennessy and Caroline Anstey, *Diminished Responsibility? The Essence of Cabinet Government,* Strathclyde/Analysis Papers, No.2 (Department of Government, University of Strathclyde, 1991).
10. His biographer, Simon Heffer, argues that the St George's Eve speech 'embraces all the main themes' that dominated Powell's political life in the 1960s and 1970s. Simon Heffer, *Like the Roman: The Life of Enoch Powell* (Weidenfeld, 1998), p.334.
11. Wood (ed.), *A Nation Not Afraid,* pp.144–5.
12. I am grateful to my friend John Alderdice, Convenor of the Liberal Democrats in the House of Lords, for bringing Seamus Heaney's poem 'The Cure at Troy' to my attention.
13. Conversation with Steve Kelly, 30 October 2011; Stephen F. Kelly, *You've Never Had It So Good: Recollections of Life in the 1950s* (History Press, 2012), chapter 8, 'A "Success Story Nation",' pp.201–23.
14. Anthony Trollope, *The Prime Minister* (Chapman & Hall, 1876) (Trollope Society/Folio edn, 1991), p.605.
15. Julian Barnes, *The Sense of an Ending* (Jonathan Cape, 2011), p.60. I am grateful to Sean Magee for bringing this passage to my attention.

16. Baruch Spinoza, *Tractatus Politicus*, chapter 1, section 4. I am grateful to Dr Stuart Aveyard of the School of History and Anthropology at Queen's University, Belfast, for including this in his PhD thesis 'No Solution: British Government Policy in Northern Ireland under Labour 1974–79' (2010) as I had not encountered it before.

17. Keith Thomas, *The Ends of Life: Roads to Fulfilment in Early Modern England* (OUP, 2009), p.2.

18. Keith Jeffery and Peter Hennessy, *States of Emergency: British Governments and Strikebreaking since 1919* (Routledge, 1983).

19. Norman St John-Stevas (ed.), *The Collected Works of Walter Bagehot, Volume Three* (The Economist, 1968), p.277. The concept appears in Bagehot's obituary of Lord Palmerston in *The Economist*, 21 October 1865.

CHAPTER ONE

1. Donald M. Frame (translator), *The Complete Works of Montaigne: Essays, Volume II* (Hamish Hamilton, undated), p.304. I am grateful to Ned Pennant-Rea for bringing this essay to my attention.

2. Ibid., pp.303–4.

3. *The Times*, 29 March 1947.

4. Peter Hennessy, *Whitehall* (Secker and Warburg, 1989), pp.152–4.

5. *Social Insurance and Allied Services*, Cmd 6404 (HMSO, 1942).

6. The fruits of the programme took written form in Peter Hennessy, *The Secret State: Preparing for the Worst 1945–2010* (Penguin, 2010), chapter 8, 'The Human Button: Deciders and Deliverers', pp.310–59.

7. Abbot Parry OSB (translator), *The Rule of St Benedict* (Gracewing, 1990).

8. The National Archives, Public Record Office, CAB 130/16, GEN 163, 1st Meeting, 8 January 1947. See also Peter Hennessy, *Cabinets and the Bomb* (British Academy/OUP, 2007), pp.36–59.

9. Ibid., p.69; House of Commons, *Official Report*, 12 May 1948, col.2117 (HMSO, 1948).

10. 'Communist MP Sees Atom Secrets', Chapman Pincher, *Daily Express*, 13 May 1948.

11. Peter Hennessy, *What the Papers Never Said* (Portcullis Press, 1985), pp.24–7.

12. Chapman Pincher, *Treachery: Betrayals, Blunders and Cover-Ups: Six Decades of Espionage*, (Mainstream, 2011), pp.628–42.

13. House of Commons, *Official Report*, 20 December 1956, col.1493.

14. Bernard Crick, *The Reform of Parliament* (Weidenfeld, 1964).

15. Martin Gilbert, *Never Despair: Winston S. Churchill 1945–1965*, (Heinemann, 1988), p.1354.

16. Crick, *The Reform of Parliament*. See chapter 9, 'What Is to Be Done?' pp.192–203.

17. Anthony Sampson, *Anatomy of*

Britain Today (Hodder, 1965). The first of the line appeared as *Anatomy of Britain*, (Hodder, 1962); the last as *Who Runs This Place? The Anatomy of Britain in the 21st Century* (John Murray, 2004).

18. Peter Hennessy, 'Foreword' in Anthony Sampson, *The Anatomist: The Autobiography of Anthony Sampson* (Politico's, 2008).

19. Ibid.

CHAPTER TWO

1. 'Paul Samuelson', obituary, *The Times*, 14 December 2009.

2. J. M. Keynes, *The General Theory of Employment, Interest and Money* (Macmillan, 1936), p.383.

3. Lord Rothschild, *Meditations of a Broomstick* (Collins, 1977), p.171.

4. Gabriel Almond, *The American People and Foreign Policy* (Harcourt Brace, 1950), p.138.

5. E. P. Thompson, *The Making of the English Working Class* (Vintage, 1966), p.12.

6. Richard J. Aldrich, 'Intelligence within BAOR and NATO's Northern Army Group', *Journal of Strategic Studies*, Vol.31, No.1, February 2008, p.112; Keith Jeffrey, *MI6: The History of the Secret Intelligence Service 1909–1949* (Bloomsbury, 2010), p.665.

7. Paul Addison, *No Turning Back: The Peacetime Revolutions of Post-War Britain* (OUP, 2010), pp.1–2.

8. See the photograph of the Queen with Harold Wilson at Balmoral in Philip Ziegler, *Wilson: The Authorised Life of Lord Wilson of Rievaulx* (Weidenfeld,1993), between pages 146 and 147.

9. Conversation with Lord Bragg of Wigton, 8 August 2011.

10. Anthony Kenny, *A New History of Western Philosophy* (OUP, 2011), p.xvi.

11. I think this line was argued by the great French historical sociologist Raymond Aron.

12. Kenny, *A New History of Western Philosophy*, p.ix.

13. Winston Churchill, *Great Contemporaries* (Thornton Butterworth, 1937), p.72.

14. Richard E. Neustadt and Ernest R. May, *Thinking in Time: The Uses of History for Decision-Makers* (Free Press, 1986).

15. Ibid., chapter 14, pp.247–70, which bears this title.

16. Jonathan Steinberg, *Bismarck: A Life* (OUP, 2011).

17. A. J. P. Taylor, *Bismarck: The Man and the Statesman* (Hamish Hamilton, 1955), p.35.

18. Henry.A.Kissinger, 'Otto von Bismarck, Master Statesman', *New York Times*, 31 March 2011.

19. Neustadt and May, *Thinking in Time*, p.251.

20. *Review of Intelligence on Weapons of Mass Destruction: Report of a Committee of Privy Counsellors*, HC 898 (Stationery Office, 14 July 2004).

21. 'What's Wrong with

Government?' Royal College of Defence Studies seminar, 7 April 2011.

CHAPTER THREE

1.   Lord Hurd was speaking on a panel, of which the author was also a member, at a meeting of the Cambridge University Land Society in the Travellers' Club, Pall Mall. It was a 'Chatham House Rules' occasion but Lord Hurd has given me permission to quote him.

2.   Ibid.

3.   Private information.

4.   Rt Hon.William Hague MP, 'The Best Diplomatic Service in the World: Strengthening the Foreign and Commonwealth Office as an Institution', Locarno Rooms, Foreign and Commonwealth Office, 8 September 2011.

5.   Geoffrey Moorhouse, *The Diplomats: The Foreign Office Today* (Jonathan Cape, 1977), pp.3–4.

6.   Philip Collins, 'The speech: What he said and what he meant', *The Times*, 6 October 2011.

7.   Vice Admiral Style has given me permission to attribute his remarks.

8.   *Securing Britain in An Age of Uncertainty: The Strategic Defence and Security Review*, Cm 7948 (Stationery Office, October 2010).

9.   *A Strong Britain in an Age of Uncertainty: The National Security Strategy*, Cm 7953 (Stationery Office, 19 October 2010), pp.9–10.

10.   Rosebery was speaking at the City of London Liberal Club on 5 May 1899. Antony Jay (ed.), *The Oxford Dictionary of Political Quotations* (OUP, 1996), p.312.

11.   Ibid. The rectoral address was delivered on 16 November 1900.

12.   Peter Hennessy, 'The Itch after the Amputation? The purposes of British Intelligence as the Century Turns: An Historical Perspective and a Forward Look', in K. G. Robertson (ed.), *War, Resistance and Intelligence: Essays in Honour of M. R. D. Foot* (Leo Cooper, 1999), p.228.

13.   Charles de Gaulle, *War Memoirs Volume One: The Call to Honour, 1940–1942* (Collins, 1955), p.9.

14.   He has used this image in conversations with the author.

15.   Sir Jeremy Greenstock, 'Freedom, Order and Shifting Sands', St Michael and St George Lecture, Locarno Rooms, Foreign and Commonwealth Office, 22 June 2011. I am grateful to Sir Jeremy for sending me a copy.

16.   Quoted in Barbara W. Tuchman, *The Proud Tower: A Portrait of the World before the War: 1890–1914* (Hamish Hamilton, 1966), p.31.

17.   The National Archives/Public Record Office, CAB 131/7, DO (49) 48, 'The Size and Shape of the Armed Forces: The Harwood Report', 21 June 1949.

18.   TNA, PRO, DEFE 5/40, COS (52) 361, , 'Chiefs of Staff Report

on Defence Policy and Global Strategy', 15 July 1952.

19. *Defence: Outline of Future Policy,* Cm 124 (HMSO, April 1957).

20. *Statement on the Defence Estimates 1965,* Cm 2592 (HMSO, February 1965).

21. House of Commons, *Official Report,* 16 January 1968, cols 577–620.

22. *Statement on the Defence Estimates 1975,* Cm 5976 (HMSO, March 1975).

23. *The United Kingdom Defence Programme: The Way Forward,* Cm 8288 (HMSO, June 1981).

24. *Options for Change* (HMSO, 25 July 1990).

25. *Front Line First: The Defence Costs Study* (HMSO, 1994).

26. *The Strategic Defence Review,* (Stationery Office, July 1998); *Delivering Security in a Changing World,* Cm 6041 (Stationery Office, 2002).

27. House of Commons Defence Committee, *The Strategic Defence and Security Review and the National Security Strategy,* Sixth Report of Session 2010–12, HC 761 (Stationery Office, 3 August 2011), pp.3–12.

28. Private information.

29. TNA, PRO, CAB 129/100 FP (60) 1, 'Future Policy Study 1960–70', 24 February 1960. See also Peter Hennessy, *Having It So Good: Britain in the Fifties* (Penguin, 2007), pp.576–95.

30. Ronald Robinson and John Gallagher, *Africa and the Victorians: The Official Mind of Imperialism* (Macmillan, 1961), p.463.

31. He has used the distinction in conversation with the author.

32. Major-General Mungo Melvin, 'Soldiers, Statesmen and Strategy', Royal United Services Institute, 16 November 2011. See also House of Commons Public Administration Select Committee, *Who Does UK National Strategy?* First Report of Session 2010–11, HC 435 (Stationery Office, 18 October 2010).

33. *Central Organisation for Defence,* Cmnd 476 (HMSO, July 1958)

34. TNA, PRO, DEFE 7/1898, 'The Higher Direction of Defence', 20 February 1963.

35. The plan was laid out in *The Central Organisation for Defence,* Cmnd 2097 (HMSO, July 1963).

36. *The Central Organisation of Defence,* Cmnd 9315 (HMSO, July 1984).

37. *Defence Reform: An Independent Report into the Structure and Management of the Ministry of Defence* (Stationery Office, June 2011).

38. TNA, PRO, PREM 11/2688, 'Reorganisation of Central Machinery for Politico-Military Planning Intelligence', Trend to Wilson, 13 March 1967; Trend to Wilson, 20 July 1967.

39. *Report of the Committee on Representational Services Overseas* (HMSO, 1964).

40. *Report of the Review Committee on Overseas Representation 1968–1969* (HMSO, 1969).

41. *Review of Overseas Representation: Report by the Central Policy Review Staff* (HMSO, August 1977).

42. Peter Ackroyd, *Venice: Pure City* (Vintage, 2010), p.384.

43. Joseph S. Nye, *Soft Power: The Means to Success in World Politics* (Public Affairs, 2004).

44. See George Robertson's 'Introduction' to *The Strategic Defence Review*, July 1998.

45. Conversation with Sir Kevin Tebbit, 30 April 2011.

46. Hague, 'The Best Diplomatic Service in the World'.

47. William Le Queux, *The Invasion of 1910: With a Full Account of the Siege of London* (Eveleigh Nash, 1906).

48. Philip Larkin, 'Aubade', in Archie Burnett (ed.), *Philip Larkin: The Complete Poems*, (Faber, 2012), pp.115–16

CHAPTER FOUR

1. I am very grateful to the Trustees of the Michael Quinlan Memorial Lecture, the former Lord Speaker, Baroness Hayman and the Mile End Group for the invitation to deliver a lecture on 'Cabinets and the Bomb' at the House of Lords on 2 February 2011 which gave me a platform for an earlier version of this chapter and a hugely knowledgeable audience on which to try it out. Ronald Knox, *God and the Atom* (Sheed and Ward, 1945), p.9.

2. Evelyn Waugh, *The Life of Ronald Knox* (Chapman and Hall, 1959), p.303.

3. TNA, PRO, CAB 134/940, HDC (55) 3, 'The Defence Implications of Fall-out from a Hydrogen Bomb: Report by a Group of Officials', 8 March 1955.

4. See Peter Hennessy, *The Secret State: Preparing for the Worst, 1945–2010* (Penguin, 2010).

5. Ibid., chapter 7, 'London Might Be Silenced: The Last Redoubt', pp.258–309.

6. For a reconstruction of the simulated countdown aboard HMS *Vanguard* that day see ibid., chapter 8, 'The Human Button: Deciders and Deliverers', especially pp.343–5.

7. TNA, PRO, CAB 130/3, GEN 75/1, 'The Atomic Bomb: Memorandum by the Prime Minister', 28 August 1945. See Peter Hennessy, *Cabinets and the Bomb* (British Academy/OUP, 2007), pp.36–8.

8. Hennessy, *The Secret State: Preparing for the Worst, 1945–2010*, p.80.

9. A. J. P. Taylor, *War by Time-Table: How the First World War Began* (Macdonald 1969), p.121.

10. Professor Nye was speaking at a seminar in Moscow. See Gordon S. Barrass, *The Great Cold War: A Journey Through the Hall of Mirrors* (Stanford University Press, 2009), pp.373–4.

11. Reginald Maudling, *Memoirs* (Sidgwick and Jackson, 1978), pp.113–18; Edmund Dell, *The Chancellors: A History of the Chancellors of the Exchequer, 1945–90* (HarperCollins, 1996), pp.290–98.

12. Conversation with Lord Stockton, 13 April 2011.

13. Conversation with Rear Admiral Simon Lister, 15 August 2011.

14. Sir Michael left an enduring testament to his special feel for the nuclear weapons question with his *Thinking About Nuclear Weapons: Principles, Problems, Prospects* (OUP, 2009).

15. Peter Hennessy, *Cabinets and the Bomb* (British Academy/OUP, 2007).

16. Downing Street Press Briefing, afternoon 4 December 2006, 'Press Briefing from the Prime Minister's Official Spokesman on: Trident'. http://www.number10.gov.uk/output/page10534.asp

17. *The Future of the United Kingdom's Nuclear Deterrent*, Cm 6994 (Stationery Office, 4 December 2006).

18. Michael Quinlan, 'Introduction' in Hennessy, *Cabinets and the Bomb*, p.ix.

19. See Hennessy, *Cabinets and the Bomb*, pp.36–59. The key documents are TNA, PRO, CAB 130/3, 'The Atomic Bomb: Memorandum by the Prime Minister', GEN 75/1, 28 August 1945; TNA, PRO, CAB 130/2, GEN 75/8th Meeting, 18 December 1945; ibid., GEN 75/15th Meeting, 25 October 1946; TNA, PRO, CAB 130/16, GEN 163/1st Meeting, 8 January 1947.

20. House of Commons, *Official Report*, 12 May 1948, col.2117 (HMSO, 1948).

21. See Hennessy, *Cabinets and the Bomb*, pp.167–209. See especially TNA, PRO, CAB 130/212, 'Atlantic Nuclear Force', MISC 16/1st Meeting, 11 November 1964; TNA, PRO, CAB 130/213, MISC 17/7, 'Atlantic Nuclear Force: The Size of the British Polaris Force', 20 November 1964; ibid., MISC 17/3rd Meeting, 'Defence Policy', 21 November 1964; ibid., MISC 17/4th Meeting, 'Defence Policy', 22 November 1964; TNA, PRO, CAB 128/39, CC(64) 11th conclusions, 26 November 1964; TNA, PRO, CAB 148/18, OPD(65) 5th Meeting, 29 January 1965.

22. See Hennessy, *Cabinets and the Bomb*, pp.256–81. See especially TNA, PRO, PREM 15/2038, M/17/2, 'Defence Expenditure, Minutes of a Meeting held at 10 Downing Street on … 30 October 1973'. 'Chevaline was a two-stage missile carrying three nuclear warheads … on a platform known as a bus. The bus was a very sophisticated space vehicle equipped with small jets which could change its orientation so that each of the three warheads could be released on a different trajectory … The bus also carried a variety of penetration aids and decoys to offer so many indistinguishable targets that an opposing ABM system [the anti ballistic missile screen around the Moscow region codenamed GALOSH] would be overwhelmed attempting to deal with them all.' 'Peter Jones', obituary, *The Times*, 18 November 2010.

23. See Hennessy, *Cabinets and the Bomb*, pp.285–322. See especially TNA, PRO, CAB 128/55, CC(74)

47th conclusions, 20 November 1974.

24. See Hennessy, *Cabinets and the Bomb*, pp.326–8. See also TNA, PRO, CAB 130/1109, 'Cabinet Nuclear Policy Committee', MISC 7 (79) 1st Meeting, 24 May 1979; 2nd Meeting, 10 July 1979; 3rd Meeting, 19 September 1979; 4th Meeting, 5 December 1979; TNA, PRO, CAB 130/1129, MISC 7 (80) 1st Meeting, 2 June 1980.

25. *Agreement Between the Government of the United States of America and the Government of the United Kingdom of Great Britain and Northern Ireland for Cooperation on the Uses of Atomic Energy for Mutual Defence Purposes*, 3 July 1958, Cmnd 470 (HMSO, July 1958). It is reproduced in Jenifer Mackby and Paul Cornish (eds), *US–UK Nuclear Cooperation After 50 Years* (CSIS Press, 2008), pp.371–82.

26. Sir Hermann was speaking in *A Bloody Union Jack on Top of It*, broadcast on BBC Radio 4, May 1988. The transcript of the programme is reproduced in Peter Hennessy, *Muddling Through: Power, Politics and the Quality of Government in Postwar Britain* (Gollancz, 1996), pp.99–129. The Bondi quote is on p.128.

27. House of Commons Defence Committee, *Strategic Nuclear Weapons Policy*, 4th Report, Session 1980–81, HC 36 (HMSO, 1981). Michael Quinlan gave evidence to it on 29 October and 4 November 1980.

28. *Defence Open Government Document 80/23* (Ministry of Defence, July 1980).

29. For the most recent government statement see *Securing Britain in an Age of Uncertainty: The Strategic Defence and Security Review*, Cm 7948 (Stationery Office, October 2010), pp.38–9.

30. Hennessy, *Cabinets and the Bomb*, p.viii.

31. Sir Michael Perrin recalling the meeting and its aftermath on BBC2 *Timewatch*, 29 September 1982. See Peter Hennessy, 'How Bevin saved Britain's Bomb', *The Times*, 30 September 1982.

32. TNA, PRO, CAB 130/2, GEN 75/15th Meeting, 25 October 1946.

33. Hennessy, *Cabinets and the Bomb*, pp.87–125. The full Cabinet discussed the H-bomb three times: TNA, PRO, CAB 128/27 CC(54) 47th conclusions, 7 July 1954; ibid., CC(54) 48th conclusions, 8 July 1954; ibid., CC(54) 53rd conclusions, 26 July 1954.

34. Hennessy, *Muddling Through*, pp.105–6.

35. Hennessy, *Cabinets and the Bomb*, pp.105–11; TNA, PRO, CAB 129/69, C(54) 249, 'United Kingdom Defence Policy. Memorandum by the Chiefs of Staff', 31 May 1954.

36. Labour's election manifesto, *The New Britain*, claimed: 'The [1962] Nassau Agreement to buy Polaris know-how and Polaris missiles from the USA will add nothing to the deterrent strength of the western alliance, and it will mean

utter dependence on the US for their supply. Nor is it true that all this costly defence expenditure will produce an "independent British deterrent". It will not be independent and it will not be British and it will not deter.' The manifesto went on to pledge: 'We shall propose the re-negotiation of the Nassau agreement.' Iain Dale (ed.), *Labour Party General Election Manifestos, 1900–1997*, (Routledge/Politico's, 2000), pp.123–4.

37. Hennessy, *Cabinets and the Bomb*, pp.167–72. TNA, PRO, CAB 130/212, MISC 16, 1st Meeting, 'Atlantic Nuclear Force', 11 November 1964.

38. Ibid.

39. Hennessy, *Cabinets and the Bomb*, pp.197–201. TNA, PRO, CAB 128/39, CC(64) 11th conclusions, 26 November 1964.

40. Hennessy, *Muddling Through*, p.115.

41. Sir Kevin was speaking at a RUSI seminar on 'Cabinets and the Bomb', 2 September 2009.

42. Quinlan, *Thinking About Nuclear Weapons*, p.30.

43. Cm 6994, p.5.

44. Sir Frank advanced this argument with me in conversation.

45. Tony Blair, *A Journey* (Hutchinson, 2010), pp.635–6.

46. Quoted in Matthew Parris, 'House of Lords Library Note … Prospects for Nuclear Disarmament and Strengthening Non-Proliferation' (House of Lords, 15 January 2010), p.8. Mr Brown delivered his speech in New York on 24 September 2009.

47. Private information.

48. TNA, PRO, PREM 11/565, 'Events Leading up to the Use of the Atomic Bomb, 1945', Cherwell to Churchill, 29 January 1953.

49. The Coalition, *Our Programme for Government: Freedom, Fairness, Responsibility*, p.15.

50. Private information.

51. *Securing Britain in an Age of Uncertainty: The Strategic Defence and Security Review*, (Stationery Office, October 2010).

52. Ibid., p.38.

53. Ibid.

54. Dr Liam Fox, Secretary of State for Defence, Written Answer, House of Commons, *Official Report*, 3 December 2010, col.1061.

55. *Securing Britain in an Age of Uncertainty*, p.39.

56. Private information.

57. Private information.

58. Liam Fox, Secretary of State for Defence, House of Commons, *Official Report*, 18 May 2011.

59. *The United Kingdom's Future Nuclear Deterrent: The Submarine Initial Gate Parliamentary Report* (Ministry of Defence, 18 May 2011).

60. Ibid., p.5.

61. Ibid., p.6.

62. Hennessy, *Cabinets and the Bomb*, p.343. Sir Michael Quinlan in conversation with Sir John Willis and the author, National Archives, Kew, 6 May 2004.

63. Sir Lawrence was delivering the vote of thanks after my Liddell Hart Lecture at King's College London on 1 November 2011.

64. Jean Monnet, *Memoirs* (Collins, 1978), p.451.

65. Hennessy, *The Secret State: Preparing for the Worst, 1945-2010*, p.311, plus private information.

66. Private information.

CHAPTER FIVE

1. I delivered the bulk of this chapter as the Sir Timothy Garden Lecture 2011 at Chatham House, the Royal Institute of International Affairs on 23 June 2011. I am very grateful to Sir Tim's widow Sue, Baroness Garden of Frognal, for her permission to include it in *Distilling the Frenzy* (letter from Baroness Garden, 15 September 2011). Much of the text was originally published in *INTERLIB*, journal of the Liberal International British Group, No.2, 2011, pp.4–8. Michael Quinlan, 'Shaping the Defence Programme: Some Platitudes', 1 December 2008, unpublished paper in Sir Michael Quinlan's private archive. I am very grateful to Lady Quinlan for her permission to quote from it.

2. Antony Jay (ed.), *The Oxford Dictionary of Political Quotations* (OUP, 1996), p.372.

3. Fernand Braudel, *A History of Civilizations,* (Penguin edn, 1995), pp.xxxvii–xxxviii.

4. Mary Douglas, *How Institutions Think* (Routledge, 1987), pp.21, 25.

5. Christopher Andrew, *The Defence of the Realm: The Authorised History of MI5* (Allen Lane,

Penguin Press, 2009), pp.27–8; TNA, PRO, CAB 16/232, Conclusion of Committee of Imperial Defence Sub-Committee, April 1909; CAB 2/12 CID (103), 24 July 1909; CAB 161/8, Report and Proceedings of CID Sub-Committee.

6. Franklyn Arthur Johnson, *Defence by Committee: The British Committee of Imperial Defence 1885-1959* (OUP, 1960), pp.65, 71, 92, 97, 120–32.

7. Hew Strachan, *The First World War, Volume I: To Arms* (OUP, 2001), p.25.

8. Johnson, *Defence by Committee,* p.131.

9. Keith Jeffery and Peter Hennessy, *States of Emergency: British Governments and Strikebreaking since 1919* (Routledge, 1983), pp.10–39.

10. The 1920 Act is reproduced as Appendix I in ibid., pp.270–72.

11. Ibid., pp.102–29.

12. Ibid., pp.32–3.

13. House of Commons, *Official Report,* 12 November 1919, col.143.

14. Johnson, *Defence by Committee,* pp.192–3; *Report of the Sub-Committee of the Committee of Imperial Defence on National and Imperial Defence* [Salisbury Committee], Cmd. 2029 (HMSO, 1924).

15. David Marquand, *Ramsay MacDonald* (Jonathan Cape, 1977), p.523.

16. F. H. Hinsley, *British Intelligence in the Second World War: Its Influence on Strategy and Operations, Volume I* (HMSO, 1979), p.36.

17. Ibid., p.37.

18. Percy Cradock, *Know Your Enemy: How the Joint Intelligence Committee Saw the World* (John Murray, 2002), p.12.

19. Ibid., p.298.

20. Noel Annan, *Changing Enemies: The Defeat and Regeneration of Germany* (HarperCollins, 1995); Cradock, *Know Your Enemy*, pp.12-14.

21. See Peter Hennessy, *The Prime Minister: The Office and Its Holders since 1945* (Penguin, 2001), pp.329, 554; TNA, PRO, PREM 13/2688, 'Reorganisation of Central Machinery for Politico-Military Planning and Intelligence', 1967–1968, Trend to Wilson, 13 March 1967.

22. *Social Insurance and Allied Services, Report by Sir William Beveridge*, Cmd. 6404 (HMSO, 1942), p.6.

23. Ibid.

24. Angus Calder, *The People's War: Britain 1939–1945* (Granada, 1971), p.609.

25. TNA, PRO, T 236 (no piece number), Rowe-Dutton to Eady, 26 January 1948.

26. Peter Hennessy, *Never Again: Britain 1945–51* (Penguin, 2006), p.370.

27. For the fullest and most up-to-date survey of this see Michael S. Goodman, *Spying on the Nuclear Bear: Anglo-American Intelligence and the Soviet Bomb* (Stanford University Press, 2007).

28. See Catherine Haddon, 'Union Jacks and Red Stars on Them: UK Intelligence, the Soviet Nuclear Threat and British Nu-

clear Weapons Policy, 1945–70', unpublished PhD thesis, Queen Mary, University of London, 2008.

29. Peter Hennessy, *Cabinets and the Bomb* (British Academy/OUP, 2007), p.331.

30. Private information.

31. Peter Hennessy, *Having It So Good: Britain in the Fifties* (Penguin, 2007), pp.573–95.

32. TNA, PRO, CAB 129/100, FP (60) 1, 24 February 1960, 'Future Policy Study 1960–70'.

33. TNA, PRO, CAB 134/1929, FP (60) 1st Meeting, 23 March 1960; Hennessy, *Having It So Good*, pp.591–2.

34. Private information.

35. TNA, PRO, PREM 15/927, 'Review of Government Strategy by CPRS: Meetings of Ministers to Discuss Strategy in Economic and Foreign Affairs, Part 3', Rothschild to Heath, 18 July 1972.

36. Jon Davis, *Prime Ministers and Whitehall 1960–1974* (Hambledon Continuum, 2007), pp.121–4.

37. TNA, PRO, CAB 184/57, 'International Oil Questions', Rothschild to William Armstrong, 21 September 1971. I am very grateful to my research student, Rosaleen Hughes, for steering me through the thickets of energy policy and the CPRS during the Heath years.

38. TNA, PRO, CAB 184/58. Rothschild to Heath, 27 April 1972.

39. TNA, PRO, CAB 134/3607, ES (73) 18, *An Energy Policy for Britain: A Report by the Central Policy Review Staff*, 9 May 1973.

40. TNA, PRO, CAB 134/3609, ES (73) 35, Ministerial Committee on Economic Strategy, 'First Report from the Task Force on Oil Supplies: Memorandum by the Secretary of State for Defence', July 1973.

41. Leonardo Maugeri, *The Age of Oil: The Mythology, History, and Future of the World's Most Controversial Resource* (Praeger, 2006), p.112.

42. Ibid., p.114.

43. I recall him saying that at the time.

44. King, 'Finance: A Return from Risk'.

45. Sir Nicholas Stern, *The Economics of Climate Change* (HM Treasury, 30 October 2006).

46. *The DCDC Global Strategic Trends Programme 2007–2036*, 3rd edn (Ministry of Defence, 2007), p.xiii.

47. *National Risk Register* (Cabinet Office, 2008), p.5. I owe my appreciation of this omission to Sir David Omand, former Co-ordinator of Security and Intelligence in the Cabinet Office.

48. Conversation with Sir Richard Mottram, 23 February 2009.

49. *The DCDC Strategic Trends Programme: Global Strategic Trends out to 2040*, p.95; for a summer 2011 analysis of the state of fusion research see 'Fusion power: next ITERation', *The Economist*, 3 September 2011, pp.72–3.

50. The 22 July 2009 letter is reproduced in *British Academy Review*, Issue 14, November 2009, pp.8–10.

51. The 8 February 2010 letter is reproduced in *British Academy Review*, Issue 15, March 2010.

52. Robert Skidelsky, *John Maynard Keynes: The Economist as Saviour 1920–1937* (Macmillan, 1992), p.401.

53. Lord Rees of Ludlow, 'The Next Half-Century: A Scientist's Hopes and Fears', 2008 Ditchley Foundation Lecture, 12 July 2008 (Ditchley Foundation, 2008), p.1.

54. Lord Rees of Ludlow, 'The World in 2050', The Lord Speaker's Mile End Group Lecture 2009, House of Lords, 18 June 2009.

55. Ibid.

56. Charles Clarke, 'Inaugural Lecture... as Visiting Professor of Politics at the University of East Anglia', 20 January 2011.

57. John Buchan, *The Thirty-Nine Steps*, first published 1915 (Penguin edn, *The Complete Richard Hannay*, 1992), p.2.

58. Sarah Bakewell, *How To Live: A Life of Montaigne in One Question and Twenty Attempts at an Answer* (Vintage, 2011), p.29.

CHAPTER SIX

1. William Hague, 'Securing our Future: The Role of Secret Intelligence in Foreign Policy', Foreign and Commonwealth Office, 16 November 2011.

2. Ibid.

3. The National Archives, Public Record Office, CAB 158/30, JIC (57) 101, 'Terms of reference for the Joint Intelligence Committee',

P. H. Dean, 1 October 1957. See also Peter Hennessy, *Having It So Good: Britain in the Fifties* (Penguin, 2007), pp.487–9; Percy Cradock, *Know Your Enemy: How the Joint Intelligence Committee Saw the World* (John Murray, 2002), p.262.

4. TNA, PRO, PREM 13/2688, 'Reorganisation of Central Machinery for Politico-military Planning and Intelligence, 1967–1968'.

5. *A Resilient Nation: National Security – The Conservative Approach* (Conservative Party, January 2010).

6. Peter Hennessy, *The Secret State: Preparing for the Worst, 1945–2010* (Penguin, 2010), p.384.

7. Cradock, *Know Your Enemy*, pp.12–13; F. H. Hinsley, *British Intelligence in the Second World War* (abridged edn, HMSO, 1993), p.8.

8. The Cabinet Office has kindly supplied me with a summary of the 'key recommendations' of the Rimmer–Martin Report, *Supporting the National Security Council (NSC): The Central National Security and Intelligence Machinery* (Cabinet Office, 2011).

9. Hague, 'Securing Our Future', and Sir Peter Ricketts, IISS Seminar on the National Security Council, 30 November 2011.

10. House of Lords, *Official Report*, 12 December 2011, GC 259.

11. Private information.

12. Hennessy, *The Secret State*, p.382.

13. Private information.

14. Sir Percy liked to describe the JIC in these terms when talking to my students on the 'Cabinet, Premiership and the Conduct of Central Government' course at Queen Mary, University of London in the 1990s. See also his *In Pursuit of British Interests: Reflections on Foreign Policy under Margaret Thatcher and John Major* (John Murray, 1997), p.40.

15. Private information.

16. Private information.

17. Private information.

18. Private information.

19. Private information.

20. *Supporting the National Security Council*.

21. Ibid.

22. Ibid.

23. *Review of Intelligence on Weapons of Mass Destruction: Report of a Committee of Privy Counsellors*, HC 898 (HMSO, 2004), pp.7–16.

24. *Supporting the National Security Council*.

25. House of Lords, *Official Report*, 12 December 2011, GC 259–60.

26. Matt Lyus and Peter Hennessy, *Tony Blair, Past Prime Ministers, Parliament and the Use of Military Force*, Strathclyde Papers on Government and Politics, No.113 (Department of Government, University of Strathclyde, 1999); Colin Seymour-Ure, 'British "War Cabinets" in Limited Wars: Korea, Suez and the Falklands', *Public Administration*, Vol. 62 (Summer 1984), pp.181–200; Peter Hennessy, *The Prime Minister: The Office and Its Holders since 1945* (Penguin, 2001), chapter 6, pp.102–47.

27. Anthony Trollope, *The Prime Minister* (Chapman & Hall, 1876)

(Trollope Society/Folio Society edn, 1991), p.603.

28. House of Commons, *Official Report,* 1 December 2011, 'Libya Crisis', Written Statement, 75 WS.

29. Sir Peter Rickett, *Libya Crisis: National Security Adviser's Review of Central Co-ordination and Lessons Learned* (Cabinet Office, 1 December 2011).

30. Ibid., p.7.

31. See Eliot A. Cohen, *Supreme Command: Soldiers, Statesmen, and Leadership in Wartime* (Free Press, 2002).

32. Ricketts, *Libya Crisis,* p.19.

33. Ibid., p.31.

34. Ibid., p.6.

35. International Institute of Strategic Studies seminar, 30 November 2011.

CHAPTER SEVEN

1. W. E. Gladstone, *Gleanings of Past Years,* Vol. 1 (John Murray, 1879), p.245.

2. In fact, Attlee's words were slightly different. At a meeting of the Parliamentary Labour Party in 1954, Attlee doodled his way through a long and impassioned speech about the perils of the H-bomb from the eloquent Welsh MP Harold Davies. When he finally subsided, Attlee removed the pipe from his mouth, put down his pen and said: 'We'll watch it; meeting adjourned.' Douglas Jay, *Change and Fortune: A Political Record* (Hutchinson, 1980), p.237.

3. Winston S. Churchill, *Great Contemporaries* (Thornton Butterworth, 1937), pp.137–40.

4. John Grigg, *Lloyd George: From Peace to War 1912–1916* (Methuen, 1985), p.474.

5. Peter Hennessy, *Cabinets and the Bomb* (British Academy/OUP, 2007), pp.128–47.

6. Macmillan diary, entry for 17 February 1963. Western Manuscripts Division, Bodleian Library, University of Oxford.

7. Conversation with Dr Paul Addison, 19 April 2011.

8. Ernest Gellner, *Anthropology and Politics: Revolutions in the Sacred Grove,* (Blackwell, 1995), chapter 7, 'James Frazer and Cambridge Anthropology', pp.102–17.

9. J. G. Frazer, *The Golden Bough: A Study in Magic and Religion,* 3 vols (Macmillan, 1890–1900), Vol. 1, pp.1–2.

10. House of Lords, *Official Report,* 3 December 2010, col. 1707.

11. Lord Attlee, 'What Sort of Man Gets to the Top?' *Observer,* 7 February 1960, reproduced in Frank Field (ed.), *Attlee's Great Contemporaries: The Politics of Character* (Continuum, 2009), pp.103–8.

12. Anthony Trollope, *The Prime Minister* (Chapman & Hall, 1876) (Trollope Society/Folio Society edn, 1991), p.567.

13. Ibid., p.603.

14. Peter Hennessy, *The Hidden Wiring: Unearthing the British Constitution* (Gollancz, 1995), p.165. See also footnote 26 on p.241 of that book.

15. Ibid., p.92.

16. Henry A. Kissinger, 'Otto von Bismarck, Master Statesman', *New York Times,* 31 March 2011.

17. Churchill, *Great Contemporaries,* p.137.

18. *The Cabinet Manual: A Guide to Laws, Conventions and Rules on the Operation of Government* (1st edn, Cabinet Office, October 2011).

19. TNA, PRO, CAB 21/1638, 'Function of the Prime Minister and His Staff, 1947–1948'.

20. B. W. Hill, *Sir Robert Walpole: 'Sole and Prime Minister'* (Hamish Hamilton, 1989), Chapter 8, 'Cutting Each Other's Throats', pp. 191–225.

21. R. J. Q. Adams, *Balfour: The Last Grandee*(John Murray, 2007).

22. Private information.

23. For the thinking behind this see the White Paper *Central Organisation for Defence,* Cmd 6923 (HMSO, October 1946).

24. Sidney Low, *The Governance of England* (Fisher Unwin, 1904), p.12.

25. Robert K. Massie, *Dreadnought: Britain, Germany and the Coming of the Great War* (Jonathan Cape, 1992), p.629.

26. Peter Hennessy, *The Prime Minister: The Office and Its Holders since 1945* (Penguin, 2001), pp.60–2.

27. TNA, PRO, CAB 16/8, 'Report and Proceedings of the Committee of Imperial Defence appointed to consider the Question of Foreign Espionage in the United Kingdom', 24 July 1909.

28. House of Lords, *Official Report,* 25 July 1911, cols 641–7; House of Commons, *Official Report,* 18 August 1911, cols 2251–60.

29. Hennessy, *The Prime Minister,* p.68.

30. Fixed-Term Parliaments Act, 2011.

31. Franklyn Arthur Johnson, *Defence by Committee: The British Committee of Imperial Defence 1885–1959* (OUP, 1960), pp.65, 71, 92, 97.

32. Hennessy, *The Prime Minister,* pp.170–71.

33. Sir Hugh MacKenzie, *The Sword of Damocles* (Allen Sutton, 1995), p.201.

34. Jonathon Coe and Richard Kelly, '*Prime Ministers Questions,* House of Commons Standard Library Note,' 6 October 2009, p.3.

35. Ibid., pp.4–5.

36. Private information.

37. The first of Mr Blair's appearances before the Liaison Committee took place on 16 July 2002.

38. House of Commons Political and Constitutional Reform Committee, http://www.publications. parliament.uk/pa/cm201012/ cmselect/cmpolcon/writev/842/ m2.htm

39. Andrew Blick and Peter Hennessy, *The Hidden Wiring Emerges: The Cabinet Manual and the Working of the British Constitution* (IPPR, August 2011).

40. *Draft Cabinet Manual* (Cabinet Office, December 2010).

41. Hennessy, *The Secret State: Preparing for the Worst 1945–2010,* p.389.

42. House of Commons, *Official Report,* 17 March 1914.

43. Anthony Trollope, *The Duke's Children* (Chapman & Hall, 1880), (OUP, 1954), p.1.

44. Private information.

CHAPTER EIGHT

1. Fred R. Shapiro (ed.), *The Yale Book of Quotations,* (Yale University Press, 2006), p.86.

2. Quoted in Jonathan Steinberg, *Bismarck: A Life* (OUP, 2011), pp.193–4.

3. Shapiro (ed.), *The Yale Book of Quotations,* p.86.

4. Walter Bagehot, *The English Constitution* (Fontana, 1963 edn; the red-covered paperback I used when I first fell under the Bagehotian spell at St John's College, Cambridge in 1966).

5. Walter Bagehot, *Lombard Street: A Description of the Money Markets* (H. S. King, 1873) (Wiley edn, 1999), p. 20.

6. W. E. Gladstone, *Gleanings of Past Years, Vol.1* (John Murray, 1879), p.245.

7. Quoted in Sidney Low, *The Governance of England* (Fisher Unwin, 1904), p.221.

8. House of Lords Constitutional Committee, *The Process of Constitutional Change* 15th Report, Session 2010–12, HL 177 (Stationery Office, 2011).

9. House of Lords, *Official Report,* 7 December 2011, GC 167–8.

10. The coalition's line was sustained by Lord Wallace of Saltaire when he replied to the Lords debate of 7 December 2011 on behalf of the government. House of Lords, *Official Report,* 7 December 2011, GC 196.

11. House of Commons, *Official Report,* 8 February 1960, col.70.

12. For what is still the liveliest account of the great constitutional crisis of 1909–11 see Roy Jenkins, *Mr Balfour's Poodle: An Account of the Struggle Between the House of Lords and the Government of Mr Asquith* (Heinemann, 1954).

13. House of Lords, *Official Report,* 7 December 2011, GC 190.

14. *The Process of Constitutional Change,* CRP 14.

15. House of Lords, *Official Report,* 7 December 2011, GC 168.

16. Ibid., GC 190.

17. *The Government Response to the House of Lords Constitution Committee Report 'The Process of Constitutional Change',* Cm 8181 (Stationery Office, September 2011)

18. House of Lords, *Official Report,* 7 December 2011, GC 189.

19. Amy Baker, *Prime Ministers and the Rule Book* (Politico's, 2000).

20. Peter Hennessy, *The Prime Minister: The Office and Its Holders since 1945* (Penguin, 2001), p.451.

21. Both these documents are reproduced as appendices in Baker, *Prime Ministers and the Rule Book,* pp.135–92.

22. Peter Hennessy, *Having It So Good: Britain in the Fifties* (Penguin, 2007), chapter 9, pp.405–57.

23. Hennessy, *The Prime Minister,* pp.433–4.

24. *Review of Intelligence on Weapons of Mass Destruction: Report of a Committee of Privy Counsellors,* HC 898 (Stationery Office, July 2004), see especially pp.146–8.

25. Enoch Powell, *Joseph Chamberlain* (Thames and Hudson, 1977), p.151.

26. Simon Heffer, *Like the Roman: The Life of Enoch Powell,* (Weidenfeld, 1998), chapter 11, pp.449–508.

27. Enoch Powell, 'Enoch Powell talks to Disraeli', *Sunday Times,* 22 December 1963. I am very grateful to Richard Ritchie for bringing this quotation to my attention.

28. The essay is reproduced in Peter Davison (ed.), *Orwell and Politics,* (Penguin, 2001), pp.397–411.

29. Ibid., p.398.

30. Ibid., p.409.

31. I had my most recent stab at this in an address during 'A Celebration of Advent', organised by Christian Responsibility in Public Affairs at St Michael's Church, Chester Square in London on 1 December 2011.

32. Winston S. Churchill, *The World Crisis: The Aftermath* (Thornton Butterworth, 1929). Churchill called his opening chapter on the Armistice and after 'The Broken Spell', pp.17–31.

33. Anthony Trollope, *The Prime Minister* (Chapman & Hall, 1876) (Trollope Society/Folio Society edn, 1991), p.567.

34. Quoted in the diary of McCallum Scott, entry for 5 March 1917. See Paul Addison, 'The Religion of Winston Churchill' in Michael Bentley (ed.), *Public and Private Doctrine: Essays in British History Presented to Maurice Cowling* (CUP, 1993), p.245.

CHAPTER NINE

1. Sir Michael made this observation over lunch in the library of the mansion in Ditchley Park on 9 July 2011 shortly before the annual general meeting of the Ditchley Foundation.

2. Conversation with Alf Dubs, 15 February 2012. Lord Dubs has given me permission to quote him.

3. House of Lords House of Commons Minutes of Evidence Taken Before The Joint Committee On The Draft House of Lords Reform Bill, Draft House of Lords Reform Bill, 30 January 2012, HC 1313-xv.

4. Roy Jenkins, *Mr Balfour's Poodle: An Account of the Struggle Between the House of Lords and the Government of Mr Asquith* (Collins, 1954).

5. *Freedom Fairness Responsibility: Our Programme for Government* (Cabinet Office, May 2010).

6. Ibid.

7. *Invitation to Join the Government of Britain: The Conservative Manifesto 2010* (Conservative Campaign Headquarters, 2010), p.67.

8. *Change That Works for You: Building a Fairer Britain* (Chris

Fox/Liberal Democrats, 2010), p.88.

9. *A Future Fair for All: The Labour Party Manifesto 2010* (Labour Party, 2010), p.94.

10. I heard him say it myself on a private occasion (he said his view was 'no secret').

11. Private information.

12. Walter Bagehot, *The English Constitution* (1867; Fontana 1963 edn), pp.137, 149.

13. Adapted from Sir Walter Scott's poem 'Young Lochinvar out of the West'.

14. Nick Clegg interviewed by Jon Snow, *Channel 4 News*, 5 April 2011.

15. N. D. Kondratiev, 'The Long Waves in Economic Life', in *Readings in Business Cycle Theory* (Blakiston, 1944). The Marxist Kondratiev first advanced his theory in 1926. See David S. Landes, *The Unbound Prometheus: Technological Change and Industrial Development in Western Europe from 1850 to the Present,* (CUP, 1969), pp.232–3.

16. Aldous Huxley, *Beyond the Mexique Bay* (Chatto and Windus, 1934), p.83. Huxley wrote: 'The commonest, one might call it the natural rhythm of life is routine punctuated by orgies.'

17. G. R. Searle, *A New England? Peace and War 1886–1918* (OUP, 2004), pp.405–24.

18. Bernard Donoughue and G. W. Jones, *Herbert Morrison: Portrait of a Politician* (Weidenfeld, 1973), pp.429–31.

19. Jenkins, *Mr Balfour's Poodle*, p.282.

20. Enoch Powell and Keith Wallis, *The House of Lords in the Middle Ages: A History of the English House of Lords to 1540,* (Weidenfeld, 1967), pp.1–11.

21. Letter from Lord Cunningham of Felling to the author, 5 March 2012.

22. Draft House of Lords Reform Bill, HC 1313-xv.

23. James Callaghan, *Time and Chance* (Collins, 1987), p.502.

24. House of Lords, *Official Report,* 3 December 2010, cols.1706–9.

25. Fact sheet produced by the House of Lords Appointments Commission for a House of Lords briefing on its work, 8 February 2012.

26. Ibid. Briefing Paper on 'The Nomination and Assessment Process'.

27. Private information.

28. *House of Lords Reform Draft Bill*, Cm 8077 (Stationery Office, May 2011), pp.11–12.

29. Ibid., pp.5–6.

30. Simon Heffer, *Like the Roman: The Life of Enoch Powell* (Weidenfeld, 1998), pp.509–13, 517, 520–21.

31. Kenneth O. Morgan, *Michael Foot: A Life* (HarperPress, 2007), pp.259–61.

32. *House of Lords Reform Draft Bill,* p.11.

33. House of Lords, *Official Report,* 21 June 2011, col.1194.

34. Ibid., cols.1193–94.

35. Ibid., col.1194.

36. On 12 September 2011.

37. House of Lords House of Commons Minutes of Evidence Taken Before The Joint Committee on the Draft Lords Reform Bill,

Draft House of Lords Reform Bill, 10 October 2011, HC 1313-1.

38. House of Commons, *Official Report*, 17 May 2011.

39. 'Chamber Music', unpublished diary on House of Lords Reform, entry for 17 May 2011.

40. House of Lords, *Official Report*, 16 May 2011, col. 1142.

41. House of Lords, *Official Report*, 17 May 2011, col.1277.

42. Ibid.

43. Ibid., col. 1280.

44. 'Chamber Music', diary entry for 18 May 2011. Lord Peston has given me permission to quote him.

45. Peter Riddell, *Parliament under Blair* (Politico's, 2000).

46. House of Lords House of Commons Oral Evidence Taken Before the Joint Committee on the Draft House of Lords Reform Bill, Draft House of Lords Reform Bill, 24 October 2011, HC 1313-iii.

47. Andrew Adonis, *Parliament Today* (Manchester University Press, 1993).

48. House of Lords House of Commons Minutes of Evidence Taken Before the Joint Committee on the Draft House of Lords Reform Bill, Draft House of Lords Reform Bill, 5 December 2011, HC 1313-x.

49. House of Lords House of Commons Joint Committee on Conventions, Conventions of the UK Parliament, HL Paper 265-1, HC 1212-1 (Stationery Office, 2006).

50. House of Lords House of Commons Minutes of Evidence Taken Before the Joint Committee on the Draft House of Lords Reform Bill, Draft House of Lords Reform Bill, 30 January 2012, HC 1313-xv.

51. House of Lords House of Commons Minutes of Evidence Taken Before the Joint Committee on the Draft House of Lords Reform Bill, Draft House of Lords Reform Bill, 10 October 2011, HC 1313-i.

52. House of Lords House of Commons Minutes of Evidence Taken Before the Joint Committee on the Draft House of Lords Reform Bill, Draft House of Lords Reform Bill, 23 January 2012, HC 1313-xiv.

53. Ibid.

54. Bill of Rights 1688, Article 9.

55. George Steiner, *My Unwritten Books* (Weidenfeld, 2008), p.137.

56. House of Lords, House of Commons, Minutes of Evidence Taken Before the Joint Committee on the Draft House of Lords Reform Bill, Draft House of Lords Reform Bill, 16 January 2012.

57. Ibid.

58. Ibid.

59. Ibid.

60. HC 1313-iii.

61. HC 1313-x.

62. He did so in my hearing.

63. House of Lords Select Committee on the Constitution, Meeting with Nick Clegg MP, Deputy Prime Minister, 1 February 2012.

64. House of Lords Select Committee on the Constitution, *Referendums in the United Kingdom*, 12th Report of Session 2009–10, HL 99 (Stationery Office, 2010), p.27.

65. House of Lords Library Note, *Public Attitudes Towards the House of Lords and House of Lords Reform*, Ian Cruse, 11 November 2011.

66. Private information.

67. Roland Watson, 'Tory Peers in revolt. Anger over Lords reform threatens coalition's entire legislative programme', *The Times*, 20 February 2012.

68. Dominic Grieve to Ivor Richard, 7 November 2011.

69. Iain Dale (ed.), *Labour Party General Election Manifestos, 1900–1997* (Routledge/Politico's, 2000), p.275.

70. David Butler, *British General Elections since 1945* (Blackwell, 1989), p.37.

71. The National Archives, Public Record Office, CAB 134/4540, H (HL) (81) 2, 'Protection of the House of Lords. Memorandum by the Secretary of State for the Home Department', 29 January 1981.

72. Ibid.

73. Ibid.

74. Ibid.

75. Joint Committee on the Draft House of Lords Bill. Written Evidence of Lord Goldsmith QC, EV 109.

76. House of Commons, *Official Report*, 3 April 1911, cols.1894–5.

77. Lord Pannick QC, Could the Parliament Act 1911 be used by the House of Commons to insist on reform of the House of Lords? Joint Committee on the Draft House of Lords Bill. Written Evidence of Lord Pannick QC.

78. Private information.

79. James Forsyth, 'Irreconcilable Differences', *The Spectator*, 25 February 2012.

80. Private information.

81. House of Commons Oral Evidence Taken Before The Public Administration Committee, *Strategic Thinking in Government*, 22 February 2012, Rt. Hon Oliver Letwin MP, HC 1625-iv.

CHAPTER TEN

1. Martin Gilbert, *Never Despair: Winston S. Churchill 1945–1965* (Heinemann, 1988), p.835.

2. Winston S. Churchill, *Great Contemporaries* (Thornton Butterworth, 1937), pp.16–17.

3. Gilbert, *Never Despair*, p.835.

4. John Colville, *The Churchillians*, (Weidenfeld, 1981), p.121.

5. Gilbert, *Never Despair*, p.835.

6. Paul Addison, *Churchill on the Home Front, 1900–1955* (Jonathan Cape, 1992), p.439.

7. Henry Pelling, *Winston Churchill*, (Macmillan, 1974), p.33. See also p.49.

8. John Ramsden, *Man of the Century: Winston Churchill and His Legend since 1945* (HarperCollins, 2002).

9. Roy Jenkins, *A Life at the Centre* (Macmillan, 1991), p.57.

10. Roy Jenkins, *Asquith* (Collins, 1964).

11. Roy Jenkins, *Mr Attlee: An Interim Biography* (Heinemann, 1948).

12. Roy Jenkins, 'Gladstone and

Books' in Peter Francis (ed.), *The Grand Old Man: Speeches and Sermons in Honour of W. E. Gladstone* (Monad Press, 2000), p.25.

13. *The Oxford Dictionary of Quotations,* second edn (OUP, 1968), p.209.

14. Quoted in John Lukacs, *The Future of History* (Yale, 2011), p.78.

15. Jenkins, *Gallery of 20th Century Portraits,* p.260.

16. Ibid., p.256.

17. Harold Macmillan, *Riding the Storm, 1956–1959* (Macmillan, 1971), p.197.

18. D. R. Thorpe, *Supermac: The Life of Harold Macmillan* (Chatto, 2010), p.57.

19. Barbara Tuchman, *The Guns of August* (Constable, 1962).

20. Alistair Horne, *Macmillan 1957–1986* (Macmillan, 1989), p.383.

21. Peter Catterall (ed.), *The Macmillan Diaries Vol.II: Prime Minister and After 1957–1966* (Macmillan, 2011), p.510. Diary entry for 22 October 1962.

22. Peter Hennessy, *The Prime Minister: The Office and Its Holders since 1945* (Penguin, 2001), pp.129–30.

23. Ibid., p.130.

24. TNA, PRO, CAB 158/29, JIC (57) 62, 'The Possibility of Hostilities short of Global War up to 1965', 20 September 1957. I am grateful to Dr Alban Webb for bringing this assessment to my attention.

25. Quoted in Lukacs, *The Future of History,* p.4.

26. I have heard him quoted by Geoff Mulgan, author of *Good and Bad Power: The Ideals and Betrayals of Government* (Allen Lane, The Penguin Press, 2006).

27. Churchill, *Great Contemporaries,* p.61.

28. Fernand Braudel, *A History of Civilizations* (Penguin edn, 1995), p.xxxviii.

29. This was a 'Chatham House Rules' occasion but Lord Butler has given me permission to cite him.

30. Ibid.

31. Hennessy, *The Prime Minister,* pp.228–47; the Butler Report, *Review of Intelligence on Weapons of Mass Destruction: Report of a Committee of Privy Counsellors,* HC 898 (Stationery Office, 14 July 2004), p.160.

32. Sir Joseph Pilling, *The Review of the Government's History Programme* (Cabinet Office, 2009 though not published until 2011).

33. I have discussed this with some of those involved.

34. Margaret Gowing, *Britain and Atomic Energy 1939–1945* (Macmillan, 1964); Margaret Gowing assisted by Lorna Arnold, *Independence and Deterrence: Britain and Atomic Energy 1945–1952, Volume 1 Policy-Making; Volume 2 Policy Execution* (Macmillan, 1974).

35. Christopher Andrew, *The Defence of the Realm: The Authorized History of MI5* (Allen Lane, Penguin Books, 2009); Keith Jeffery, *MI6: The History of the Secret Intelligence Service 1909–1949* (Bloomsbury, 2010).

36. Sir Lawrence Freedman, *The*

Official History of the Falklands Campaign. Vol.I The Origins of the Falklands War; Vol.II War and Diplomacy (Routledge, 2005).

37. W. K. Hancock, *Country and Calling* (Faber, 1954), pp.196–7.

38. Peter Hennessy, *Whitehall* (Pimlico, 2001), p.139.

39. Churchill, *Great Contemporaries*, p.72.

40. Quoted in Lukacs, *The Future of History*, p.24.

41. William Hague, *William Pitt the Younger: A Biography* (HarperCollins, 2004).

42. William Hague, *William Wilberforce: The Life of the Great Anti-Slave Trade Campaigner* (HarperPress, 2007).

43. Rt Hon. William Hague, MP, 'The Best Diplomatic Service in the World: Strengthening the Foreign and Commonwealth Office as an Institution', Locarno Rooms, FCO, 8 September 2011.

44. 'Saturday interview', 'I've often been wrong, but I was absolutely right about the euro', 'Rachel Sylvester and Alice Thomson meeting William Hague', *The Times*, 10 September 2011.

45. Hague, 'The Best Diplomatic Service in the World'.

46. Ibid.

CHAPTER ELEVEN

1. The National Archives/Public Record Office, PREM 16/1858 'Security. Disclosure of Official Information; Francis and Younger Reports on Security and Privacy; White Paper on Official Information; Part 7.

2. For an account of the Agadir crisis see Robert K. Massie, *Dreadnought: Britain, Germany and the Coming of the Great War* (Jonathan Cape, 1992), chapter 39, 'Agadir', pp.715–43.

3. Home Office, *Departmental Committee on Section 2 of the Official Secrets Act 1911, Vol.1, Report of the Committee*, Cmnd 5104 (HMSO, 1972).

4. Lord Hurd of Westwell speaking on *One Hundred Years of Secrecy*, first broadcast on BBC Radio 4, 16 August 2011.

5. Sir Bernard Ingham speaking on *One Hundred Years of Secrecy*.

6. TNA, PRO, PREM 19/357, 'Security: Review of Adequacy of Leaks procedure', Bancroft to Whitmore, 15 January 1980.

7. Ibid., Whitmore to Bancroft, 18 January 1980.

8. Ibid., Thatcher to Whitelaw, 4 August 1980.

9. Ibid., Ingham to Pattison, 21 July 1980.

10. TNA, PRO, CAB 175/36, 'Cabinet Office Civil Emergencies Book July 1973'. I am grateful to Rosaleen Hughes for persuading the Cabinet Office to declassify this document in 2011.

11. Nicholas Wilkinson, *Secrecy and the Media: The Office and*

*History of the United Kingdom's
D-Notice System* (Routledge,
2009)

12. Keith Jeffery and Peter Hennessy,
*States of Emergency: British Gov-
ernments and Strikebreaking since
1919* (Routledge, 1983).

13. TNA, PRO, HO 322/778,
'Relations with the Press: Open
Government Issues; Peter Hennessy's Articles on Civil Defence
in "The Times", November 1979',
Sir Frank Cooper to Sir Robert
Armstrong, 2 November 1979;
Armstrong to John Chilcot, 12
November 1979. My articles ran
as 'Whitehall brief' columns between 13 and 23 November 1979
culminating in a leading article,
'Open Planning for Emergencies', which I penned and was
published on 26 November 1979
(all nicely preserved in the Home
Office file).

14. *The Labour Way Is the Better
Way: The Labour Party Mani-
festo 1979*, reproduced in Iain
Dale (ed.), *Labour Party General
Election Manifestos, 1900–1997*
(Routledge/Politico's, 2000). The
Polaris replacement section is on
p.236.

15. TNA, PRO, PREM 16/2246,
'SECURITY: Proposed Article by
Peter Hennessy on Strategic Nuclear Deterrent', Hunt to Stowe,
12 April 1979.

16. Ibid. Jim Callaghan scribbled his
comments on the minute on 13
April 1979.

17. Ibid. Hunt to Stowe, 12 April
1979.

18. Private information.

19. Samuel Brittan, *Steering the*

*Economy: The Role of the Treas-
ury* (Pelican, 1971).

20. Peter Hennessy, 'Abrasive Touch
for a Silky Machine', *Times Higher
Education Supplement*, 19 January 1973.

21. Peter Hennessy, 'The Think Tank
gets a man with a talent for saying what he means', *The Times*,
January 1975.

22. *The Civil Service, Vol.1, Report of
the Committee 1966–68* (HMSO,
1968).

23. TNA, PRO, PREM 16/762, Allen
to Armstrong, 7 November 1974.

24. Ibid.

25. Ibid. Armstrong to Wilson, 8
November 1974.

26. Ibid. Wilson's scribble is undated.

27. Ibid., Armstrong to Allen, 8
November 1974.

28. Peter Hennessy, *Whitehall* (Secker and Warburg, 1989), p.xvii.

29. *One Hundred Years of Secrecy.*

30. TNA, PRO, PREM 16/762, Hennessy to Haines, 8 December
1974.

31. Ibid., Haines to Armstrong, 12
December 1974.

32. Ibid. Armstrong to Haines, 13
December 1974.

33. Ibid.

34. Ibid., Haines to Hennessy, 17
December 1974.

35. TNA, PRO, PREM 16/1858,
'Peter Hennessey', Stowe to Callaghan, 4 July 1978.

36. Ibid. Callaghan's comments are
undated but Ken Stowe receives
the minute back on 10 July 1978.

37. Frank Field, 'Killing a Commitment: The Cabinet v The Children', *New Society*, 17 June 1976.

38. TNA, PRO, PREM 16/1113,

'SECURITY: Leak of an Article in *The Times* on Child Benefit Rates: Sir Douglas Allen's Report; Proposal for Privy Councillors to examine the security of Cabinet documents'. See also PREM16/1449, 'SECURITY: Leak of Cabinet Information on the Child benefit Scheme: Article in New Society magazine, 17 June 1976; reports by Metropolitan Police; Committee Privy Councillors (Chairman: Lord Houghton of Sowerby) on Security of Cabinet Documents; II', 'Child Benefit Leak – Report by Sir Douglas Allen', undated.

39. Frank Field speaking on *One Hundred Years of Secrecy*.

40. Bernard Donoughue, *Downing Street Diary Volume Two: With James Callaghan in No. 10* (Jonathan Cape, 2008), p.61.

41. Hennessy, *The Prime Minister*, p.451.

42. TNA, PRO, PREM 16/1856, 'Security. Disclosure of Official Information: Franks and Younger Reports on Security and Privacy; Implementation of Reports by the Faulks and Phillimore Committees; Reform of Official Secrets Act; Official Information Bill; Part 5'.

43. TNA, PRO, PREM 19/593, 'SECURITY, Leaks about Civil Contingencies Unit (CCU) to Peter Hennessy of *The Times*'; investigation. Armstrong to Whitmore, 14 November 1980.

44. Ibid.

45. Peter Hennessy, 'Echoes of the General Strike in hardliners' plan: Cabinet split on use of civilian volunteers during stoppages', *The Times*, 19 November 1980.

46. TNA, PRO, PREM 19/593, Armstrong to Whitemore 19 November 1980, Whitmore to Thatcher 20 November 1980.

47. TNA, PRO, PREM 19/953, Payne and Stevens to Armstrong, 9 February 1981.

48. Ibid. Armstrong to Bancroft, 10 February 1981.

49. Ibid. Bancroft to Armstrong, 19 February 1981.

50. House of Lords, *Official Report*, 17 January 2012, col. 534.

51. Ibid., col. 537.

CONCLUSION

1. House of Lords, *Official Report*, 8 September 2011, col.403.

2. Quoted in Thomas L. Friedman and Michael Mandelbaum, *'That Used to be Us': What Went Wrong with America – and How It Can Come Back* (Little Brown, 2011), p.328.

3. Michael Howard, *War and the Liberal Conscience* (Hurst, 2008), p.vii.

4. Michael Howard, 'The Transformation of Strategy', *RUSI Journal*, August–September 2011, Vol.156, No.4, p.16.

5. John Rentoul, *Tony Blair: Prime Minister* (Little Brown, 2001), pp.526–7.

6. *A Strong Britain in an Age of Uncertainty: The National Security Strategy* (Stationery Office, October 2010), pp.9-10.

7. Rt Hon. William Hague, MP, 'The Best Diplomatic Service in the World: Strengthening the Foreign and Commonwealth Office as an Institution', Locarno Rooms, Foreign and Commonwealth Office, 8 September 2011.

8. Sam Coates, 'Voters back veto as coalition is put to the test: Angry Clegg raises danger of 'pygmy' Britain', *The Times*, 12 December 2011.

9. He has used the line more than once in conversation with the author.

10. *The Oxford Dictionary of Quotations,* Second edn (OUP, 1968), p.14. The OED takes as its source Pappus Alexandr., Collectio, lib viii, prop 10, ξ xi (ed. Hulsch, Berlin, 1878).

11. Antony Jay (ed.), *The Oxford Dictionary of Political Quotations* (OUP, 1996), p.185.

12. Quoted in David Hannay, *The Quest for a Role* (I.B. Tauris, 2012 forthcoming).

13. Conversation with Lord Waldegrave of North Hill, 27 July 2011.

14. *The Disturbances in Brixton*, Cmnd 8427 (HMSO, 1981); see also: *After the Riots: The Final Report of the Riots, Communities and Victims Panel* (Stationery Office, 2012)

15. http://www.ons.gov.uk/ons/datasets-and-tables/data-selector.html?cdid=IHXW+dataset=bb+table-id=15.

16. Jonathan Sacks, 'We've been here before. And there is a way back', *The Times*, 12 August 2011.

17. Howard Jacobson, 'They may be criminals, but we're the ones who have created them', *Independent*, 13 August 2011.

18. Ibid.

19. Peter Hennessy, *Whitehall* (Pimlico, 2001), pp.313-14; TNA, PRO, PREM 19/484, 'HOME AFFAIRS. Civil disorder: disturbances in Brixton, Bristol, Liverpool, Manchester and London districts…'

20. Simon Russell Beale, 'The Symphony: Beethoven and Beyond', BBC4, 10 November 2011.

21. A. H. Halsey and Josephine Webb (eds), *Twentieth Century British Social Trends* (Macmillan, 2000), pp.226-7.

22. House of Commons, *Official Report,* 17 March 1914.

23. Jeremy Greenstock, 'Freedom, Order and Shifting Sands', St Michael and St George Lecture, Locarno Rooms, Foreign and Commonwealth Office, 22 June 2011.

24. Nick Curtis, 'Strong sentiments', *Evening Standard*, 15 September 2011.

25. Avner Offer, *The Challenge of Affluence: Self-Control and Well-Being in the United States and Britain since 1950* (OUP, 2006); Avner Offer, Rachel Pechey, Stanley Ulijaszek, 'Obesity under Affluence Varies by Welfare Regimes: The Effect of Fast Food, Insecurity, and Equality', *Economics and Human Biology*, Vol.8, No.3, December 2010.

26. Johan Huizinga, *The Waning of the Middle Ages*, first published 1924 (Penguin, 1979), p.318.

27. Ibid., p.25.

28. Linda Gottfredson, 'Intelligence', *New Scientist*, 2 July 2011, p.iv of special supplement.

29. George Steiner, *My Unwritten Books* (Weidenfeld, 2008), 'School Terms', p.122.

30. Quoted in George Lukacs, *The Future of History,* p.26.
31. William Shakespeare, *Henry IV Part 2,* Act 3, Scene 1, line 76.
32. Alan Judd, *Uncommon Enemy* (Simon and Schuster, 2012), p.150.

INDEX